DYNAMICS OF WOMEN LEADERSHIP

DYNAMICS OF WOMEN LEADERSHIP

H.G. Joshi

ACE BOOKS INDIA
NEW DELHI

ACE Books India
4649-B/21, Ansari Road
Darya Ganj, New Delhi - 110 002

Dynamics of Women Leadership

First Published 2010
ISBN 978-81-909743-4-9

[The responsibility for the facts stated, conclusions reached etc., is entirely that of the author. The publisher is not responsible for them, whatsoever.]

Sole Distributors
EKTA BOOKS DISTRIBUTORS
4649-B/21, Ansari Road
Darya Ganj, New Delhi - 110 002
Ph.: 23263193 / 9811582579 / 09435116718
Fax: 011-23263193
Email: ektabooks@yahoo.com
www.akanshapublishinghouse.com

PRINTED IN INDIA

Published by ACE Books India, New Delhi and Printed at
Harmain Offset Press

Contents

Preface

> "A strong leader knows that if he develops his associates he will be even stronger."
>
> —*James F. Lincoln*

As is generally understood, leadership is an inherent quality of a person. But, it can be developed and built. We all know women constitute nearly half of the human population on this earth. But they were/are treated as weaker sex in almost all societies. Though many women emerged as able leaders in different societies in different course of history, they are still underestimated as a leader. Since politics is the major field where ample opportunities are there of proving one's leadership qualities, power and authority, we have taken women leadership in the field of politics in the present study.

As an established fact, women constitute about a half of the total human population on this earth. Amidst plenty of others, she plays important role for reproduction of human species. But she is considered weaker sex and discriminated on various accounts in almost all societies with varying degree and magnitude all across the world.

Recent years have witnessed a worldwide concern for women. Ways back the world community devoted the year of 1975 to women and, during the course of that year, further decided to have a World Decade to promote their cause: to fight against discrimination based on gender, denial of opportunities to participate in public life outside their homes, exploitation, illiteracy, inferior jobs and poor wages, and generally a lower status compared to that of men. The Decade succeeded in creating awareness about these issues, both among men and women. It also prompted governments to devise special policy measures and to initiate constitutional reforms to improve the situation of women. These have brought about noticeable changes but still there is a far way to go, and the situation is not the same in all the countries.

It is also remarkable that women in politics have historically been under-represented in Western societies compared to men. Many women, however, have been politically elected to be heads of state and government. Most prominent may be the female leaders of world powers such as Prime Minister of India Indira Gandhi, Prime Minister of the United Kingdom Margaret Thatcher, Prime Minister of Israel Golda Meir, Chancellor of Germany Angela Merkel, Prime Minister of Canada Kim Campbell, Prime Minister of France Edith Cresson, President of India Pratibha Patil, President of the People's Republic of China Soong Ching-ling (AKA Rosamond Soong), and Director of the Cultural Revolution, dictator Jiang Qing, Prime Minister of Pakistan Benazsir Bhutto, Prime Minister of Bangladesh Begum Khaleda Zia and Sheikh Hasina.

Politics is one field where the evidence of increasing participation by women is still not very impressive in most of the countries in the region. This is so on two counts: the number of women politicians is relatively smaller compared to men, and the majority of women are believed to be indifferent to politics as is exhibited by their participation in voting, in public demonstrations, in debates and discussions. Whatever participation in politics is there, it is to be found mostly among the women from the urban elite groups. The women in rural, illiterate, and non-elite strata are mostly outside the pale of politics.

The present book intends to portray women leadership in general and in the field of politics in particular. We have gathered information about some countries where women leadership has vehement potential but it faces several hurdles.

Women leadership in the context of politics is highlighted taking instance of different countries in South and Southeastern Asia and Australia. Facts and figures derived from different research projets are also cited to elucidate the nature and trends of women leadership. The main topics included in this work are—Introduction; Women Leadership in Philippines; Women in Politics in Malaysia; Women in Politics in Thailand; Women Leadership in Australia; Women Leadership in Some South Asian Countries; Bibliography etc.

I express my gratitude to various scholars for borrowing their research findings with the sole aim of disseminating their erudition to a wider readership. I am equally grateful to all those who have extended whole-hearted help in making relevant material available for the present study. I am thankful to my colleagues and friends for their guidance and help in different stages while working on this project. My publishers also deserve all appreciation for materialising this venture.

—HGJ

1

Introduction

> "A strong leader knows that if he develops his associates he will be even stronger."
>
> —*James F. Lincoln*

As is generally understood, leadership is an inherent quality of a person. But, it can be developed and built. We all know women constitute nearly half of the human population on this earth. But they were/are treated as weaker sex in almost all societies. Though many women emerged as able leaders in different societies in different course of history, they are still underestimated as a leader. Since politics is the major field where ample opportunities are there of proving one's leadership qualities, power and authority, we have taken women leadership in the field of politics in the present study.

Recent years have witnessed a worldwide concern for women. The world community devoted the year of 1975 to women and, during the course of that year, further decided to have a World Decade to promote their cause: to fight against discrimination based on gender, denial of opportunities to participate in public life outside their homes, exploitation, illiteracy, inferior jobs and poor wages, and generally a lower status compared to that of men. The Decade succeeded in creating awareness about these issues, both among men and women. It also prompted governments to devise special policy measures and to initiate constitutional reforms to improve the situation of women. These have brought about noticeable changes but still there is a far way to go, and the situation is not the same in all the countries.

Women in politics have historically been under-represented in Western societies compared to men. Many women, however, have been politically elected to be heads of state and government. Most prominent may be the female leaders of world powers such as Prime Minister of India Indira Gandhi, Prime Minister of the United Kingdom Margaret Thatcher, Prime Minister of Israel Golda Meir, Chancellor of Germany Angela Merkel, Prime Minister of Canada Kim Campbell, Prime Minister of France Edith Cresson, President of India Pratibha Patil, President of the People's Republic of China Soong Ching-ling (AKA Rosamond Soong), and Director of the Cultural Revolution, dictator Jiang Qing.

The first women other than monarchs to hold head of state positions were in socialist countries. The first was Khertek Anchimaa-Toka of the Tuvan People's Republic from 1940-1944, followed by Sükhbaataryn Yanjmaa of the Mongolian People's Republic 1953-1954 and Soong Ching-ling of the People's Republic of China from 1968-1972 and 1981. Following the socialist countries, the Nordic countries have been forerunners in including women in the executive branch. The second cabinet Brundtland (1986-1989) were historical in that 8 out of 18 cabinet members were women, and in 2007 the second cabinet Stoltenberg (2005-present) was more than 50% women. Some current female politicians that have reached top positions in the Nordic countries are the President of Finland, Tarja Halonen and Deputy Prime Minister of Sweden, Maud Olofsson. In 2003 Finland had a historical moment when all top leaders of the country were women and also represented different political parties: Social democrat Tarja Halonen was President, Riitta Uosukainen from National Coalition Party was Speaker of the Parliament and after the parliamentary elections of 2003 Anneli Jäätteenmäki from Center party was on her way to become the first female Prime Minister of Finland. The world's first elected female president was Vigdís Finnbogadóttir of Iceland, whose term lasted from 1980 to 1996.

In 2005, Ellen Johnson-Sirleaf of Liberia became Africa's first elected female head of state.

It was not until World War I and the first socialist revolutions that the first few women became members of governments. Alexandra Kollontai became the first female to hold a minister position, as the People's Commissar for Social Welfare in Soviet Russia in 1917. Nina Bang, Danish Minister of Education from 1924-26, was the world's second full female cabinet minister.

The first female head of government was Evgeniia Bosh, the Bolshevik military leader who held the People's Secretary of Internal Affairs position in the Ukraine People's Republic of the Soviets of Workers and Peasants from 1917-1918, which was responsible for executive functions. Nevertheless, development was slow and it was not until the end of the 20th century that female ministers stopped being unusual.The first government organization formed with the goal of women's equality was the Zhenotdel, started by the government of Soviet Russia. According to a 2006 report by the Inter-Parliamentary Union, 16% of all parliament members in the world are female. In 1995, the United Nations set a goal of 30%.

The top ten countries are Rwanda with 56.3%, Sweden (47.0%), Cuba (43.2%), Finland (41.5%), the Netherlands (41.3%), Argentina (40.0%), Denmark (38.0%), Angola (37.3%), Costa Rica (36.8%), Spain (36.3%). Cuba has the highest percentage for countries without a quota.

According to the same report, nine countries have no women parliament members.

The US House of Representatives contains 77 women, and the US Senate contains 16. Eight states have female governors. However the state of affairs cannot be said glorius despite many women leaders' presence on the scene.

Politics is one field where the evidence of increasing participation by women is still not very impressive in most of the countries in the region. This is so on two counts: the number of women politicians is relatively smaller compared to men, and the majority of women are believed to be indifferent to politics as is exhibited by their participation in voting, in public demonstrations, in debates and discussions. Whatever participation in politics is there, it is to be found mostly among the women from the urban elite groups. The women in rural, illiterate, and non-elite strata are mostly outside the pale of politics.

But these are impressionistic observations. In most cases, information is not available about the actual extent of women's participation in politics. How many of them are active, in what kind of politics, and at what level? What are the distinguishing attributes of those who participate and those who do not? Is the non-participation due to legislative restrictions or due to social and cultural prohibitions? These and similar other questions need a systematic probing across cultures to arrive at meaningful generalisations that would guide further policy and social action.

The dominant socio-cultural trait impeding women's participation is the stereotyped roles of men and women, and the image that politics is the realm of men. The socialisation of both career politicians and ordinary citizens is a key to understanding both the demand and supply sides of the political game. Evidently, career politicians tend to come from a family environment which is liberal and supportive of women's public participation. While domestic chores may be an obstacle to political work, they can be overcome, especially with a helpful family. The politicians tend to be educated people, with their involvement in an array of extra-curricular activities, ranging from student activism to social welfare work and more explicit political work, as a lead up to their political career. It is the gradual broadening of personal experiences beyond the introspection of the formal daily regimen which establishes the root of political preparation.

Several queries arise regarding women's progression to power, particularly concerning their own autonomy and capability: did they jump on their husband's or family's political bandwagon rather than build their own political vehicle? Are they really well-informed about politics beyond the party political platform? Are they cause oriented, party-oriented, or self-oriented? Are they genuinely motivated to help foster women's participation in politics or are they mere opportunists? And finally, are these questions all gender-specific?

From another standpoint, the picture gained from the interviews with ordinary citizens depends upon a cluster of different interests. The elite and middle income groups, especially from urban areas, have relatively easy access to information and mass media which can shape their political opinions. They may then exercise their voting rights upon a broad base of information and may move beyond voting for personalities to voting for political parties. The lower income group, especially in rural areas and low income settlements, tends to be less well-informed and have less access to information. If they vote, they are not likely to be well versed in party policies but would go along with personalities or follow the voting patterns of local leaders, their own families, or their peers.

To them, it is the daily bread and local issues which count. Gender would seem to take second place, if it occurs to them at all. On the more positive note, it is encouraging that the studies support the contention that mere illiteracy is no impediment to political awareness. A large group of illiterate women in South Asia exercise their voting rights extensively. Politicians could not afford to be condescending towards the illiterate people. In other words, illiteracy is not a synonym for political ignorance or inaction.

Women do exercise their power despite their being uneducated in the conventional sense. However, this does not contradict the point that educated women are better empowered in the sense that they are enabled to take on political career and assume positions of power.

This pervasive image of politics is compounded by the 'dirty politics' rubric. To make political power more accessible to the low-income groups and to the women of those groups will be the challenge for future. Equally important is the role of women in helping sanitise the political games. In fact, some country studies indicate that women candidates are preferred because of their image of 'being clean'. It is evident that there are too few women at the higher level of political decision-making.

At the bottom or local level, some countries provide encouraging signs with greater participation of women. In the midst of all this, there is the tentative spread of women's participation in different political arenas. However, as indicated in the studies, the mere fact that there are more women in parliaments, and in political parties, does not mean that they will promote the cause of women's rights and women's public participation. Suitable linkages between groups of women with different political attitudes and orientation need to be created. At the same time, the scope of the word 'politics' itself may need further scrutiny and may be broadened so that non-formal community level politics be included. There is the additional issue of affirmative action to promote women in politics. On the one hand, this implies goals and aims to help women rather than actual quotas in parliament. On the other hand, some may wish to advocate specific quotas reserving political places for women. The country studies diverge on whether such affirmative action is required. There is also at stake the type of elections and nominations open to women in politics. These differ between countries. It is interesting to note the comment concerning Australia, for example, which suggests that there is less access to the lower house of parliament via the single member electorate but more access to the Senate which has a proportional representative system. Behind the scenes, there is the complexity of pre-selection procedures which may obscure women's interest for the imputed greater good of the party.

Women's contribution in the political sphere is rather small. Women are not just invisible, they are conspicuously absent in this area of decision making. They are neglected, and they are themselves indifferent to politics. The notion continues that "Politics is the realm of men", and that "politics is dirty power game—a preoccupation of the rich." This turns a majority of women, if not all, away from politics. Thus, they mostly remain aloof from politics and their voices are not adequately heard by political decision makers. Politics remains one of the men's strongholds.

Various studies and researches show the complicated nature of low participation of women in politics. Even in egalitarian, democratic and industrially developed societies women political leaders have not come to the fare. Though the nature of politics, type of political system or ideology, and structure of political institutions are contributing factors to determine the degree of women's participation, the socio-cultural and historical conditions appear to have stronger influence. Politics, too, is socially, culturally, and historically bound. In general terms, however, women do hold some measures of influence and power. But their influence, and power, are usually exercised in informal and personal settings and not in the public spheres. Women as a category, in most societies, do not have formal power or publicly recognised authority equivalent to that held by men. Certainly, women's formal power varies by class, culture, race, religious sects, etc.; but it is always less than that of men in the same position.

The public-private dichotomy is still very much prevalent and it hampers women's active participation in politics. Politics being 'public' affairs and women being mainly in 'domestic' domain, it is difficult for many women as well as men to overcome this dichotomy, and break the notion of division of labour by sex. There is a need to change this set notion into a more flexible one raising awareness that "Personal is Public". Linkages need to be explicitly shown and understood as to how the familial and personal matters are relevant to politics, and vice versa. The definition of politics needs re-examination. The word politics in a narrow sense, implies formal partisan politics at national, provincial, and municipal levels. Although the formal partisan or parliamentary politics is a part of politics, it is not synonymous with politics *per se.* Grass-roots level community activities, in fact, have political elements and implications, but they are often excluded from the limited interpretation of 'politics'. The formal, parliamentary politics is in fact possible on the basis of various 'political' actions at different levels.

Accumulation and culmination of such actions enable many politicians and policy makers to initiate action and lead them to make certain decisions. In the context of women's participation in politics, this community level or grass-roots politics is the area where women are actively involved and are making contribution. This is often the entry point to formal politics for many politically active women.

Remarkably, in spite of the significant role that the community level grass-roots activities can play even in the large framework of formal or mainstream politics, and in general development process, the merger of the two—micro and macro—politics seems to be difficult. Politicians and those involved in mainstream formal politics regard grass-roots level activities as politically unimportant, as these are outside of the conventional type of politics. But the grassroots and community level workers and activists tend to have a negative view and attitude towards the formal/mainstream politics, and appear to be apolitical or sometimes even anti-politics. Thus, innovative methods and techniques used at the grass-roots level to mobilise women into community activities, and knowledge and experience gained in that process, are not properly tapped and utilised for bringing them into the mainstream politics. Linkage between micro and macro level politics remains an issue to be tackled. The role of government/public administration in politics is not to be underestimated. The politicians and government/ public administrators are closely linked as policy decision-makers and policy implementors. Government administration is one of the entry points for many politicians. But for women, this does not yet appear to be the case.

There are several entry points for politicians. Perhaps the most notable is the family connection, particularly for women. However, this is not exclusively so for women politicians. Many male politicians are also backed by politically well-counted families. But what is significant for women politicians or candidates is that often they can receive sympathy votes when something wrong happens to their fathers or husbands, such as their assassination/ death or dismissal, or imprisonment.

However, one should not underestimate the capability of such women candidates/politicians and their efforts to make themselves good and sincere politicians. (In fact, women politicians often have image and reputation that they are sincere, clean and diligent). Furthermore, some women, in fact, decide themselves to become politicians even at their young age, regardless of the family's political connection. The image of women politicians is not always a correct reflection of reality. The image perceived by ordinary people, or projected by the media, is usually divided into two extremes: women politicians are seen as either 'man-like' 'iron-lady', or as 'amateur', 'soft (indecisive)', 'housewife-come-politicians'. Or else they are identified through kinconnections i.e. Mr. X's daughter, or Mr. Y's wife or widow, etc. They are rarely quoted as their individual selves, and are not taken as they are. Accurate portraits of their lives as politicians and women, and objective review of their work and achievements as professional politicians are needed. By documenting the work and life-histories of some successful and capable women politicians, and disseminating such information in popular form, one can present a role model for ordinary women citizens, and change the stereotyped image of women politicians.

The candidate selection process within political parties is not clear to many and is unknown to outsiders. The decision-making on this matter is still in the hands of a few (mostly men). This makes it difficult for ordinary citizens to understand how people can become politicians. Thus, the notion of politics being the preoccupation of the rich and elite is sustained.

To gain access to high level political decision making, one needs to have an extraordinary strength of will and determination. It may mean sacrificing personal pleasure and happiness. Women politicians have to work twice as hard as their male counterparts in order to be recognised and to make their presence felt. Yet to be real representatives of the majority of women, they are required to be sensitive to the problems of the silent majority, who are usually not well articulated, and who are not always politically beneficial to many politicians. How to make politicians, both males and females, gender sensitive, and how to make the present political system gender responsive is indeed a serious question.

At the same time, one needs also to think and devise the ways of sending those who are truly representative of the people to parliament or to other political decision making bodies. Organisation of concerned women, and well-co-ordinated and innovative support system for women politicians/candidates may be evolved to meet this end. Strengthening the linkages between women politicians and women's organisations is also needed. There are several issues that the studies raise; some of these require further empirical research, others call for affirmative action. Both social scientists and social workers will find the studies useful and stimulating.

The present book intends to portray women leadership in general and in the field of politics in particular. We have gathered information about some countries where women leadership has vehement potential but it faces several hurdles.

2

Women Leadership in Philippines

Geographically, Philippines is part of Southeast Asia. It is an archipelago composed of 7,000 islands. The biggest island is Luzon in the north and the second biggest is Mindanao in the South. Between Luzon and Mindanao are smaller islands which constitute the Visayan group of islands. Palawan is the longest and biggest island on the western part of the archipelago. Samar and Leyte lie on the eastern side of the Philippines.

The northernmost province of the Philippines is the Batanes group of islands separated from the southernmost tip of Taiwan by the Bashi Channel, while Batanes is separated from the northernmost tip of Luzon by the Balintang Channel. The bodies of water that surround the Philippines are the South China Sea on the West and the Philippine Sea on the East, which opens to the Pacific Ocean, while the Southern tip of the Mindanao island is bound by the Celebes Sea. The Sulu Sea surrounds the Sulu group of islands and its broader eastern portion separates Mindanao from the Visayas. This portion is also known as the Mindanao Deep. The countries that surround the Philippines are a portion of southern mainland China to the Northwest, Taiwan to the North, Vietnam to the West, Sabah, which is considered part of Malaysia, to the Southwest and the Celebes and the Indonesian group of islands to the South. Eastward, beyond the Philippine Sea, are the Micronesian group of islands is the Pacific Ocean.

In fact, for administrative purposes, the Philippines is divided into 15 regions including the national capital region and two autonomous regions, one in Luzon and one in Mindanao. Each region is composed of several provinces. There are 78 provinces all over the Philippines. Each province is administered by local officials headed by a governor. Most cities have their own separate city charter and are governed separately from the province by officials headed by a mayor.

The different municipalities within a province have their own municipal mayors and sets of officials but are supervised by the governor of the province. For economic development planning purposes, the various units of government within a region select their respective representatives to work together as the Regional Development Council. The autonomous regions are governed separately by their respective organic laws. Each province is divided into electoral districts proportional to the population. Each district elects a representative to the National legislature. The Senators are elected for the whole country.

According to a 1989 official estimate which indicates that the country's population is 60,097,000. According to the earlier 1980 census the population was 48,098,460. It showed the urban population to be 17,943,897 (37.3%) and the rural population 30,154,563 (62.7%). In the 1989 estimate, the urban population was 25,321,600 (42.13%) and the rural 34,665,388 (57.87%). In the earlier census the population distribution according to sexes was 24,128,755 (50.17%) males and 23,969,705 (49.83%) females. In Metropolitan Manila where the survey in this study was mostly done, the population as of the 1980 census was

5,925,884 out of which 2,855,712 (48.2%) were males and 3,070,172 (51.8%) were females. In region 11 in which the city where the Mindanao survey was made is located, the population in 1980 was 2,270,949. There were 1,148,920 (50.6%) males and 1,122,209 (49.4%) females.

Concerning women's entry into the labour force, the 1998 statics on the number of employed persons grouped according to the major industries and distribution of sexes are as follows: total persons employed: 21,497,000; male, 13,654,000 (63.5%); female, 7,843,000 (36.5%). The distribution is represented in the following table on next page.

Statistics on population distribution according to sex showed that in both the 1980 Census and the 1989 estimates, there were more males in the labour force than females by over a million. In Metropolitan Manila, in the 1980 Census, however, women outnumbered men by almost a million.

With regard to the employment distribution of women in the major industry group, there were more males employed than females. The areas with a higher number of females than males are wholesale and retail trade. As far as the major occupation group is concerned there appeared to be more females employed in the professional, technical and related work as well as in sales and services.

Major industry group	*Both sexes*	*Male*	*Female*
Agriculture, fishery and forestry	9,920,000	7,413,000	2,507,000
Mining and quarry	157,000	143,000	14,000
Manufacturing	2,238,000	1,192,000	1,046,000
Electricity, gas and water	95,000	80,000	15,000
Construction	858,000	842,000	13,000
Wholesale and retail trade	2,9722,000	1,034,000	1,939,000
Transportation, storage and communication	1,049,000	1,001,000	48,000

Financing insurance, real estate business services	—	—	—
Community, social and personal services,	379,000	241,000	138,000
Industry not adequately defined or not reported	3,827,000	1,703,000	2,1244,000

Major occupation group	*Both sexes*	*Male*	*Female*
Professional, technical and related workers	1,198,000	446,000	753,000
Administrative, executive and managerial workers	171,000	128,000	43,000
Clerical workers	899,000	411,000	489,000
Sales workers	2,867,000	982,000	1,904,000
Service workers	1,944,000	775,000	1,169,000
Agricultural animal husbandry, and forestry workers, fisherman hunters	9,798,000	7,307,000	2,491,000
Production and related workers, transport equipment operators and labourers	4,619,000	3,625,000	994,000
Occupation not adequately defined	1,000	1,000	0

The lack of employment opportunities, underemployment, and low salary scales in the country have attracted Filipinos to job openings, overseas. It is also the official policy of the government since 1970 to export manpower services to foreign countries.

Records showed that women like the men had availed of the opportunity to work aboard. Women overseas workers represented 36 per cent of the total deployment in 1980. This increased to 46.4 per cent in 1986 out of a recorded 414,461 workers deployed. There were 477,764 overseas workers deployed in 1988 and the deployment of women continued to increase. But the estimate is that there are more overseas Filipino workers than officially recorded by the concerned government agency. It is sad to state, however, that most Filipino women working abroad are hired as domestic help when many of them are degree holders and professionals in the Philippines. There are also documented accounts of the travails and abuses that many women have been subjected to in their place of work.

Historically, the Philippines had been linked with the island of Borneo because of the affinity of the Muslims of Mindanao and Maynilad with the Muslims of Borneo. Certain theories also link the country with the Sri-Vijayan and the Mahjapahit empires although there is insufficient proof of this. But what is accepted is that the Philippines was peopled with migrants from Indonesia and the Malay Peninsula in ancient times-which explains the vestiges of Malayo-Indonesian influence in the Philippine cultural heritage.

The original inhabitants of the Philippines were the Negritoes or the Aetas. But since the waves of migration to the Philippines occurred at different times, the Aetas were pushed back to the mountainous interior.

By the 14th century Islamised people came to the Philippines and began to spread their religion. The Muslims soon established strong kingdoms in the Sulu Islands and later in the Maguindanao territory along the Polangui River. Other kingdoms were also established in a portion of Mindoro and in Maynilad in Luzon. Those tribes that were not converted to Islam moved to the hinterland and remained in the periphery. The larger portion of the Philippines was then occupied by non-Islamic tribes while the Islamised tribes confined themselves to their territory, largely in Mindanao.

Historical accounts indicate that among the non-Islamised people, women had more freedom in their social relations and enjoyed a higher social status. Some attained political equality with men and occupied position of leadership. Historical and folkloric accounts mention the rules of Princess Urduja of Pang asinan and Queen Simla. We further learn that among some tribes, women acted mostly as priestess known as the *babaylan.* The Babaylans were said to have wielded power and influences over the tribe. In Muslim kingdoms, however, social customs and more for women changed and they were treated with reservation.

By the 16th century, the Spaniards claimed to have discovered the Philippines and maintained their colonisation of the island for 333 years. They established a centralised colonial administration, integrated the territory under their rule and spread Catholicism. They also gave the Islands the name Filipinas which was later transformed by the Americans to Philippines, the name by which it is known today. Only the Muslims resisted conversion to the new religion. Spanish laws were also applied to the colony. Those that affected women were the Spanish Marriage Law of 1870, the Spanish Code of Commerce of 1885 which became effective in the Philippines on 1 December 1888, the Spanish Civil Code of 1885 which applied to the colony on 7 December 1889, and the Spanish Penal Code that took effect on 14 July 1887.

Under the Spanish colonial rule, the application of Spanish laws affecting women, compounded by the religious influence and the customs and tradition of Spain, moulded women into suppressed beings, subservient, servile, self-sacrificing, and serene. Married women were expected to obey their husbands and to be dependent on them. They could not engage in trade or make purchases without the consent of the husbands. But there was a double standard of morality: liberal for men and rigid on the women. Under the influence of Catholicism and the tutelage of the friars and the ecclesiastic, the Filipinos acquired very conservative values as demanded by religion, the customs, and the laws. Nobody rebelled against the system and the socialisation of women went in this direction throughout the Spanish period and even beyond. When the Spanish colonial government introduced popular education in the 17th century, there were separate schools and orphanages for girls. The curriculum for girls' schools included reading, writing, arithmetic, religion and courses in social deportment and housekeeping such as needle-craft and cooking. In the boys' schools, however, aside from the basic four 'Rs', education also included courses such as Spanish, geography, history and practical agriculture. Women as a general rule, were not encouraged to obtain higher education because the roles expected of them were only geared for motherhood and housekeeping. Worse, most women did not have the freedom to choose their husbands. Parents did the matchmaking. During the Spanish period, women who managed to improve their educational training and assert themselves, as history has recorded, did so through their own effort. The majority of the women in the Philippines under Spanish colonial rule, however, were subjected to the prevailing and value orientations of the period. Spanish rule ended on 10 December 1898 when the Philippines was ceded to the United States. The American defeated the Spaniards in the American-Spanish War that broke out in May 1898 in Cuba. Upon the assumption of American sovereignty over the Philippines, Spanish laws were supplanted by organic laws which the U.S. Congress promulgated to apply to the Philippines together with the instructions of President William McKinley to the Second Philippine Commission on 7 April 1900. The American colonial government after establishing the administrative machinery in the islands, organised the public schools system intended to provide universal education for the colony. Higher education was also established and was open to all. The concept of equality which goes with democratic principles was something new to the Filipinos and the women. But the educational institutions run by the ecclesiastics continued their functions of administering education for girls.

Many parents still preferred that their daughters obtain an exclusive type of education characterised by the conservatism of the old school. It took some time before women began to appreciate the new freedom offered to them. But the courageous ones who availed of higher education and trained for the professions were considered exceptionally adventurous and possessed with an indomitable will. However, while education was opened for all and women were provided with the opportunity to develop their talents and assert themselves, not all women immediately ventured into the new pastures. Besides, while equal opportunity was presumably available to them, the limitation lay in the fact that gender classification had already been made for the different professions. For instance, women were welcomed as nurses, teachers, midwives, pharmacists, pianists, secretaries, opera singers, but not as doctors, engineers, lawyers accountants, architects or into other professions dominated by men. The study of law was associated with the preparation for a government or public career or for the judiciary. Women were not encouraged to take a masculine profession such as law. For a woman to become a lawyer was therefore, considered a challenge.

While some women took up the study of law during the earlier period of American rule, this was not the case in the medicine, engineering and dentistry; these were taken up in the later part of the American period. Marriage and raising a family remained the full-time career of women including those whose educational training and skills would qualify them to practice their professions. The prevailing attitude was for the man to provide the needs of the home and the family and the woman to first take care of the children and the home. This was fortunate for women whose husbands were good providers, but woeful for those whose husbands were incompetent. But the sad part was that in reality women worked to provide for the needs of the family but very seldom were they openly given the recognition for doing so.

The honour always went to the men even when they could hardly fend for themselves. For peace and good relations to be maintained in the home, the wise wife could never give the impression that her husband was "under the *says* (skirt)" or henpecked. And it was worse of course if she showed that she was more intelligent than him.

The experience during the World War II under enemy occupation and the difficulty, violence and atrocities that the people had undergone may have contributed to certain changes in the outlook that brought about cultural liberation for most Filipino women. The Japanese military occupation had suppressed people's activities because of the fear and suspicion that these would subvert their authority. Many men were arrested and executed on the mere suspicion that they were members of the Filipino underground movement against the Japanese. To be safe, therefore, as well as to be above suspicion, the men stayed at home while the women worked for their livelihood.

Most women in the urban centres were engaged in handicraft, dressmaking and small trade to earn money, while many others, who were widowed during the war were forced to fend for the economic survival of the family. Women in the rural areas were the ones doing the farming, fishing and raising of livestock because it was not safe for the men to be visible in the fields when the Japanese military patrols would come by. But like the men, the women, too, were exposed to the hazards of being suspected by the Japanese military of aiding the underground movement. Women during the period were also victims of unabated atrocities and crimes which were never brought to justice.

However, there were also women freedom fighters who fought side by side with men against the Japanese in some areas in Luzon. It has been documented that some towns and municipalities in Central Luzon were freed from the Japanese because of the struggle of the Hukboing Bayan Laban sa Hapon (HUKBALAHAP) to which these women belonged. It was this need to ensure the safety of the men and the survival of the family that led women to achieve a liberated outlook and to recognise that their place was not merely in the home nor their role simply to raise children. Having discovered their capabilities, many women after the war showed their assertiveness in fields where only the men used to thrive, such as in business and in the practice of their professions.

The post-war educational curricula continued the policy of equality for both men and women and universal education. Women began their entry into the professions that were previously dominated by men. Several women enrolled in the colleges of medicine, engineering, law, commerce and accountancy, architecture and other courses in the hard sciences like physics, chemistry, mathematics and statistics.

Statistics on literacy indicate that 89.40 per cent of Filipinos are literate. But even with a professional degree, a large number of women continued in the professions of teaching, nursing, midwifery, secretaries, sales clerks. Today it is encouraging to note that women have entered almost all professions, including those that were regarded as men's preserve. There are women in the military service and the police force. Records of the professional board examinations in the country reveal that women are in the following professions: agricultural engineers, engineers, architects, certified public accountants, chemical engineers, chemist, civil engineers, criminologists, customs brokers, dentists, dieticians, nutritionists, doctors, electrical engineers, electronics and communications engineers, foresters, geodetic engineers, geologists, lawyers, mechanical engineers, medical technologists, metallurgical engineers, midwives, mining engineers, nurses, optometrists, pharmacists, physical and occupational therapists, sanitary engineers, social workers, sugar technologists, veterinarians, as well as in other professions that do not need government board examinations. But women in the practice of their professions are still faced with the basic problem of how to gain the same level of recognition as men in the same field and how to obtain higher positions and salary scales. There is also the need for more women to develop skills in the scientific and technological professions. One reason why women do not train in these areas is their own cultural bias that the hard sciences are difficult and are only for men. Some parents are also guilty of harbouring a social bias thus discouraging their female children from taking degrees that are difficult. It is presumed that when they marry they may not really practice their professions. Women today, However, have reached a level of cultural and professional liberation that makes them compete with men without qualms.

From pre-colonial Philippines to the present, women have played an important role in the development and emergence of the Filipino nation. As exemplified by the pre-Hispanic *babaylan* or *katalonan* – the chief priestess in the barangay, the women of the revolution, to the women of the 19th century suffragist movement until the present day women leaders, history presents a moving tableau of Filipinas asserting their God-given right to participate in the development of community and nation equal with men.

Women in politics and public policy gradually increased in number starting 1938 when universal suffrage was finally won until the most recent 11th Congress of the Republic of the Philippines. Still their number remains a measly 10 percent of the total number of elected representatives and senators of the Philippine Congress.

It is commonly observed that most if not all women in national politics in the Philippines, past and present, belong to the elite class and to established political clans. "All are college educated and endowed with special expertise." At first their politics start in political campaigns with no legislative agenda specific for women's concerns. In time, however, largely in part to the existence of a strong women's movement in the Philippines, women's issues and concerns are increasingly incorporated in political platforms and the legislative agenda of women candidates and legislators.

Although there is perceptible trend towards greater participation of women both in elective and appointive positions, women are still very much in the minority. The enactment of the Party-list Law (RA 7941) raised hopes for the 12 marginalized sectors: labor, peasant, fisherfolk, urban poor, indigenous cultural communities, elderly, handicapped, women, youth, veterans, overseas workers and professionals. The implementation of the law however revealed both generic weaknesses and absence of viable mechanisms for government agencies to fully implement the law.

From the day the Bill of Rights was introduced in the Philippines during the American colonial period which allowed the people to exercise the freedom of speech, of association and assembly for redress of grievances, women's political participation has been quite visible. When women were granted the right of suffrage in 1935, which was the gain made by the demonstrations and lobbies by the women suffragettes, some women did not just stop at voting and campaign participation but also launched their candidacies for elective offices despite the odds that they had to face.

Women politicians have come a long way since then. Filipino women have competed strongly in a profession considered the preserve of astute men where competence is not the only criterion; one has also to be adept in the art of statecraft and in political manipulation. Through the years, women got themselves elected to almost all positions available in the Philippine political system such as seats in the Philippine Legislatures, governorships of provinces, mayorships of cities and municipalities, lesser political positions in provincial and city or municipal councils, as well as headships of barangay councils, the smallest units of government. Finally, a woman for the Presidency was legitimised by the Filipino people after 7 February 1986.

Since the post-war period women have also occupied positions in the Cabinet and some administrative functions in the bureaucracy. Women have been appointed to the Judiciary-from the Justices of the Supreme Court down to the lesser courts all over the country. Women have also participated in the drafting of the Philippine Constitutions, of 1973 and 1987. In the contemporary period women have organised peasant and labour movements to pressurise the government for the creation of policies that are beneficial to their groups. In the period of the' 70s, a few women organisations came up in opposition to the authoritarian rule of President Marcos.

Presently, more women's organisations have evolved not only to pressurise government for welfare policies for women but to take sides in crucial issues facing the nation. Women are also organising themselves in rural areas both the livelihood and for political purposes. Today's women's organisations all over the country have the opportunity to network and dialogue among themselves, to report on the nature of their work and achievements and identify the problems that women face in their respective areas. It appears that the process of networking allows women to be more assertive.

At the same time, it provides support for a more united position to push for legislative policies beneficial to them. But while such organisations have taken a more intelligent direction, it is not clear how women's issues and concerns are taken up by career women politicians. While the Filipino women's role in politics gives the impression that a lot has been achieved by the nature of their political participation, this study has gone on a more realistic inquiry on what the situation of women's participation in contemporary formal politics actually is.

The study has looked into the role of career women politicians in the national legislature and as local officials as well as ordinary women citizen's participation in politics.

The data for the present studty are based on the sample of common women citizens is made up of total of 350 interviewees. One hundred and fifty of the total number represent the middle class and the other 200 represent the lower class. Seventy-five per cent of the middle class women citizens come from Metro Manila and 25 per cent from a city in Mindanao. Of the lower class women, 25 per cent come from a small community in Metro manila known as the dumping place of garbage gathered from the city, an area which purportedly has 400 poor families whose means of livelihood is scavenging. The second 25 per cent of the respondents are household helpers and shop helpers in Metro Manila.

Finally, the last 50 per cent of the respondents are women who belong to organised groups like the urban poor, the peasant women's group, women in the labour force, and women who identified themselves as the poor fisherfolk community. The respondents were receptive to the survey although in certain cases some aspects of the questionnaire had to be explained to them. The most difficult part of the survey was fixing appointments. The second difficulty was getting back the filled-in questionnaire.

Because of its lengthiness it required time for the respondent to sit down and reflect on the nature of the questions asked. For this reason, the researcher had to simplify the questionnaire into two pages for the women of the lower class who were not highly educated. The survey made in the city in Mindanao was done by a research associate who is an instructor of political science in a university in the area who spoke the local language.

There was no problem communicating with the women politicians and the middle class respondents in English or for them to answer the questionnaires in their original form. Most respondents, however were sensitive to the question on their monthly income which was often left unanswered. But the researcher disregarded that as a criterion for classifying the respondent into middle or lower class. In the Philippines one can easily tell the social status of a person (upper, middle or lower) without using the income statistic as the immediate criterion.

The kind of lifestyle and the educational and professional status of a person will place her in the middle class category. The same can be said of the respondents belonging to the lower strata of society.

The survey questionnaires were received from UNESCO in November 1988 and were administered from that period until March 1989. However, it was necessary to continuously administer some questionnaires to obtain better answers. For instance, the survey on the organised women's groups among the lower strata was done in two attempts in order to find out how these groups would respond as compared to those who were sedentary and not organised. The research that had to be done on the performance of women legislators also took time to complete because of the voluminous material we examined in the archives of the Philippine Legislature. Collating the data is a long and tedious process.

Women in Politics

The Philippine Constitution of 1935 embodied the democratic principles of the American Constitution and the different Organic Acts that applied to the Philippines during the American colonial administration. President William McKinley's Instructions to the Second Philippine Commission and the subsequent laws that governed the Philippines provided for the application of the Bill of Rights in the country. The Bill provided safeguards for the right to life, liberty and property of the individual. It also granted people the freedom of speech, of the press, and the rights to assemble peacefully to petition the government for redress of grievances. The principle of equality before the law which democracy promised also implied that women should enjoy equal rights and protection under the law as men. But when elections were authorised by the Philippine Bill of 1902 and later by the Jones Law, women were not allowed to vote. In protest, women leaders organised rallies and demonstrations and milder forms of pressures so that the right of suffrage could be granted to them. This came, supposedly, in 1933 with Commonwealth Act No. 4112. And yet they were unable to vote. When the Tydings-McDuffie Law in 1934 authorised the writing of the Philippine Constitution, Women did not stop their lobbying. They wanted assurance that the right of suffrage for them would be included in the Constitution. The idea was however, not accepted by the delegates. Even President Quezon was reluctant. But finally when the draft of the Constitution was made, it was provided that women's suffrage would be granted it, in a plebiscite to be held two years after the adoption of the constitution, no less than 300,000 women possessing the necessary qualifications would vote affirmatively on the question. The women mobilised their forces in 1937 to give an affirmative answer in the plebiscite and at the same time voted for the first time for the local officials in this election. The final provision in the Constitution provided for universal suffrage for every Filipino who could comply with the voting requirements. This was the first successful women's political participation in the country. When women gained the right of suffrage they also, in effect, gained the freedom to participate in almost all kinds of political activity. While voting was women's basic entry into the political arena, there had been no law that prevented them (i) from campaigning for a particular candidate or candidates of their choice; (ii) from contributing to campaign funds of candidates, or (iii) from engaging in information drives on their ideas of good government. Women were considered qualified candidates for offices that men had occupied. The 1935 Constitution as well as the subsequent Philippine Constitutions of 1973 and 1987 had uphold women's right for political equality. They had the right to organise and conduct peaceful demonstrations and rallies and exercise the freedom of press and speech to promote whatever interests they wished. The 1987 Constitution has an explicit provision that the state should reorganise the role of women in nation building and ensure fundamental equality before the law for men and women (Art. II, Sec.14).

The 1987 Constitution also recognised the rights of non-governmental organisations to be consulted and to recommend policies that government would adopt. (Article XIII, Section 15 and 16). Women's organisations could recommend to government bodies as well as to the Legislative body the policies. The Legislature also allowed the representation of sectoral representatives by which a seat could be allocated for a women's representative, (Article VI, Section 5). Women could organise political parties or be members of political parties and complete in the elections in the country.

Even during the authoritarian rule of President Marcos, women were allowed to participate in government as politicians and party members as well as members of the bureaucracy. The 1973 Constitution had upheld the political participation of women. The only women's groups which the government had suppressed were those that were perceived to be leftist or those suspected of attempting to subvert or overthrow the government.

Today the government recognises the empowerment of the people and has institutionalised this in the Constitution. It is a very optimistic development as far as women's organisations are concerned.

Supplementary Legislations

Aside from the provisions protecting women's participation in politics there are other Constitutional aspects that ensure the protection of their rights. In the 1987 Constitution, Article XIII, Section 14 provides that:

> The state shall protect the working women by providing safe and healthful working conditions, taking into account their maternal functions, and such facilities and opportunities that will enhance their welfare and enable them to realise their full potential in the service of the nation.

This provision is further strengthened by Article XIII, Section 3 which says that:

> The state shall afford full protection to labour, local and overseas, organised and unorganised, and promote full employment and equality of employment opportunities for all. It shall guarantee the rights of all workers to self-organisation, collective bargaining and negotiations, and peaceful concerted activities, including the right to strike in accordance with law.

Regarding women's representation in the Legislature, Article VI, Section 5(2) provides that:

> For three consecutive terms after the ratification of the Constitution, one-half of the seats allocated to party-list representation shall be filled as provided by law, by selection or election from the labour, peasant, urban poor, indigenous cultural communities, women, youth, and such sectors as may be provided by law except the religious sector.

Executive Order No. 198 issued on 18 June 1988 implemented the provision. However, out of two women nominees only one was granted approval by the Commission on

Appointments. The confirmed representative assumed her functions but died while in office.

Other provisions giving importance to women are included in Article IV on Citizenship. Section 1 considers as citizens of the Philippines "those whose fathers or mothers are citizens of the Philippines; and Section 3, "those born before 17 January 1973 of Filipino mothers who elect Philippine citizenship upon reaching the age of majority. Section 4 also states that citizens of the Philippines who marry aliens shall retain their citizenship unless by their act or omission they are deemed under the law to have renounced it. The provision for Social Justice through Health (Article XIII Section 11) states that the state shall adopt an integrated and comprehensive approach to health development which shall endeavour to make essential goods, health and other social services available to all the people at affordable cost. There shall be priority for the needs of the underprivileged sick, elderly, disabled, women and children. The state shall endeavour to provide free medical care to paupers. The family is also protected under the Constitution (Article XV and Article II Section 12). The signing of the revised Family Code of the Philippines by President Corazon Aquino on 17 July 1987, was considered significant because it provided more adequate legislation to protect women and the family in the context of Filipino culture. President Aquino also signed the National Code of Marketing of Breastmilk Substitutes. The Agrarian Reform Law embodied in Republic Act 6657 signed on 10 June 1988, recognised rural women as qualified women members of the agricultural labour force and assured them equal rights to ownership of land, equal shares of the farm produce and representation in the advisory or appropriate decision-making bodies. There are other laws for the protection of women. For example is the Civil Code of the Philippines which was enacted in 1949. The Code had adopted principles that liberalised the rights of women. It declared that a 21-year-old woman is qualified to perform all acts of civil life unless the law specified the limitation. The Code also allowed mixed marriage between a Christian and a Muslim. There is also a General Banking Law or Republic Act No. 337 enacted in 1948 which allowed a married woman in her own right and in her own name to make deposits and withdraw the same and to receive dividends and interests from such deposits. Aside from the Labour Code which protects workers including women, there are other laws too for the protection of women and children. Republic Act No. 679, enacted in 1952, regulated the employment of women and children. Republic Act No. 1561, enacted in 1956, granted maternity leave to government employees under temporary appointment who had rendered less than two years of service.

Republic Act No. 2714, enacted in 1960 established a Women and Minors Bureau in the Department of Labour to monitor violations of the Labour Code on the protection of women and minors. Women were recruited to the Auxiliary Corps in the Armed Forces of the Philippines authorised by Republic Act No. 3835 which was enacted in 1963. While it was a gain for women because they had made a breakthrough in a profession exclusively reserved for men, they were to be discharged the moment they got married. In 1984, Presidential Decree No. 1910 was issued wherein the woman auxiliary could not be removed from service upon her marriage, if she had already completed at least three years of military service. During the rule of President Marcos Presidential decrees were issued in the interests of women and children. Among them was P.D. No. 148 in

1973 which amended the Women and Child Labour Law; P.D. 442 in 1974 or the Labour Code; P.D. 491 in 1974 which created the National Council; and P.D. No. 639 which was the Child and Youth Welfare Code.

The protection of women in the Labour Code is embodied in the provisions which prohibit discrimination in terms and condition of employment on account of sex upholds the principle of equal pay for men and women, the requirement of adequate physical facilities in the place of work, sufficient rest and meal periods, restrictions on hazardous jobs for women that require night work except in allowable cases. Discrimination practised by the employer which could lead to his prosecution include: his stipulation that single status be a condition for employment, denial of benefits provided in the code, discharge of women employees to prevent the enjoyment of benefits, discharge of women on account of pregnancy, or the refusal to allow women to return to their work for fear of another pregnancy. The Workmen's Compensation Law providing security and compensation for workers and dependents against injuries and death in the course of employment also include women workers and their dependents. But despite all these protective measures and threats of penalty to the employers who violate them, discrimination against women workers still takes place.

The Philippines' participation in the United Nations Conference on Women which adopted or forwarding Looking Strategies for the Advancement of Women in 1975 in Nairobi takes the credit for having spurred the awareness for the welfare and advancement of women in the country. The National Commission on the Role of Women (NCRW) through Presidential Decree No. 633 was created as a result of the UN initiative. At the same time, a Philippine Target and Strategies for full Participation of Women in

Socio-Economic Development (1980-1985) was implemented through the Letter of Instruction No. 1066 on 18 September 1980. Under the Aquino Administration, a Philippine Development Plan for Women has been incorporated into the National Economic development Authority (NEDA) Medium Term Plan for 1987-1992 in order that women's socio-economic interests be promoted as part of the economic development of the country. President Aquino had issued Executive Order No. 348 directing the various government agencies and bureaux to implement this plan from 1987 to 1992.

Various government agencies have adopted some women's programmes and assigned them to certain bodies within their agencies for implementation. The Department of Labour and Employment has the Bureau of Women and Young Workers; the Department of Agriculture has the Bureau of Agricultural Extension; the Department of Social Welfare has the Bureau on Women. Agencies like the Philippine Overseas Employment Agency and the Overseas Workers Welfare Administration are assigned to take care of overseas workers and their problems including those of women workers. In the two Houses of the Philippine Congress there are several pending bills in the interests of women particularly some concerning protective measures for overseas workers. Non-governmental organisations concerned with women's issues are also working on bills for women that they would like the legislators to pass into laws.

Women's movements in the Philippines can be classified according to their motivation-those that are politically motivated or those that are welfare oriented; or according to its class character-those led by elite women or those led by women of the masses; and also according to its ideological underpinnings those that have nationalist objectives or those that are feminist inspired. Feminism and the women's movement is a current concern.

When the women of the 1930s mobilised to be granted the right of suffrage under the law the move was political. It was also inspired by feminism and was led by an elite group of women. While it was feminist in character the women at that time were not aware of the term. Feminism is defined as

> awareness of women's oppression and exploitation in society, at work and within the family and conscious action by women and even by men to change this situation. Anyone who recognises the existence of sexism or discrimination on the basic of gender or male domination and patriarchy and who takes some action against it is a feminist.

When peasant women joined men in demonstrations against the government in the 1930s and in the earliest post-war period over the issues of land tenancy, land distribution, exploitation of peasants by the landlords and the inimical sharing system, the motivation was to promote the welfare of the peasants and the tillers of the soil against the landlords, interests. The peasant movement was a mass-oriented movement that expected government to work for a social justice policy for the peasants. Its ideological underpinning was nationalism and socialism. Socialism in the Philippines also expresses the working class aspiration to control the mode of production. The same can be said of women participation in the labour demonstrations during the same period. Often times peasants and workers supported each other in mass actions against the government initiated by either group.

During the Japanese occupation of the country from December 1941 to February 1944, the women who joined the HUKBALAHAP were motivated by nationalism and self-preservation. But all these women did not come from the peasant and the rural working class. Some of them belonged to middle class homes in the provinces and were college educated. But they were forced to take up arms to protect themselves and their families from the enemy and other forms of abuses. Like the men, many of them fought bravely in the field against the Japanese. After the war, however, the ideological underpinning became more prominent. Women were carried into the mainstream of socialist ideology because of the government's neglect to offer a solution to the land question and the exploitative landlord-peasant relation which was to the detriment of the latter. The same was true with women in the labour unions owing to the perennial unfair labour practices.

Another aspect of how women have organised themselves in the Philippines is the formation of civic associations to take care of the welfare of certain deprived groups in society. There are hundreds of groups of this nature, led by elite and wealthy women who have so much to offer. Charity and civic works also have helped these philanthropic women give direction to their lives. Together with these groups are the religious organisations which also perform civic and welfare functions. But while there are several women's groups of this kind all over the country, they cannot be characterised as part of a women's movement because each group works by itself and not in the context of a sustained co-ordinated effort, as a united grouping of women making a civic and welfare effort to develop the country.

The most popular group of women are the career politicians, who have not, however, organised themselves to be one in purpose. Each is a person distinct and separate from the other. The only common line among them is that they are all involved in introducing certain recommendations which they think should constitute the policies to be applied either to their respective communities or to the whole country. The other notable aspect is that they are in a profession which throws them into constant competition and possible conflict with men. Women career politicians are continuously increasing in number since independence.

During the Marcos rule, the women's movement made further strides. Ideological discussions were often conducted by study groups along socialist lines. The women who were involved in the political movement were indifferent to the idea of voting or participation in the referenda conducted several times during the period. By holding referenda, Marcos had extracted his alleged mandate from the people. Women's political participation was manifested by the public demonstrations and rallies that they conducted to oppose the dictatorship. They risked a great deal because of the suppressive policy of the government against any opposition to the regime. In fact some women were reported to have been arrested and tortured and some even died.

The women who participated in the movement against the dictatorship came from all walks of life. Their involvement was most significant, for it meant that they had to forget their own safety and the safety of their families while putting up their political opposition. Some participants in these movements have rejoined the women's movement under the Aquino administration. There was also a change in the names of the women's organisations. Their movement today has become more attractive even for the less adventurous because the environment has become comparatively less suppressive. There are also incentives for women's organisations to obtain fundings for their projects from foreign donors.

Some women groups which participated during the EDSA Revolution on 22-25 February 1986 were not there to support Mrs. Aquino or the military faction that broke away. The primary reason was to oust the dictator. But certainly some groups, particularly the religious and the cause-oriented were Cory Aquino's loyalists. Some women, however, moved away from the cause-oriented groups after the Aquino government was established.

Under the Aquino administration there has been a more intelligent direction of the women's movement; there exist now more opportunities for networking and dialogue among women's organisations from all over the Philippines. Women can discuss their problems and possible solution and take common stands regarding women's issues. There has been more education and discussion about gender issues and feminism as a women's ideology. The less education ones were organised by their more intelligent sisters and oriented to the current political ideological, welfare and gender issues. There has been extensive efforts to organise women from all walks of life—the urban poor, the peasant women, women in factories, women in fishing villages, domestic helpers from overseas who come home, the indigenous women, even the enlightened prostitutes and entertainers, women in the media, and almost any sector where there are women.

But while women were organised and given education and orientation to make them understand gender issues and feminism, not all of them have fully absorbed its significance. The issues that lower class women understand easily are those concerned with welfare and benefits. This conclusion is derived from the researcher's participation in three big workshops of hundreds of women from all walks of life held in different place in Metro Manila at different dates within the period of the research. The biggest umbrella organisation for women groups from all over the Philippines is the Women's Action Network for Development (WAND) composed of 76 women organisations representing various sectors. Another umbrella organisation is the General Assembly Binding Women for Reforms, Integrity, Equality Leadership and Action (GABRIELA) composed of ten women's organisations. Religious institutions have their own network composed of poorer women groups. The agenda of these three broad networks of women's organisations include women's development and welfare, gender issues and women's empowerment. But there are other organisations that are not part of these broad networks. College and universities have also organised women's centres within their units. Six universities in Metro Manila have done this, so far. A conservative estimate would place the number of women's organisations in the country at 300. Some organisations, however, have their regional chapters or units.

Women from various sectors have agreed to organise as a result of a political consciousness—that only as organised groups can they be effective in their endeavour. When organised, women can become a potent political forces. They had proved this during the period of the dictatorship and in the outing of that dictatorship. Under the Aquino administration the women's movement has also taken more important political positions. Among these are (i) the issues of the U.S. military bases in the Philippines which some women groups would like to see terminated, (ii) the ban on nuclear weapons, (iii) the promulgation of the agrarian reforms law which the rural and nationalistic women's groups would like implemented effectively, and (iv) the position on what to do with the Marcos's stolen wealth as well as the country's foreign debts. In a general sense, the women's movement has taken up these issues as national concerns. Recently, women leaders of some organisations have also taken the initiative to associate gender issues and feminism with the greater national issues at hand.

Women participation in politics in the Philippines has taken five forms: participation by voting; campaigning for a particular candidate; becoming candidates themselves; assuming positions in the Cabinet or the bureaucracy; and organising and mobilising women for political empowerment as earlier discussed. The record showed that the number of women voters was 492,032 in 1937 when they first cast their votes on the plebiscite issue of women's suffrage and the election of local officials. By 1988, the number increased to 13,650,000. A study made by Luzviminda Tancangco indicated that voter turn-out among women was higher than among men in 18 out of 22 elections since 1947. In the 1988 election according to the Commission on Election statistics, it was 79.29 per cent for women while for men it was only 68.64 per cent. Generally there were more women voters than men.

The Tangcangco study also indicated the role of women as campaigners in the various elections held in the Philippines. Campaigns were done not only on an informal basis as among friends and relatives but by a more formal organisation of women. Cited were the Women for Magsaysay for President Movement in 1953; the Blue Ladies for Marcos in 1969; the Osmena Women's League and the Osmena Pearls in 1981. During the 1988 Snap election, there were groups known as the Cory's Crusaders, the UNIDO Ladies, the Volunteers for Cory and Doy, and the Antipolo Ladies for Cory and Doy. Women as campaigners were considered useful, not only as distributors of campaign material but also as charming entertainers, party hostesses, and persuasive vote getters. In the 1987 Congressional election, the Umbrella organisation known as GABRIELA campaigned for the candidacies of the Alliance for New Politics (ANP) which included a women candidate. Unfortunately, she did not win.

There was also an all women's political party, the *Kababaihan Para sa Inang bayan* (KAIBA) formed in time for the 1987 Congressional elections. The GABRIELA and other women groups supported KAIBA candidate who won a seat in 1987 Congressional election. But the votes for her did not all come from women's organisations. The elites in her district also supported her. The KAIBA is the first attempt by women to form an all-women's political party. Since 1946, the government was sympathetic to the participation of women in the Cabinet and other government bodies. There has been a woman appointee to the Cabinet of almost all the presidential administrations that had served the country. But the position that the lady cabinet member has perennially held is the portfolio for social work, a position often associated with woman's service for the needy and the helpless. Under the Marcos administration, aide from the social work portfolio occupied by women, the Ministry of Human Settlements was headed by Mrs. Imelda Marcos which had control of all the agencies of the government that attended to the social services in the country or what was termed at that time as "the 11 basic needs of the people". When the Aquino administration assumed office, Mrs. Aquino appointed three women cabinet secretaries and eight women undersecretaries out a total of eight Cabinet secretaries and 66 undersecretaries. But as the government continued in office, the women Cabinet members were replaced by men. At the time of writing this report, there is only one woman sitting in the Cabinet, two women Justices in the Supreme Court, and three women as heads of constitutional offices. Women have been candidates in the various local elections held in the country since 1947 and have served in various capacities—as provincial governors, mayors of cities and municipalities, women council and provincial board members, and many as heads of their *barangays.* Mrs. Imelda Marcos was appointed Metro Manila Governor with jurisdiction over four cities and 13 municipalities from 1978 up to the fall of her husband in 1986. Her control over the Metropolitan Manila local governments and the various agencies under the umbrella of the Ministry of Human Settlements which provided 11 basic social services to the country made her very powerful. The local election of 18 January 1988 had the most number of women candidates—5,517 in all. The number of positions to be contested was 16,904. Finally the election results showed that 1,678 women were elected out of 5,517 candidates, in other words, 30 per cent of them got elected, thus occupying 10 per cent of seats. Candidacy to the positions in the Philippine Legislature has also been attractive to women. Electoral contests in this area were considered difficult and expensive but records show that a number of women were able to hurdle the election challenge and win seats in the House of Representatives and the Philippine Senate. A representative to the House is elected by the constituents district. During the First Congress (1946-1949) there was one woman representative from the lone district of Bukidnon; during the Second Congress (1949-1953) another woman won a seat from the lone district of Bataan; for the third Congress (1953-1957) a woman won a seat from the First district of apiz; for the Fourth Congress (1957-1961) another lone woman won a seat representing a province in the Bicol region; during the Fifth Congress (1961-1965) there were two women representatives, one from the Third district of Albay and the other the First district of Pampanga; during the Sixth Congress (1965-1969) there were six women winners—from the lone district of Batanes, the First district of La Union, the Third district of Albay, the First district of Pampanga, the Third district of Iloilo and the Second district of Layte; for the Seventh Congress (1969-1972) two women won seats, one from a district in Iloilo and the other from a district in Pangasinan.

The records of the Philippine Senate show that since 1955, women Senators have been elected to the Senate. Senators are elected at large by the nation's electorates. The first woman Senator was elected during the 1955-1961 Senate; another woman Senator won during the 1959-1967 term. A woman Senator won for the 1963-1969 term while there were two women senators who won seats during the 1967-1972 Senate. One woman Senator was elected during the 1965-1971 Senate. She was re-elected in the 1971 Senatorial election. But while it was encouraging that women had broken the barriers in national politics, their membership in the National Legislature did not even constitute one per cent of the total membership. The incumbent members of Congress in 1972 were not able to finish terms of office because President Marcos declared martial law on 21 September, 1972, abolishing the Congress.

It was not until July 1978, that the new unicameral Congress known as the Interim Batasang Pambansa was convened after an election. Ten women won seats during the 1978-1984 Assembly and another ten for the 1984-1989 Assembly. But this second Assembly was abolished after the Snap election of 7 February 1986. Mrs. Corazon Aquino was legitimised as the new President by the support of people power which ousted President Marcos. The next

Congressional election was on 11 May 1987, under the 1987 Philippine Constitution. Twenty-one women gained seats, in the bicameral Congress, 18 in the House of Representatives, two in the Senate and one appointed as a sectoral representative.

Women career politicians generally come from elite and middle class families. Seventy per cent of the women who won seats in the three National Legislatures being studied have an elite background. To be an elite in the Philippines means one must come from a traditionally rich family which has been prominent in the community where it originated and must also be known nationally. Members of the family must have served in important private and government offices in the past or hold such positions at present by virtue of their prestige and prominence. Most elite families were also known to have provided leadership in their respective communities. While elites are the recognised rich people in the community, it is difficult to measure how much wealth they have. But one criterion is that the public are aware of their business interests in the community and the nation.

Middle class socio-economic background means that the family or the person is not wealthy but has college education. Expertise through education allows the person to have a lucrative position in the place of work. The person can afford to own a house, enjoy all the basic luxuries of living, maintain a car or two, send children to decent schools and have the gadgets that are the hallmark of modern living. Thirty per cent of women in the three National Legislature under consideration can be classified as middle class.

Those who served in the Constitutional Commission of 1986 considered themselves competent professionals. While they preferred to be classified as middle class and all were working women, a closer examination had shown that 33 per cent could be designated as elites. An examination of the composition of each Philippine legislature revealed that 70 per cent of the women members of the Interim Batasang Pambansa of 1978-1984 could be classified as elite. The social background of the women members in the 1984-1986 Batasang Pambansa indicated a 90 per cent and 10 per cent middle class origin. In the present Congress 62 per cent women can be classed as elite.

Elections in the Philippines have been so expensive despite a rule against election expenditures, that only the rich and those with money can afford to compete. Prestige and popularity are not sufficient factors in winning. Wealth counts very much. Wealthy women, who can afford to compete in the national elections, do so by virtue of their birth, marriage to rich husbands who are supportive of their political inclination and through their own business acumen to make money. Records show that a few of these women members of the Legislature were holding high positions in business corporations before their election. Some of these business holdings are established nationwide but most are confined to their region of origin and to Metro Manila. Several women are closely related to other known politicians in the country who have served in the past and the present governments. It is interesting to know that at least four of the incumbent women in Congress are related to three or four other members of the same Congress. Women politicians are not to be blamed for this kind of situation. Elite politics have often brought this about. As has been stated earlier, people with money have a better chance of winning the elections. It turns out, therefore, that wealthy elites belonging to the same clan will have a better chance of winning as long as they are distributed in different electoral district. Patronage politics prevails in the country and women politicians have benefited by this practice both in the national and local levels of government. But it must also be noted that politics in the country has encouraged a bandwagon mentality. Politicians capitulate to a particular presidential candidate because of the prospect that a wealthy person will have a surer chance of winning. And when the presidential candidate finally wins and holds the reins of power, politicians polarise around the presidency.

This happened in 1986. In the 1987 and 1988 elections the general sentiment in the country was to oust the politicians identified with the Marcoses. Several people from the cause-oriented groups became political candidates overnight to provide an alternative leadership so that people could choose from among them and get rid of these politicians identified with the previous regime. The majority of the winners in both the Congressional and the local elections held in 1987 and 1988, respectively, were from the cause-oriented groups which belonged to the broad coalition of groups supporting President Corazon Aquino. Several women winners in these elections were identified with the pro-Aquino coalition. As has been indicated, these two elections encouraged more women to be candidates and women came to occupy political seats. Women politicians at the local level of government come from families considered prominent and well-to-do in the locality where they were elected to office. Most of these families are considered the elites of the community. Before their election to office, many were involved in socio-civic activities by which they had gained recognition from the residents. Several had been engaged in activities that involved public service to the community. It must be noted that 75 per cent of the local women politicians were working women before they assumed elective office. Their husbands can be described as stable businessmen or professional practitioners with substantial earnings. Both husbands and wives are members of almost all the available civic and social organisations in the community, the kind of people to whom the poorer residents can turn for financial assistance or any other help when in need or in case of an emergency. They stand ready and willing to give their money and time to charity work and extend a helping hand to others.

They are also willing to spend their funds during elections. But while the women politicians in the local government are generally recognised as the prominent women and the elite of the community, the socio-economic-economic status of at least 75 per cent would be middle class and only 25 per cent would fall under the category of the traditionally known elites. Some women politicians in the local government cite their parents as farmers or people engaged in some form of agricultural activity.

As farmers they owned substantial land to be able to send some children to college. Most local women politicians gained their status after they set up their own homes. Not all of them were rich. People elected them to office in recognition of what they had done for the community or for what they are capable of doing. In local communities people also give recognition to the intellectual capacity, kindliness and humility of candidates. If the candidates possess these traits they have a chance of getting elected even if they are not rich. It must also be taken into consideration that in the local election of 18 January 1988, the President's supporters carried almost all the candidates under the yellow banner to victory. But in the subsequent poll for the election of barangay officials in April 1989, voters were reportedly less enthusiastic.

Almost all women career politicians had actively participated in social organisations and in civic and charity works. They had shown assertiveness and assumed leadership roles during their student days or in the practice of their professions. Women who became national leaders generally belonged to the families with access to politicians and politics or had members of their families in government service or engaged in active political careers.

They also had friends who were politicians or relatives of politicians. When young, they had been exposed to political discussions or matters related to government and politics, and as members of the community they had displayed a strong sense of social consciousness and political awareness and concern. Women national legislators have interesting academic profiles. A majority had obtained their education from exclusive schools in the country. Several had pursued special studies or degree programmes abroad. Those who had served in the Interim Batasang Pambansa of 1978-1984 had the following academic qualifications: Master of Arts degree in Education—2; four-year college degrees in Education, Commerce, Bachelor of Arts, and in Economics—8; graduation with honours, *magna cum laude,* and *cum laude*—2. Women legislators elected during the 1984-1986 Batasang pambansa included three lawyers, one with a Master of Law and another in Education; one was a social worker while another graduated with Bachelor of Economics, *magna cum laude;* one had gone through special courses in languages, painting and designing in a European school; and two were High School graduates but with experience in government service and public life.

The Constitutional Commission had two women lawyers, one media woman with a doctorate in English, one registered nurse with a doctorate in public health, one nun, and one civic leader with training in music. The incumbent women legislators elected for the 1987-1992 Congress have the following degrees: two medical doctors, two with PhD. degrees, two with M.A. degrees, two educators, 11 with B.A. or B.S. degrees, and two college undergraduates. Women legislators who may have appeared lacking in formal academic degrees have compensated such shortcoming by their wealth, experience, social status and powerful political access. The ages of the national level women politicians ranged from 35 to 70 years. Of the local level women politicians, two had completed degrees in social work, ten had done Bachelor of Arts, five had graduated with bachelor of Science degrees and eight with Bachelor of Science in Education, one had a doctorate in Education, nine had law degrees, one finished secretarial science and two were high school graduates. Most of the degree holders had worked in some office or enterprise before recruitment to politics. A few were self-employed.

Prior to entering politics, some women had worked as teachers, office managers, radio announcers, company cashiers, sales representatives, and social workers. Some were self-employed running their own businesses and were primarily housewives until they were convinced of joining politics. Almost all had been active in socio-civic work. Some had taken part in campaigns for particular candidates in the past, usually for relatives or close friends.

A majority of the incumbents were involved in the activities of the cause-oriented groups in their communities after the Ninoy Aquino assassination. Most said they were anti-Marcos. Those who are not currently in power but were former politicians, are engaged in private business. Ninety-five per cent of the local women politicians are married and their ages range from 22 to 66. Ninety per cent of them are Catholic. Most of those who are married have adult children who are already engaged in their own professionals or have families of their own.

All women career politicians hire helpers, housekeepers, cooks and drivers and other household staff, perhaps to compensate for their absence and for their lack of time to attend to household chores for the family. It is the practice in the Philippines for affluent households to have helpers. But it is significant that some of these important national women politicians said that they tried to cook for the family when they had the time.

Fortunately it is easy to hire help in the Philippines especially when the helpers know that they will be in the employ of important people of the community. In the performance of their duties, women politicians are often dependent on technocrats. A competent technical man is helpful, or else it is a folly for a woman to be in politics when not trained in the administrative and political requirements of the job. Wise women politicians also have media men and image builders in their employ.

In most cases, women career politicians' entry into politics, especially at the national level, was a result of the encouragement of male relatives or friends who had access to politics or were in politics themselves. Those with family connection has either their father, grandfather, uncle, brother, husband or cousins in politics. Some of these male politicians have already established reliable mass bases in their respective communities. It is presumed that women were encouraged to join in politics by those predisposed to political power. There is also a prevailing attitude that politics runs in the family. Some women politicians were assured of mass support through their relatives in politics who had access to a well-organised political machine and party support. The women's own social experience and good public relations contributed to their getting and gaining votes.

In fact, the reasons that have influenced some politicians' entry into politics can be summarised as follows: it was pure chance that they were community's civic leaders; the desire to change the status quo where politics was controlled by traditional politicians (referring to the Marcos group); the Ninoy Aquino assassination; dictates of the people; pressure of time (referring to the need to take a political position in a crisis); persuasion by friends among the cause-oriented groups; the desire to fight Marcos and his cronies; the desire to render service to the people; to prove one's capability for leadership; to test one's popularity with the people; to speak on behalf of the youth (youth representative); and to bring people closer to the political leader.

They had overlooked one reason, namely to promote and protect women's interests.

The new women politicians mentioned some of the obstacles they faced in their entry into politics: the lack of finances for campaigns; the fact that they were virtually unknown or did not have political leaders to help their cause; and the difficulty in contending with other politicians with well-established national statures. The most serious problem was the constraints and responsibilities demanded of politicians, and at the same time, their responsibilities to the home and family.

While in office, the obstacles included intrigues from oppositions, letters of threats sometimes from insurgents, and black propaganda from rivals. Women politicians also have to contend with the pressures of internal politics. At the time of their election the women in the present Congress were members of the different political parties which constituted the coalition that supported Mrs. Aquino. The distribution was as follows: UNIDO-4; UNIDO-LP-1; LP-Salonga-1; PDP-Laban-5; LB-DP-Laban-2; NP-1; LB-1 and Kaiba-1. Four women legislators launched their candidacies as Independents. The sectoral representative for women and the disabled did not belong to any political party nor did she agree to affiliate with any. She was a Presidential appointee. The other woman representative appointed by the President was not confirmed by the Commission on Appointments. She took her case to the Supreme Court but lost. After two years in office some of these women changed their party affiliations following the prevailing political polarisation taking place in the Senate and the House of Representatives.

Ninety per cent of the incumbent women politicians in the national and local governments did not have lengthy careers in politics. In the past administrations, at least 20 per cent of the national-level women politicians had built their political careers by first serving in the elective local government positions before launching their candidates for national elective offices. Some of these women had been re-elected and had learned the political game in the process. A few local women politicians in the past had been in office for several terms and had gradually become competent at their jobs. There were cases where the so-called local political dynasties had dominated leadership for several years and where the local elective positions had been held by one family or one clan; women members, thus were no exception as office holders.

In the Philippines there is no marked discrimination against a woman politician as has been shown in our earlier discussion and by historical political experience. It is interesting to note that the role models cited by the women politician in the survey were all male politicians who have a track record for their statesmanship and able leadership tested through years of public service. The reasons for their choice can be summarised briefly: competence, outstanding achievements, leadership, political ideas, personality, dynamism, dedication, concern for the poor, concern for victims of military abuses, and statesmanship.

Notably, women politicians believed that their political support came from friends, the youth, the general public, from women, and also men. Most of the women incumbents are not members of organised women's groups. But they think that individual women politician can still be effective in mobilising support for themselves even if they are not members of groups or political parties. In a real sense, women are not proportionately represented in politics and the respondents think that there should be greater representation in decision-making for the women today.

They agree that in politics women must be treated on equal terms with men; they think that few women occupy higher positions in the bureaucracy because few are prepared to carry out the work requirements in the higher echelons; there seemed to be a feeling that women are often underestimated in their competence and capacity. Many disagreed with the idea of setting a quota for women politicians. There is still a need for women to wield real influence in government.

The major obstacles that women politicians have to overcome is the belief that women are weak in facing problems. One handicap is that their projects cannot be implemented owing to a lack of funds. What they need is support so that their work can have some impact in their community.

The other negative perceptions about women politicians are: they cannot sustain themselves in a crisis; their freedom of movement is limited even in simply going around and knowing the constituency; they cannot travel around without a companion; they may be soft in making decisions that require toughness; they may become pregnant and this will obstruct their political duties and functions; it will be difficult for them to compete with male machismo; there is still a prevailing bias against women even if the male will not admit it. It was conceded that sometimes some women cannot help but feel inferior to men. As an exercise in self-appraisal women career politicians attributed their success in politics to patience and perseverance, sincerity, loyalty to the constituency, and an attitude of sympathy towards the people. The implication in this appraisal is that these attributes are generally missing in men.

Those women who had felt a sense of insecurity when they were new in politics were able to master it and had adjusted to the demands of the office. However, even women politicians themselves are not united in their attitude regarding choices between a man and a woman politician. Some may still prefer to support a male politician depending on his competence. They think that an ideal woman politician is one who is competent tough, dynamic, energetic, and knowledgeable. She must be strong willed, decisive, good and strong.

Performance Appraisal

It is pertinent to note that there is no denying that women politicians take their jobs seriously. The legislative output of women legislatures during the period 1978-1984, was affected by the prevailing trend at the Batasang Pambansa where cabinet bills were given more priority while one individually introduced bills had difficulty of passage. It must also be noted that President Marcos had continued issuing Presidential Decrees until February 1986. Women legislators' accomplishments during the period included the introduction of bills of local application that dealt with the changing of names, creation of municipalities, setting up of health centre or hospitals, upgrading of the status of schools, related welfare projects and livelihood projects. Only two women legislators introduced bills on women whereas they often became co-authors of bills that male legislators had sponsored. For the period 1978-1984 a total of 1100 bills were introduced or co-authored by the women members of the Assembly and only 103 became actual Batas Pambansa.

The women legislators had also contributed to the passage of 174 resolutions. During the 1984-1986 Batasang Pambansa, a total of 488 parliamentary bills and 196 resolutions were initiated or co-authored by women legislators. This second Batasan was prematurely abolished in February 1986, and no bill sponsored by women became a law. Among the women members a former Justice of the Supreme Court introduced the most number of viable bills.

Significantly, during the 1978-1984 Batasan, one lady legislator introduced extremely relevant bills, whose subject matters have continued to be of concern to the country till today, namely: an act governing the public inspection of the assets and liabilities of all the members of the Batasang Pambansa for the purpose of public transparency. There was also an act making *Tagalog* as the *lingua franca* in the Philippines; another act required that drugs and other medical substances be sold under their generic names instead of their brand names; and finally an Act requiring locally manufactured cigars and cigarettes to carry the label, "smoking is dangerous to health".

Unfortunately none of these Acts ever saw the light of day. They were tabled and forgotten. Records of the Congress which opened in July 1987 indicated that at the end of the First Regular Session, 11,000 bills were introduced in the Lower House, of which only 53 became laws. Women members had affixed their names to 1,517 bills and to 160 resolutions either as sponsors or co-authors. The sectoral representative for women had passed a resolution making the month of March the month for women. With regard to legislations concerning women, a total of 152 bills were introduced as of December 1988. Of these, 126 were sponsored by male members of the Lower House; only 26 were introduced by female members.

They related to the need for day-care centres, standardised salaries for domestic helpers equal rights for women with men, more protection for women in family relations, protection against illegal recruitment for overseas work, ban on mail order brides, maternity benefits for both parents, protection for nurses working overseas, population issues, social problems and protection for women workers. In relation to the general Congressional output as of February 1990 the Lower House introduced 28,091 bills, of which 208 became laws while the Senate introduced 1,420 bills, of which 41 became laws. Women legislators indicated that upon their assuming office, they tackled the following issues: environment, human rights, ban on nuclear weapons, American military bases, pornography, foreign debt, economic problems, rights of government employees, agro-based industrialisation, improvement of the investment climate, food production, agricultural improvement, agrarian reform, education, health and the question of autonomy for local governments. What is sad about these efforts is that these bills which became laws and which related to what the women had worked for, were all authored by the male members of Congress.

Further, the women at the local level of government listed the following tasks to which they had given priority: beautification and health service in the barangays; establishment of the Philippine National Red Cross blood bank, and an emergency hospital, improvement of the puericulture centres, promotion of family planning, visits to districts, creation of training programmes for out-of-school youth, creation of jobs, programmes for government employees who opted for early retirement, creation of fast track development programmes as counter-insurgency measures, and the creation of women related activities for community development. Many women politicians appeared to have common goals and plans to beautify and develop their respective communities, promote youth development, protect and promote the safety of people especially in insurgency prone areas, promote health facilities and services and give assistance to the oppressed and displaced inhabitants in conflict zones.

In nutshell, there are three crucial issues in Philippine politics today: what to do with the US bases in the country; how to immediately implement the Agrarian Reform. Law as the government's centre-piece for social justice; and how to prevent political corruption. On the issue of the U.S. Bases, two women legislators took anti-bases positions while two other women legislators preferred to study the matter thoroughly to determine what preparations needed to be made in case of a pull-out. On the agrarian question, one woman legislator opted for a pro-peasants agrarian reform law while another was opposed to the provisions that would deprive the landlords of most of their land. Two women legislators were also linked to certain vested interests and commercial transactions that were questionable.

The sample of the common women citizens is composed of women from both the middle and the lower class. The middle class women come from the urban centres—75 per cent from the Metropolitan Manila area and 25 per cent from a city in Mindanao. The lower class women in the sample belong to three groups: (i) organised women workers in the industry, the urban poor, the peasant women, and some women coming from a community of fisherfolk; (ii) women helpers in shops and restaurants and domestic helpers in households; and (iii) housewives from a barangay community within Metro Manila who live near a garbage dump.

The age of the middle class women ranges from 25-65 years. Ninety per cent are married. They have three to six children between the ages of 2 and 35. Some children are already professionals. These women have completed their college education. Ninety per cent are working women, while 10 per cent used to work but quit their jobs upon marriage and are plain housewives. They are, however, involved in socio-civic activities in their communities. The husbands are college graduates and professionals. They have a lucrative employment or are self-employed, which means that they have their own business or are practicing their professions.

The professional women described their work as teachers, secretaries, medical technologists, nurses, doctors, marketing trainers, sales representatives, cashiers, office managers, government employees, dentists, and private office employees. The self-employed women said they were business women, beauty salon operators, dressmakers, farmers, doctors, dentists and optometrists. The majority are Catholics, the rest are Protestants, born again Christians, Evangelical Christians and Aglipayan. There are two Muslim women from Mindanao City. Almost all these women are members of social, civic, religious and political associations. The civic associations are the parents-teachers, the homeowners and the community beautification club.

In the lower class category, few of the women workers have completed college and have to settle for the jobs available to them in the factories. Some are college undergraduates or high school graduates. Some domestic and shop helpers have finished high school but most have not. A majority are migrants to Manila from the province. The women from the dump site have not finished high school, most not even their elementary education. Ninety per cent of the industry workers are single women. The domestic and shop helpers are all single women. The ages of these two groups range from 18 to 30 years. The urban poor and the rural women are married and have children. Their ages range from 25 to 55 years and they have children between 2 to 25 years. Many indicated that their religion was either Catholic or born again Christians but others did not divulge their faith. The husbands of these women are as little educated as they are. The husbands have no fixed jobs except those who are peasants and fishermen. The rural women come from towns close to Metro Manila.

Middle class women have an adequate exposure to the media and to all kinds of information available in the country. Almost all reported that they read newspapers, watch the news on television, listen to talk shows nearly everyday and to the news on the radio when necessary. They listed at least 17 newspapers as their daily source of news on the radio when necessary. They listed at least 17 newspapers as their daily sources of news, a majority of which are published in English. Many indicated that they read not only the front page news but also the columns of noted columnists and even the editorials. The talk shows on television that they patronize are those that deal with the political issues of the day. They also watch the entertainment portion of the television shows. They cited three international news magazines as their frequent source of foreign news aside from the foreign section of the daily newspapers.

On the other hand, the women workers in the industry have more media exposure than the rest of the lower class groups. They read newspapers in the vernacular at least three times a week. Ten per cent said that they read the front page news of newspapers in English and sometimes they listen to talk shows on television if they had the time. It is presumed that most homes in the urban centres even those of the poorer segment of society, try to afford a television set. The transistor radio is the common source of news for the common people.

Members of the organised peasant and fisher women groups and the rural women as well as the poor urban women indicated that they always listened to the news on their transistor radios. Besides, they listened to their favourite radio commentator almost everyday. The domestic and shop helpers prefer to watch the entertainment programmes on television whenever they have the opportunity. Those who can listen to the radio prefer soap operas. The women near the garbage dumpsite do not seem to have access to media and information, unlike the other groups. Most do not even have a radio but if they do their preference is for soap operas which they refer to as radio dramas.

There is no problem with the voting participation of middle class women. Only 2.6 per cent stated that they had intentionally refused to vote in certain elections. The reason given was that they felt that no one deserved their vote. This is an indication of strong political awareness. However, political indifference was also shown by 5.3 per cent of the respondents who said it would not make any difference if they did not vote. Those who had exercised their voting rights said that it was a service to the people and the country to do so. Their reasons for voting for a particular candidate are summarised as follows: the person is better qualified; his/her past service record in politics is good; the candidate has integrity, competence and good performance; the candidate is intelligent and active; and the candidate is close to the people.

The reasons given by the few who choose to vote for the party are as follows: her affiliation with the party; she agrees with the party platform; and she considers the party programme to be beneficial to the people. Most of these women indicated that they discussed politics with members of their family. Some said that their fathers and the husbands were the ones most interested in politics. Others, however, also stated that none of the family members was interested in politics. Around 8 per cent of the women said that they were the ones interested in politics in their homes. A majority of them did not favour the idea of any member of their family joining politics. The reasons given were: politics will make the family poor; it is a dirty business; it will make the life miserable for the candidate who loses; and it will be difficult to deal with some manipulative people. Those on the other hand, who think that they would like to see someone in the family enter politics gave the following reasons: those in politics can contribute to the development of the community; some members of the family are already tested politicians; there is nothing wrong in being a politician as long as young have people's support. Twenty-five per cent of the respondents personally knew some incumbent politician or those who have served in previous administration. Some are even related to them. On whether the politicians are helpful to the people, 50 per cent of the respondents answered favourably because, they said they can provide assistance during calamities and emergencies; they can give money during elections; they can help people find jobs; they can facilitate many things such as the construction of barangay schools; roads and other community facilities can be constructed with the politician's recommendation.

The other 50 per cent who don't find the politicians helpful said that the politicians are only good when they are campaigning for an office. Once elections are over they don't live up to their promises to the people.

Seventy-five per cent of the respondents don't find politics relevant to their lives. Those who said they consider it relevant gave reasons which are summarised as follows: the safety and security of the people depend on those who hold power; it is important to understand what the government is doing and should do; politicians help those who have helped them; community projects are possible through politicians' decisions.

Only 37 per cent of the women were familiar with the name of their congressional representative and with what had been done for their constituency. Most respondents could not tell what their representative really did. The most common answer was that nothing had been done yet. The reply was most interesting considering that many politicians are faulted for not attending to priority needs in the country. This may not mean an absence of political awareness but a revelation of the truth that nothing really had been done yet. Those who said that they don't know what had been accomplished could be interpreted as lacking in awareness.

Among the lower class groups of women, the workers and the organised rural women are the most political aware. Ninety per cent participate in the elections. Most said the reason was why they did so was to test the capability and the competence of the candidates. They discussed politics with their husbands and adult children. None, however, wanted any member of the family to be in politics because it was a matter remote to their status. They considered politicians useful because they could complain about their problems to them. But they also regarded politics as an obstacle to their lives. In their view, some politicians were helpful to their problems but most were not. The two prominent women politicians whom they knew are Cecilia Munoz Palma and Charito Planas.

They also knew the name of the congressional representative of their district and what had been done for the community. The representative had provided job placements for people and given some recommendations for work. The women also gave names of their local barangay officials who, they felt had served the constituency well. The poor organised urban women are also politically aware because they knew that by organising they get better attention. Women who are domestic and shop helpers and those living near dump site seem to have a very level of political consciousness. The helpers group has exposure to media but is not interested in political questions or in what politicians do. A majority do not even register for the polls. This means that they do not participate in voting. The reason given was that they were busy with their work and it did not matter really whether they voted or not. The women near the dump site neither register nor cast their votes. But the husbands of some do vote. The dump site women think that they have derived some benefit from politicians because they were given canned goods and other foodstuffs during elections. Their knowledge of politician goes not further than their barangay captain and Mrs. Aquino. They considered Mrs. Marcos a helpful person probably because of the dole she used to give to the poor communities. The other prominent woman politician they know is Leticia Shahani. In comparison with the women helpers, the dumpsite women revealed a certain degree of consciousness about some politicians and about the benefits that accrued to them. The helpers group, on the other hand, is simply indifferent to any political happening, perhaps, because their lives seem far removed from political activity.

Middle class women have formed varied opinions about the nature of past and present political leaders. This has influenced their general perception of politicians in the country. Their comments on former politicians are summarised as follows: they were insincere; power hungry; corrupt, interested only in money; the competent among them proved to be corrupt; the leadership was corrupt. On the other hand, their views on present politicians are summarised in the following: many are a disappointment; those who cannot run their offices property should resign; they are corrupt like the previous politicians; some people around the leadership are abusive; the politicians are not doing their job; they don't know much; the job for uplifting the masses has not been given much attention; they are weak in fostering progress; they only come to the people when they need their votes; politicians are all alike—insincere and corrupt. Almost all the respondents used the word corrupt to describe politicians. The positive comments about politicians are those that refer to the person's competence. Some women recognised the competence of a few politicians but qualified their positive judgement with specific negative descriptions.

Those who prefer to vote for a woman politician rather than a man, (25 per cent of the respondents), gave the following reasons: women are sensitive to human problems; they may be less corrupt than men; they can be depended to keep their promises; they are God-fearing and more sincere; women can be better organised as managers; they can be firm unless pushed by power politics. Other reasons given are those concerning the need for equality between men and women. Women should be given more representation in decision-making; those who think of giving equality for women, would always vote for women in a political competition with men. Some women also think that to minimise corruption in the country, women should be given a heightened political role.

Those who have doubts about what women can do as politicians, gave the following reasons: politics is dirty business and women have no place in it; women may be weak and fickle and can be easily influenced; women decided with the heart and not with the mind; they should not be in politics because they are more needed at home; women are most happy while at home. These respondents constituted only 10 per cent of the group of middle class women. The rest of the respondents said they would vote for either a man or a woman depending on their qualifications. Women workers and rural women agree with middle class women on their perception of politicians. However, these organised women's groups are more determined to support women politicians for two major reasons: (1) that women politicians will surely help women first, and (2) that they would know how to get alone with people and understand their problems.

Women citizens have participated in various political activities in their communities. Aside from casting their votes during elections a few have been involved in other ways. Two per cent of the 350 middle and lower class respondents have served in the polls as watchers for particular candidates and as canvassers of the electoral returns. Only 70 per cent have voted in the elections regularly while 30 per cent have not. The reasons for not voting include: boycott by 2.6 per cent; they did not find voting important; they were busy with their work. This apolitical group constitutes 27.4 per cent. Two per cent of the respondents are involved with political parties as members and supporters. Their membership is not limited to the pro-government party; they also belong to opposition groups, namely the KBL and the *Partidong Bayan.* Most women who had engaged in political campaigns for candidates were not formally affiliated with any political party or an official campaign organisation. Out of the 70 per cent politically participating women, 30 per cent were involved in campaigns for their friends, relatives, friends of people they knew and friends of their employers. Some women also campaigned for candidates whom they thought deserved to be elected.

Many said that they campaigned for the cause-oriented group and for Mrs. Aquino. They had also campaigned for good government in the past. But 2 per cent of the politically participating women also supported opposition candidates and the Marcos loyalist group. The other method of political participation was joining rallies and demonstrations held after the Ninoy Aquino assassination. Fifty per cent of the 70 per cent politically conscious women had taken part in these besides attending or organising private meetings to support the election bid of Mrs. Aquino. Some women joined the NAMFREL or the National Movement for Free Election with a view to safeguarding election returns against fraud. A few even experienced violent confrontation at the polls.

The politically emancipated Filipina today is the outcome of the Filipino women's struggle to free themselves of the social, cultural and legal bondage that Spanish colonial tradition invented for them for 333 years. Their status of freedom and equality is credited to the democratic tradition that American colonial administration introduced into Philippine society. The Filipino women themselves have to be credited for their boldness and courage in asserting their right of equality with men.

This outlook has proved beneficial over the years. All the gains that have been achieved in terms of policies and legislations to protect and promote women and women's concerns in the Philippines were the result of society's consciousness that whatever goods are granted to men must also be equally given to women. But it must be noted that the privileges that women enjoy owe a good dealt to the view expressed by Filipino men that women should be treated as their partners and equals. That is why there is no marked discrimination against women politics.

It is, however, an accepted reality that the elite has greater access and this for two reasons: the first; is the nature of the politics of patronage and clientelism by which the elite with their resources can easily rise to become the patron amidst a network of clientele relationships; and second, the societal expectation that a politician must be highly competent in terms of education and training to be totally acceptable to the people. With these qualifications, only those possessing the economic resources—i.e., the socio-economic elite—can gain a favourable access. Many middle class people, however, have also gained access to politics by their competence and capacity to spend money. Women politicians who have high educational training and competence as well as socio-economic resources have no problem in entering the political profession;. Thus women politicians in the Philippines are found at almost all levels of the political hierarchy, both on the national and the local scenes.

If there are fewer women than men in political positions, one reason for this is that only a small number think that politics is the right career for them. As the study shows some women still entertain the hidden fear that they may not be equal in capacity to men in running for political office. Successful women politicians in the country must have the determination to show that their political career can bear effective results. That is why in the past, women politicians have been re-elected. Even today, there are some women career politicians who were re-elected to office because of their past political experience and record. The prevalence of dynastic regional politics has not excluded the role of a woman politician who belonged to the ruling clan. Political events since 1986 made a tremendous breakthrough for women who were interested in the pursuit of a political career. Many women broke the barrier of political elitism in several regions in the country. The study has shown that at the local level, many middle class women won seats in the 1987 election for local posts. Their passport to political victory was the support extended by the cause-oriented groups.

At the same time, people were eager to bring about a political change. Even in the Congress of the Philippines which seems to have been the bastion of political elitism especially for the women politicians, the last Congressional election has shown that new names with non-elite tradition won at least 38 per cent of the seats. This is an encouraging record in comparison with the 1978-1984 and the 1984-1986 Assemblies. Over and above this, the most significant event is that a woman became the President of the Philippines. She represented, however, the apex of the elite class in the country.

Women legislators were authors or co-authors of bills and resolutions in both the House of Representatives and the Philippine Senate. Records show that with regard to the general performance of the House and the Senate, as of February 1990, there were a total of 28, 891 House bills introduced by lawmakers, but only 208 became laws; of 1,420 Senate bills, only 41 became laws. Thus a total of 249 laws was the output of the Congress after more than two years' work. It is clear that women have to work still harder to leave their mark.

There were 152 legislations introduced in the House of Representatives concerning women and women's welfare as of December 1988. Of these, 128 were sponsored by the male members of the House which means that only 26 were introduced by women. Most bills have not been calendared. The question that can be raised therefore is, how concerned are women legislators with issues that affect women and what are they doing to promote their welfare. Another question is: are women legislators influential enough to be able to sway the trend of legislation or to ensure that the bills that they had introduced would be calendared for consideration? What is the sense of urgency of the bills that they had introduced.

In terms of legislative output, women legislators have to be more alert, aggressive and assertive—the three As—for greater legislative impact. It will need determination and seriousness of purpose for every bill introduced to become a law. Women in Congress must project quality participation as legislator in order to be heard. The role of local women politicians is equally challenging. A woman officials is under close scrutiny by the people whom she is serving. In some cases, she will have to deal with the problem of insurgency. At the same time, she must be concerned with community development amidst the poverty that seems to characterise 80 per cent of the country. The effective woman official is one who can successfully meet the pressure posed by these needs.

Quality of political participation depends on the level of political awareness. This in turn, depends on which group of common women citizens one is dealing with. The degree of political awareness of a particular group hinges on the nature of their socialisation process. Political awareness can also be equated with political consciousness. The nature of women's political participation depends on the level of their political consciousness. Middle class common women citizens who have a high level of education and broader media exposure to what is happening in the country become politically active. They participate regularly in elections as voters, campaigners, canvassers, poll watcher- and as volunteers to safeguard free elections.

Some women even boycott the elections. Not only do women join rallies and demonstrations but in some cases spearhead their organisation. They also conduct political meetings, join political parties or support parties. In the elections held since 1986, middle class women have played an active role, supporting cause-oriented groups and Mrs. Corazon Aquino. There were others who favoured former politicians as well as candidates identified with the left. It must be noted that two candidates of the Partido Ng Bayan also won seats in the House of Representatives.

These women have limited educational training and exposure to media but their experience in organising and mobilising their ranks have made them politically conscious.

The other groups of women are the domestic helpers and the shop helpers who lead sedentary lives, and are not exposed to politics. The group is apolitical and does not participate in elections. The third group is the unorganised urban poor near the dump site who are extremely poor and have no media exposure. Their political socialisation is limited to their concern of what economic benefits they can obtain for survival. The group is apolitical and doesn't bother to participate in elections. The truth is that there are too many women of this kind in the country, who do not participate in any political activities. This may have a bearing on the fact that, according to the Commission on Election, reported registered voters in the Philippines i only about 25 million out of a population of over 60 million. The voting age in the Philippines is 18 years. By computing the population statistics based on age distribution, there are an estimated 29,957,851 non-voters below voting age in the country. This means that the probable voters would number a little over 30 million. It appears then, that almost five million people do not participate in elections in the country. The marginalised women are included in the estimated statistics of non-voting qualified voters.

The case of the Filipino women is unique in the sense that women are accepted and supported in politics even by the most competent men. But what women politicians need to prove is their competence and credibility, and the quality of their political performance. Gender discrimination, if any, is allayed when women can truly prove their ability as administrators, legislators, and politicians. While women politicians have expressed their concern about how to keep up with men who have an established political stature, such concern is just as natural for men politicians who are still political who are still political neophytes.

Women in politics have transcended the social and cultural constraints set on them. The fact that in the Philippines, they participate in political activity at all levels and occupy high positions in political office and in the bureaucracy, are signs of the women overcoming these constraints. But what needs to be changed are women's attitudes.

Women of the lower class who do not participate in any political activity in the community are apolitical not because of discrimination against them but because of their own personal attitude and lack of concern. If they are socialised with a new political orientation, it may still be possible for them to get involved in political activity. Poverty is not a reason for political non-participation as proved by women workers and organised rural and urban women.

When the suffragettes mobilised to assert their rights to vote, they did so out of a feeling of being discriminated against as women. While not aware of the feminist ideology at that time their action was a rebellion against voting discrimination. In other instances where women were involved in political organisations, demonstrations and other forms of political mobilisation, the reason for doing so was not to oppose gender discrimination but to assert a role in the larger issues of the country such as policies for social justice, the need for political change against authoritarian rule, support of political causes as projected by the cause-oriented groups or even support of the labour group mobilisation or adoption of anti-bases or the anti-nuke positions. These are not feminist but national issues. Women legislators themselves were not concerned with the feminist outlook, nor did they give priority to women's concerns as their primary task as lawmakers. Not too many women lawmakers in all the Congresses in the Philippines had women's issues in mind when they recommended certain legislations. The present House of Representatives records, as indicated by this study, have more bills for women introduced by male members rather than by female members. One hundred and fifty-two bills were introduced but only 26 by women for women concerns.

However, some women's organisations are concerned with orienting women members towards the feminist ideology. Thus, topics that are taken up the women's fora give priority to discussions on the role of women in relation to particular national issues. However, the most serious problems of discrimination against women are those involving men's acts of violence at home and outside and where women are exploited as sex objects. Women legislators have not seriously taken up the question of making of laws which can provide adequate protection for women who are battered or subjected to sexual indignities by perverted husbands. The family Code of the Philippines despite amendments, does not provide sufficient protection for the helpless wife.

REFERENCES

Aguilar, Carmencita T., 1987, "The Muslims in Manila Prior to Colonial Control". *Sojourn,* SEACCNA, ISEAS, February 1987.

_____, 1980, *Philippine Development Plans, Foreign Economic Policy and Development Diplomacy.* (M.A. Thesis) UP Department of Political Science.

Alzona, Encarnacion, 1934, *The Filipino Woman: Her Social, Economic and Political Status, 15665-1935.* Manila, Benipayo Press, 1934. 146 leaves.

Angeles, Leonora C., 1989, *Feminism and Nationalism: The Discourse on the Women Question and Politics of the Women Movement in the Philippines.* M.A. Thesis. UP Department of Political Science, 1989.

Aruego, Jose M., 1949, *The Framing of the Philippine Constitutions,* Volume II. Manila, Philippines: University Publishing Co.

Benavides, Enriqueta R., *The Filipino Woman's Social, Economic and Political Status.* Manila: Cultural Foundation of the Philippines. 17 leaves.

Benitez, Helena Z., 1985, Filipino Women's Participation in Politics: The Difference. It Can Make.

Cortes, Irene R., 1974, *Women's Rights Under the 1973 Constitution.* Quezon City.

_____, 1975, *Achieving for Women Full Equality Before the Law.* Quezon City.

_____, n.d., *Status of Women in Philippine Law.* University of the Philippines.

_____, n.d., *Status of Women in the Philippines.* U.P.

De Leon, Belen A., 1973, *Selection of Women as Senatorial Candidates.* Quezon City.

Greene, Justin Jay, 1970, *Women Leaders in the Philippines: Social Background and Political Attitudes.* Ph.D. Dissertation. Syracuse University.

Kalaw, Pura V., 1952, *How the Filipina Got the Vote.* Manila.

Malayang Kilusan ng Bagong Kababaihan, n.d., Makibaka. Manila.

Palanca, Isabelita, 1984, "Woman Power for Good Government". *Bulletin Today.* 17 March 1984.

Paras, Edgardo, 1950, "The civil Rights of Women in the Philippines". *Centro Escolar University Faculty and Graduate Studies Journal.* pp. 176-200.

Palma, Rafael, 1919, *The Woman and the Right to Vote.* Manila. Bureau of Printing.

Phelan, John, 1956, *The Hispanisation of the Philippines.* Princeton University Press.

Red, Isagani V., 1974, *Mass Media Exposure and Attitude Towards the Socio-Political Leadership of Women.* Quezon City.

Romero, Flerida Ruth P., 1979, *Women's Status in Philippine Society.* Quezon City: University of the Philippines Law Center.

Santos, Alfonso, Editor, 1977, *Heroic Virgins and Women Patriots: Female Patriotism During the Japanese Occupation.* Manila: National Book Store.

Subido, Trinidad T., 1955, *The Feminist Movement in the Philippines: 1905,1955.* A Golden Book to Commemorate the Golden Jubilee of the Feminist Movement in the Philippines. Manila.

Tapales, Prserfina D., 1984, *Women in the Philippine Bureaucracy: Toward an Alternative Approach to the Study of Political Participation.* Ph.D. dissertation.

3

Women in Politics in Malaysia

Modern Malaysia variously known as the real Asia, and "Asian Tiger" has had a long history.

Geographically, Malaysia covers an area of about 130,000 square miles, occupying the Malay Peninsula in the West and the state of Sabah and Sarawak in north western Borneo Island. The two regions are separated by about 400 miles of the South China sea. Peninsular Malaysia, covering 52,000 square miles, has its frontiers with Thailand; Sabah and Sarawak, together about 78,000 square miles border the territory of Indonesian Kalimantan. In 1987, the two territories contained a total population of 16.53 million, with 14.13 million in Peninsula Malaysia and 2.4 million in Sabah and Sarawak. The total female population of Malaysia is slightly higher (50.39%) than the male population. The population of Peninsular Malaysia comprises three major ethnic groups: Malays, Chinese, and Indians. The department of Statistics records the current Malay population in the Peninsula at 56.0 per cent, followed by 33.0 per cent Chinese, 10.2 Indians, and 0.9 per cent of other nationalities. The Malays are all Muslims, living predominantly in the rural areas of the Peninsula (69.2%). The majority of the Chinese and Indians are settled in the urban centres of the country. In the rural areas, the Indian population is mainly contained in oil-palm and rubber estates and plantations. Sabah and Sarawak region contains numerous other ethnic groups who are either Muslims, or Christians or animists.

Malaysia may be described as a Constitutional Monarchy, practising a democratic system of government under a monarchy and multi-party system. The Yang Di Pertuan Agong or King is the supreme head of state, elected every five years by the Council of Rulers. However, the Prime Minister heads the government with a Cabinet of Ministers and Deputy Ministers. The Prime Minister is usually the President of the political party which has scored the highest number of parliamentary seats in the National Elections. Currently, the Prime Minister of Malaysia is Datuk Seri Mahathir Mohamad, the President of the Untied Malay National Organisation (UMNO), a party with the National Front or barisan Nasional which comprises a collection of several (12) ethnic or multi-ethnic based parties. Other than UMNO, two other dominant ethnic parties, the Malaysian Chinese Association (MCA) and the Malaysian Indian Congress (MIC) represent the Chinese and Indian members of the National Front. Another party Gerakan is a multi-racial but Chinese dominated party and is also part of this coalition. At present it controls the state government of Penang. National Elections are held every five years, and State and Parliamentary elections run concurrently. Women are eligible for voting. Voters have to satisfy the requirements of citizenship and be of 21 years of age and above. Citizens who are not in the country during election day may vote by proxy. Candidates in State and Parliamentary elections have to be above 21 years but are only eligible to contest if they do not have a criminal record, have not been declared a bankrupt and at the time of elections do not hold a salaried position in the government or public services. Both female and male candidates can stand on a party ticket or contest as independents.

During the colonial period female literacy for the native Malay population was based on Qur'anic teachings in the Arab or Jawi script. Women were generally unable to read or write in Bahasa Melayu using the roman script. The Malays were generally suspicious of new educational institutions set up by the British, seeing these to be part and parcel of an attempt to gradually convert them to Christianity.

In the 1870s, the British decided to introduce qur'anic lessons in these schools in an attempt to boost their enrolment. However, the 'Hadjee' or 'Khatib' (terms used by the British for religious teachers) were not on the State payroll; parents were required to contribute to their salary. In other words, no official recognition was given to Islamic religious instruction in secular schools. Gradually, this system was introduced in all Federated Malay states in the Peninsula. By 1895, a little more than 5,000 pupils were registered in government Malay schools; the number went upto 8,000 at the turn of the century (1901), a ratio of one to three against the school-age Malay population of 6 to 12 (Loh, P., 1975:14). Malay parents however still hesitated to send their daughters to these schools so that the enrolment was predominantly male. This reflected trends of thinking about the usefulness of religious education for women; they could be retained at home under the protective wing of their mothers, would be less susceptible to unforeseen influences from strange men, could make a career from religious education (secular Malay education was not a means to upward economic mobility) and finally, would be more desirable as wives if they were to remain 'traditional', i.e. conforming to pre-existing institutions of socialisation and learning.

This traditional value orientation towards education was also prevalent in the other dominant ethnic groups. Prior to 1900, Chinese women were a rare sight in the Peninsula. Chinese male immigrants had to either bring them over from China or marry local women to establish a family life (Ward, S., 1980:133-134). By 1900, with the disintegration of the Ch'ing Dynasty, Chinese women were freer to immigrate and began to accompany their male counterparts. By the 1940s, the growth of Chinese families was significant enough in Malay to create a demand for Chinese education. Again the demand for Chinese rather than English reflected the value orientation of the Chinese which emphasised the need to uphold social values and sentiment and to preserve some kind of ethnic identity through language. However, Chinese education remained for the most hierarchical and anti-egalitarian. As explained by Loh, in Chinese society men were 'perceived as superior to women, elders to juniors and the literate to the illiterate' (1975:35). However, it has been argued that Chinese women were also very aware of the importance of education and that the strength of the Chinese value system upheld by Chinese women with the family and school increased the anti-Chinese sentiment in Southeast Asia, in particular in Malaya and Thailand (Ward, S., 1980:134).

In British Malaya, this sentiment coincided with the rise of Malay nationalism. With increasing class hierarchies developing among the Chinese in the Peninsula, the more wealthy began to break this trend of vernacular education by sending their sons and daughters to Hong Kong, Europe, England, and to the United States. The middle classes in urban centres began to patronise English medium schools which eventually provided a new alternative education for Chinese women. Indians from the middle and upper classes in urban centres began to enrol in English-medium schools while workers and labourers in the rural areas and in estates went to the vernacular schools. Most girls dropped out of the school after the completion of primary education.

In Penang and Singapore, however, the urban Muslim population of Indian-Arab origin comprising Gujaratis, Arab, Punjabis and Southern Tamils was more enthusiastic in enrolling their daughters in English-medium schools, including convents, run by various Catholic and Anglican orders. These minorities were usually more cosmopolitan and European in their orientation and attitudes. The value orientations of these English educated women emulated those of their parents: That British was best; that colonialism brought new venues for progress and development; and that the Malays were rather backward not to recognise this. Indeed with their parents firmly entrenched in the British Civil Service, British professional schemes or British Companies, most of these young women and men only interacted with those Malays who were hired as drivers, servants or gardeners. Such children formed a rather derogatory picture of the Malay educated young boy or girl who had neither hear of Enid Blyton nor taken any piano or ballet lessons.

Apparently, in those days, class rather than religion was the determining factor for acceptance of western education. The rural Malays, for the most part impoverished and hostile to foreign intruders, saw European education as an extension of European colonialism. In contrast, urban Malay and non-Malay Muslim families with their closer social and economic association with those in power emulated the British way of life. Firmly entrenched in this mode of socialisation was the accepted truth that economic and social mobility could only be achieved through English education. These families did not hesitate to send their sons and daughters to English medium schools for professionalism and economic specialisation was an important value orientation which did not allow for any kind of discrimination in gender. These regional (rural-urban) and class discrepancies in the acceptance of western education were probably most strongly maintained by members of the Malay royalty. The British set up a special public school in Kuala Kangsar, Perak, to nurture English upper class values in the children of the Malay royalty, to groom them in the style of leadership of British aristocrats in the East. Elsewhere class hierarchies permeated the schooling system where special English elite schools began to cater to those children whose parents were already entrenched in the elite structure of colonial society. Among these elite schools were the Victoria Institution in Kuala Lumpur and the Central School in Perak established in the 1880s.

No surprisingly, the seeds of political discontent and consciousness developed among those who went through vernacular education; interesting enough, for Malay women, participation in the political process began with religious education in Islam. It was here that Malay women were infused with ideas of nationalism from scholarly religious experts. Further, besides developing reading and writing skills, experience in public oration and debate built up a fair amount of self-esteem and confidence in a world of men. In a sense, in the pre-independence period before the 50s, Islamic education initially accommodated to the Adat tradition of the Malays, which was essentially secular, political and pragmatic with an in-built anti-western and anti-colonial ideology. Rather than confine Malay women to domesticity, it provided them with a professional and political platform to participate directly in the nationalist movement.

The present literacy and educational status of women in Malaysia reflects their late participation in the modern education system. It may be noted that the general adult literacy rate in Malaysia is 72 per cent; male literacy is 80 per cent and female 64 per cent (Population Census, 1980). This includes literacy in vernacular systems of education, which, had it been discontinued during the colonial period and the post-independent decades, would have deflated female literacy levels even more. Female literacy levels are expected to increase significantly by the year 2000 with 100 per cent enrolment in State primary schools for both boys and girls (Ministry of Education Statistics, 1987).

In 1987, the gross enrolment ratio for secondary education (68.68%) fell significantly behind the primary school enrolment ratio of 97 per cent. The female enrolment ratio is estimated at 68.68 per cent, in view of the fact that male-female enrolments do not vary if both lower and secondary school statistics are considered. In 1987, the Ministry of Education placed female enrolment in relation to male at 49.13 per cent for lower secondary and 50.19 per cent for upper secondary. This seems to suggest that there are 0.87 per cent more boys than girls in lower secondary school and 0.19 per cent more girls than boys in upper secondary.

Higher educational levels in universities continue to decrease more radically. However these figures do not include the number of students studying in universities abroad. Although accurate statistics are not available, it is estimated that approximately 5 per cent of Malaysian students of secondary and post-secondary education are registered at colleges abroad. This reflects massive numbers of school-leavers entering the labour force after or before the completion of secondary school.

A small fraction of school-leavers enter vocational and technical institutes and colleges after obtained the Lower Certificate of Education *(Sijil Rendah Pelajaran)* at level three of Secondary School or the Malaysian Certificate of Education *(Sijil Pelajaran Malaysia)* at level five of Secondary School. In 1987, the female enrolment an universities was 41.21 per cent and male enrolment, 58.89 per cent. The differences was less significant for colleges which showed a 49.06 per cent female enrolment. However, the female percentage of attendance at technical and vocational schools was low, contributing to 26.10 per cent in 1987. The percentage of youth entering the labour market after secondary education is more than 70 with women contributing about 50 per cent of this economically active sector. This is confirmed by trends of increase in the age at marriage for women from 18 to 25 over the last three decades. Since most girls leave secondary school at 16 to 17 years of age marriages are postponed for about three to seven years, during which time formal employment is sought for personal or family economic commitments.

However, in 1985, it was estimated that only 41.66 per cent of the economically active female population were engaged in waged employment. Hence 58.34 per cent remained unemployed. The statistics of employed women, however, referred to the registered employed so that the actual percentage of working women could be considerably higher.

Studies on leadership, political activity and public life in Malaysia have usually adopted a diachronic perspective, with a view to identifying the effects of major historical developments on the traditional leadership structure of Malaysia. They attempted to analyse the way in which colonialism in the nineteenth and twentieth centuries contributed to the crystallisation of power in the hands of the traditional Malay elites within the government bureaucracy. They indicate that the growth of a newly emergent Malay male-dominated elite, whose access to authority and influence depended on Western education, is an obvious outcrop of British colonisation.

As a new development, with the expansion of the government machinery after independence, political power and influence gradually spread amongst men and women who were either professional bureaucrats or members of political parties. Traditional rural leaders—both men and women who had actively participated in the national movement—continued to preserve their status, in the lower rungs of the political hierarchy. The changing functions of Malay rural elites merely implied tnat a multiplicity of leadership roles was undertaken by a limited number of persons for whom achieved status was enhanced by traditional respect and deference (Cf. S.H. Ali, 1964). Thus, despite important modifications, such as the shift from the village head and the *penghulu* from a grass-roots leader to a government broker, traditional elements of leadership at the village level have remained more or less constant.

More importantly, the development of the Malay bureaucracy did not change the traditional values on which the Malay leadership system was based. Notions and concepts of loyalty *(taat setia),* deference *(hormat),* consideration *(timbang-rasa)* continue to be pledged symbols of political support for Malay leaders who now amass the support of the people through the government political structure membership in a political party. Studies of political activity and leadership development have generally tended to neglect women. Only in the last few years have such studies been undertaken in the field of political sociology and political science. A work that is devoted entirely to the participation of Malay women in formal politics is Lenore Manderson's (1980) study of the Kaum Ibu (Wanita UMNO) Malaysia.

It also attempts to analyse the participation of Malay women in politics historically from the post -World War II period through 1972. She demonstrates how the movement towards independence spurred women into participating in social organisations concerned with improving the roles and status of women, where women directly competed for positions of authority and power. She argues that within the Pergerakan Kaum Ibu or Wanita UMNO, despite the participation of women in politics, their role did not change in essence but rather drew its inspirations and its mode of operation from tradition (Manderson 1980:207).

The participation of women in politics has neither presupposed nor effected change in their fundamental role. How bureaucratic structures impede women's development in formal political organisations has been described by Dancz (1983) and Karim (1983). Studying female political leadership among the Malays, Karim came to the conclusion that women still competed with each other within the marginal structures of the political system. Women's branches of political parties were appendages to the organisation rather than strong viable forces of their own. Another underlying observation of these studies was that class, professionalism, and ethnicity continued to influence women's participation in public life and political activity. Malay women leaders were 'descendents' of highly educated, wealthy or influential families from rural areas *(orang kaya* or *orang besar kampung)* (Karim, 1983).

These women enjoyed a high professional status mainly because of their family background. Thus, Malay women leaders, though few in number, were counterparts of Malay male leaders; in many instances, they were spouses of men who were already active in politics and who already had a readymade network of ties and connections with important members of society. Since the participation of Malay women in politics reflected a closed restrictive circuit of patrons and leaders; the majority of rural women continued to function as followers, notwithstanding their leadership qualities or potential skills of leadership and decision-making.

They may be able to express their interest and motivation by joining village-based organisations but their opportunities for upward mobility depend on the support from a political party. These women, however, formed the backbone of Malay politics. Their keen interest in party politics, and their active participation in the electoral system implied that they were the determinants of leadership patterns amongst women and men. This cursory examination of women in political activity and public life in Malaysia serves to provide the backdrop to this present study. Women's participation in political activity and public life necessitates a dualistic examination of women as leaders and 'followers'. The issues of patterns of decision-making among leaders and followers is an important one. To what extent do women leaders emulate party ideology or show a more general concern for the advancement of their sex is an important area of study.

Do women voters express their participation in political activity in gender terms? How are wider issues relating to ethnicity and class integrated with problems of gender? What is the future direction of leadership amongst Malaysian women and will there be a trend to utilise the democratic process as a strategy to advance women's rights vis-a-vis men? This study attempts to address some of these general issues, with the underlying concern that it can provide the main structural ingredients to the problem of resolving unequal representation of gender in political activity and public life in Malaysia.

Now it is pertinent to note that like elsewhere in South and Southeast Asia, women in Malaysia appear to have limited political roles but high potential as leaders of society. Women may develop their roles as leaders of various village-based organisations, state executive councils and national bodies, but may be unable to develop their potential to the fullest because of the political party system which reduces a women's bureau with the party to an organisation of minorities. Hence, women's participation in political and public activity often involves a struggle against conventional notions of politics, over and above other constraining factors relating to perceptions of women's domesticity by society. As ordinary citizens, women generally suffer from under exposure to political and economic, issues, communicated through discussions and dialogues, newspapers, and other sources of mass media.

Also, since they are physically and geographically less mobile than men (mainly because of the traditional domestic tasks which they continuously perform) it is often implied that women cannot indulge in or develop an interest in political and public activity to the same extent as men.

Obviously, in Malaysia, women have more extensive, clearly defined roles in the socio-economic fields than in politics. To illustrate, it is apparent that rural Malay women command a high status in their society in relation to their knowledge and skills associated with child-care, child socialisation, family health and hygiene, supplementary earnings from agriculture and petty trading (Karim, 1987). Women who are mothers become the patrons of society, for they guide and influence their children in social values that make them responsible and disciplined members of society. However, a cultural system which encourages bilaterality in social relations, where complementary tasks are viewed as non-hierarchical, may not necessarily encourage equal participation in public and political activity.

Some may face problems of acceptance within the family. The situation is probably different for women who are independent earners. They may be able to balance their roles as leaders of their homes and formal organisations more confidently, even hiring domestic help when necessary. The majority of women who are unable to seek alternative strategies for domestic responsibility, including obtaining assistance from spouses and children continue to be alienated from political activity. Effective planning and implementation of community development and women's programmes, aimed at increasing venues for the participation and training of women as community leaders, may help them further develop their potential as leaders and patrons of society.

Generally, involvement in formal organisations other than political parties and voluntary organisations has not been very encouraging. The trade union movement has not been particularly successful with issues of sexual discrimination probably because it appears as a whole, to be more concerned with problems of political and organisational autonomy and with the increasing trend of the government to establish in-house unions. The struggle for direct participation in decision-making in the public and private sector began as early as the forties when women protested against discriminatory wage practices introduced by the British in the mining, teaching, and service sector. Union agitation for reform with regard to the employment of women gained momentum during the 1950s. The war had inevitably advanced the cause of women workers and their active participation in the national movement prompted leaders to view them more seriously.

As far as urban workers are concerned a sense of solidarity had developed among all ethnic groups but this time to carry on with the fight for equality and recognition. Although the first major statement regarding women's wages was released in the Report of the Benham Committee in 1950, its long-term effects were not satisfactory. The Report recommended lower salaries for women in the government services and in many employment categories, and although it granted equal pay to women in certain occupations, including typing and clerical, these positions were to be increasingly dominated by women. The Federation of Malay Women Teachers Union (WTU) was concerned with the status of women teachers: they campaigned to abolish discrimination against married women, and for paid maternity leave and equal pay.

In 1961, under the Education Ordinance of 1957, the Education (Salaries and Appointments) Rules 1961 were introduced according to which married women could not be refused appointment or be dismissed without cause. Yet they were required to retire on marriage and be re-employed on a temporary basis. The battle for equal pay primarily waged by the W.T. Union movement brought in long-term effects only in May 1969 when the government introduced equal pay and pension rights. Although professional women gained significantly with the implementation of equal pay, may of the women's problems in the manufacturing and service sector remained untouched.

The survey on Women Citizens and Women Politicians involved the administration of a set of two questionnaires provided by UNESCO. The surveys were conducted by 22 students: 18 employed for the 'Women Citizens' component;

and four for 'Women Politicians'. Both components of the survey were conducted simultaneously over a period of approximately two months. To save costs, students were asked to make random samples of citizens and politicians from their states *(negeri)* of origin. All 12 States in Peninsular Malaysia were thus covered through a purposive sample. Within each state, students were further asked to contact both rural and urban households and women politicians equally.

Students faced extensive problems such as lack of co-operation, and interview fatigue experienced by respondents. In particular, members of the opposition were reluctant to be interviewed. Co-operation was mainly obtained from government supporters or politicians of the Government party, the Barisan Nasional.

Comments relating to ethnic and communal sentiments could not be adequately elicited through the structured questionnaire and had to be noted separately. It is also likely that statements on income were understated since politicians generally had access to many forms of resources which were not easily accounted for in cash terms. Confusion also arose in cases of women who were not earning and were dependent on their husband's income.

While it is a well known fact that women who did not earn nevertheless managed their husband's income and kept some of it for themselves. It is anybody's guess how much of this constituted their 'earnings'. Women in home-based work referred to themselves as "housewives' although they earned some income of their own. Home based production usually generated resources like food and clothing which did not constitute cash earnings but nevertheless contributed to family income in kind.

The general comment of most respondents was that the ballot was secret and that they did not necessarily have to satisfy the interviewer by answering questions. The length of the questionnaire also made many respondents wary of the whole process, causing them to contribute short vague statements about personal particulars which were to be covered in the open-ended statements.

Older women, in particular, were reluctant to take time off from farming and home-based work and became less co-operative as the interview proceeded. However, since students were asked to be patient and persuasive, all questionnaires were completed, with some containing more substantive information than others. Student investigators said that they found the study interesting and informative and realised that it was an important area of focus in social science research.

They said that despite the constraints of time, they were glad to be given the opportunity to participate in the survey. To a significant extent, the investigation into political conscientisation led to their own conscientisation and awareness. This seems to be the most important consequence of the decision to integrate the UNESCO study with the Anthropology/Sociology Compulsory Research Course on 'Survey Research Techniques and Participant Observation' given at the Universiti Sains Malaysia where the project was based.

Employment and Occupation

Female economic productivity and employment has been traditionally viewed as necessary and important in rural society, encouraging women (married or single) to continue with gainful employment. Overall trends of postponement of matrimony for the Malaysian youth accelerated by the pursuit of employment in the tertiary sector and public services has brought down the annual growth rate of the population from 3.1 per cent in 1970 census to 2.5 per annum (Fourth Malaysian Plan, 1981).

In the decade after the Independence in 1957, the Malayan Government pursued economic strategies that were aimed at improving the economic livelihood of the predominantly Malay rural population through a range of rural development programmes. Agencies also aimed at improving economic productivity and marketing techniques by encouraging resettlement in land integrated schemes. This led to vast displacements of Malay populations within the rural area. The expansion of multi-national and local-based industries in the fringe of capital towns encouraged rural-urban migration which contributed to significant increase in urban poverty amongst Malay migrants. Jobs were scarce, poor-paying and irregular. Workers were not well organised in trade unions to improve working conditions. The 31 May 1969 racial riots in Kuala Lumpur, which led Malays on the fringe of urban poverty to vent their frustrations upon the more settled Chinese populations, was an indicator that rural poverty was neither easily alleviated through integrated land development schemes, nor by encouraging rural Malays to migrate to the cities. A more viable infrastructural base was necessary, and efforts to improve agricultural techniques, managerial skills and individual participation were accelerated under the 'New Economic Policy' implemented in 1970 under the Third Malaysian Plan.

Women have contributed significantly to waged employment in the primary sectors of the economy, oriented around the production of rubber, coconut, oil-palm, tea and pineapple in small holdings, estates and plantations. The

1980 figures demonstrate a lower overall female employment in all sectors, compared to male employment but if women's employment in other agricultural activities such as rise, fruit and vegetable cultivation, is also considered the figures are considerably higher for Peninsula Malaysia, Sabah and Sarawak.

Trends in the estate sector have also been towards a gradual deployment of women between 1967 and 1980 with the exception of oil-palm production which has shown an increase in both male and female participation over the same time period.

Male-Female Labour Force Distribution in Major Production Sectors

	Peninsular		*Sabah*		*Sarawak*	
Sectors	*Male*	*Female*	*Male*	*Female*	*Male*	*Female*
Agriculture	57.5	42.5	91.1	8.9	80.5	19.5
Industry	73.8	26.2	85.7	14.3	86.4	19.6
Services	64.0	36.0	62.4	37.6	62.2	37.8

Source: Report of the Labour Force Survey by the Statistics Department of Malaysia, Table A1, 1980.

In the 1970s, with increasing urbanisation and development of the tertiary sector, imbalances in rural and urban development became more pronounced in the Peninsula. The manufacturing sector drew labour from agriculture mainly from the younger age category, an important source of labour for family small holdings and farms. Over the last two decades, in particular, the number of young men and women drifting into unskilled, low-paying occupations in the manufacturing sector has been significantly high. National statistics on the distribution of population in rural and urban areas reveal that the majority of the people continued to be rural. In 1980 while 69.2 per cent of the population was rural, only 30.7 per cent resided in urban areas. Malays constituted 65.2 per cent of the rural population and only 32.8 per cent of the urban. (Malaysian Population Census, 1980). Significantly, with most of the regular (salaried) employment opportunities concentrated in urban areas, rural-urban drift was highest among the Malays. Reliable statistics on Malay rural-urban migration are not available but estimates revealed that between 1975 and 1980 the annual average growth rate of Malay migrant workers in urban centres was approximately 5.7 per cent (Labour Department, 1982).

It is significant that the kind of industries encouraged by the Malaysian government also created a high demand for female labour. In the post-independence period, between 1960 and 1980, the government promoted the development of labour intensive industries such as electronics, textiles and garment manufacture and the assembly of electrical goods. The majority of these manufacturing concerns represented foreign multi-national corporations from Japan, South Korea, Europe and the United States. Significantly, these labour intensive occupations generated a high demand for unskilled female labour which was mainly obtained from the rural areas in the country. This implied that the majority of these young factory workers were Malays.

During the 1960-1970 decade, the manufacturing sector saw in increase of 224.1 per cent women in the labour force compared to 58.5 per cent men. In contrast, the increase in the participation of women in the agricultural sector was 26.0 per cent and that of men only 1.2 per cent. In the 1970-1980 decade, the percentage increase of women in the manufacturing sector was 227.03 per cent over the 1960-1970 decade. In comparison, the percentage increase in the number of men employed in manufacturing during this decade was 99.8 per cent (Ministry of labour, 1982). This significant increase in manufacturing created a labour shortage in the agricultural sector particularly in labour intensive activities relating to rubber tapping and rice cultivation. In 1980, manufacturing accounted for 15.8 per cent of all employment in the country, the second most significant sector next to agriculture.

In the Labour Force Survey conducted in 1974, it was reported that 1.2 million women were engaged in productive work out of a total of 2.9 million in working age group of 15 to 64. Those categorised as 'unemployed' were either housewives (1.2 million), or children of school-going age (0.5 million).

Occupational Structure of Women, Peninsular Malaysia

Occupation	*Percentage (%)*
Agricultural	39.0
Production and Related Workers	21.4
Service Workers	11.7
Clerical Workers	11.0
Sales Workers	8.7
Professional/Technicians Workers	7.9
Managerial/Administrative Posts	0.4
Total	100.0

Source: *Report of Labour Force Survey*, Department of Statistics, 1980.

In 1980, the number of women gainfully employed was estimated at 1.6 million, the majority still being agricultural (39.0%) and production workers (21.4%). Their employment status, however, was not extremely encouraging. In 1980, in urban areas where most production work was concentrated, 6 per cent of men were employers compared to 3 per cent women, and 73 per cent male employees compared to 77 per cent women. The marginal difference between male/female employment status reflected the capitalistic mode of the economy more than gender differentiation of employment since the total workforce revealed only 4 per cent in employer status compared to 57 per cent employees and 27 per cent in the category of 'own account workers'.

An update of female labour force participation according to occupational groups, covering the years 1985 to 1988. The percentage of women in the primary agricultural sector is constant at 38.96 per cent. When mining and quarrying are included, the overall distribution of women in the primary sector averages at 26.1 per cent. The secondary sector comprising skilled and unskilled workers comprises only 25.7 per cent women, with 24.6 per cent in the skilled technical, professional and executive occupation and 27.4 per cent in manufacturing, construction, transport and communication.

Female Labour Force Participation According to Occupational Group, 1985-1988

Occupation	*Female %*
1. ***Primary Sector***	
(a) Agriculture (Including Farmers, Fishermen, Logger and Related Groups)	38.96
(b) Mining (Including Mining and Quarry Workers and Related Groups)	10.36
Total (a), (b)	26.16
2. ***Secondary Sector***	
(a) Skilled Workers	24.62

	(Including Professional and Technical Workers, Administrative, Executive Managerial, Craft-Production and Storage)	
(b)	Unskilled Workers (Including Manufacturing, Construction, Transport and Communication)	27.35
	Total (a), (b)	25.7
3.	***Tertiary Sector***	
(a)	Professional (Higher Level) (Including Doctors, Lawyers, University Teachers)	24.43
(b)	Professional (Lower Level) (Including Lower and Secondary School Teachers, Nurses, Social Workers, Journalists and Librarians)	57.37
(c)	Service (Unskilled and Semi-Skilled) (Including Clerical and Sales Workers, Services relating to Food, Entertainment and Tourism)	33.36
(d)	Self-employed	27.41
4.	Workers not classified in above occupations	24.87

Compiled from relevant Government Departments and Ministries.

The tertiary professional sector (higher and lower level) reflected a relatively higher female distribution at 40.9 per cent. Significantly, the percentage of women teaching in pre-school and secondary schools is much higher than men at 57.37 per cent. This higher percentage, however, is not maintained for women in higher professional levels, including university lectures, doctors and lawyers; for her the figure drops sharply to 24.43 per cent. Service industries relating to unskilled or semi-skilled profession concerned with office work, food catering, sales, entertainment and tourism is also low at 33.4 per cent and lower still for those in self-employed business, at 27.4 per cent.

Generally, with the exception of teaching, librarianship and nursing, all other professions show women occupying less than 30 per cent of the jobs in the public and private sector (Table 3.5). The lowest percentage distributions are in engineering and science (estimated at below 20 per cent) followed by medicine (22.6%) and law 23 per cent. Women lectures also amount to less than 30 per cent (28.8%) of the teaching staff of universities. Social work and social administration, usually a popular occupation with women remains at lower percentage level of 29.4 per cent journalism at 27.6 per cent. These figures are not expected to increase significantly. Indeed a policy for a 40 per cent deployment of women in education was formalised in 1988 (Ministry of Education, 1988). The Malaysian army also announced a freeze in the recruitment of women, stating that the 10 per cent target has been achieved (Malaysian Armed Forces, 1988). The Navy does not still allow women to command ships.

Female Labour Force Distribution in Professional Occupations, 1985

Occupation	*Female %*
Medical Doctor	22,55
Lawyers	22.95
Lectures and Professors	28.83
Kindergarten, Primary and Secondary School Teachers	54.44
Nurses	100.00
Social Workers	29.42
Journalist	27.61
Librarians	75.39
Engineers	n.a.
Scientists	n.a.

Compiled from various Government Departments and Ministries.

The Bilaterality of Adat and Islam

In traditional Malay society, women's status, in relation to men, had customarily assumed an ideology of balance and equality based on the family and kinship rule of bilaterality which minimised social differences in gender. The preference for uxorilocality in the first few years of marriage and later, for neolocality, was under certain circumstances, occasionally waived for a virilocal-neolocal pattern.

Rights and control over land, other physical resources, and movable property was usually determined by *adapt* or customary law which ensured that property was divided between men and women. Islamic rules of inheritance favouring men were relatively unpopular, for it invariably led to interpersonal conflict between cognates and threatened to break up the family and kinship group. However, it was occasionally employed when the women of the family had previously been given a share of the property or voluntarily forsaken their rights after marrying men of considerable wealth and fortune (Karim, 1987). Within the family, sibling relationships were ordered according to age rather than sex principles, while parental roles tended to be complementary rather than segregated. Childrearing and socialisation were generally regarded as 'female tasks imposing a weight of domesticity upon women. But this was somewhat counter-balanced by their ability to obtain full control over the labour, skills and resources of their sons and daughters. While Islamic rituals gave men some preeminence other social activities surrounding birth, circumcision, marriage, child-birth and feasting highlighted the role of women as ritual specialists, mediators, caterers, decorators and ritual entertainers within and beyond the physical boundaries of the village. Marital status and age, rather than gender, guaranteed an individual participation in ritual or ceremonial activity. Unmarried men and women experienced ritual exclusion because it was felt that they were not fully initiated or socialised into the intricates of Malay *adat*. They were often referred to as *mentah* (uncooked, raw), a term which conveyed their marginal and inferior ritual status. On the other hand, married men and women were believed to be more 'ripe' *(sudah masak)*, or knowledgeable and experienced *(sudah rasa, ada pengalaman)*. The dichotomy of ritual exclusion—inclusion, based on marital status was symbolically expressed in the free, open sexual language used between married men and women. Laced with crude sexual imageries and metaphors it was a distinct contrast to the more subdued repartee between unmarried men and women. One of the more important effects of Islam on women was education. Islam gave women a chance for formal education and a new opportunity to develop careers as religious teachers *(ustazah)* or instructors (*guru* Koran). As explained earlier, women attended Arabic schools in villages (the *pondok* system of tutelage) or nearby towns where they could commute daily without much disruption in their family life. In the evenings, they had either further religious instruction or training in the marital arts. Those who were more interested to learn female oriented professions relating to cooking, weaving, handicraft and embroidery were encouraged to do so but interest and aptitude were important considerations for work. Women were not forced to undergo rigorous apprenticeship in 'female oriented' pursuits. An underlying consideration was how these pursuits could be used as a source of major or supplementary earnings.

The first reports of Malay women's active interest and participation in regional or national level politics was in the 1930s when a group of young Malay women was sent to be educated in Padang Panjang, Sumatra in Indonesia, in a school named Diniah Puteri Secondary School. It attracted young Malay women from rural elite families in the Peninsula, particularly the class of ulama who believed that existing local provisions for education for women in Christian English medium schools were highly unsuitable for their sons and daughters since Christian morals were included in the educational curriculum. The reaction against Christian missionary education was probably much more strongly felt by women than men, since western education was also associated with western norms and modernity which was believed to intervene with Malay values derived from *adat* and Islam. For a majority of Malay parents, the question of the choice of education did not arise; economic constraints did not enable them to educate their daughters or sons beyond primary schooling or grade VI. Others were more willing to see their daughters through local Malay medium or Arabic secondary education party because of the affordable expenses and party because they preferred to choose a more conservative approach to education.

As explained earlier, the number of Malay families who allowed their female children to be educated in Christian missionary or government English schools were clearly in the minority and these were restricted mainly to urban families who foresaw a brighter future for their children in the English medium. The choice of the Arabic school, Diniah Puteri, at Padang Panjang was not only due to its close physical proximity to Malay but also for its reputation of preserving a radical Islamic tradition of teaching where the majority of the teachers were nationalistic and anti-colonial. In accordance with the Islamic tradition of education, the students learned techniques of public oration and political debate and effectively used their knowledge of Islamic law *(fiqh)* and Philosophy *(falsafah)* to develop a political consciousness which rejected western systems of administration and power over Muslim nations. Significantly, the majority of the Indonesian students at this school were children of political detainees *(anak-anak buangan politik)* and Indonesian nationalists fighting against the Dutchcolonial rule. Feelings of nationalism and patriotism were deeply implanted in the minds of these young women and remained so after they returned to their villages in Malaya. Among the rural women who were deeply affected by the more revolutionary educational experiences in Indonesia were Aishah Ghani, Datin Sakinah Asri, and Samsiah Fakeh who together in 1945 laid the foundations for the first women's movement in Malaya called AWAS or *Angkatan Wanita Sedar* (The Movement of Conscious Women). Although the core of its leadership was formed by these politically radical women, the other members of AWAS comprised Malay women who were trained school teachers or religious instructors, the core of the rural gentry. This movement obtained warm support and encouragement from members of the Malayan National Party or *party Kebangsaan Melayu Malaya* (PKMM) formed in October 1945 by radical Malay intellectuals such as Dr. Burhanuddin Helmi, Musa Ahmad, Haji Moh, Abdullah C.D., Ahmad Boestaman and Salleh Ahmad.

From 1945 to 1948, a number of political parties were banned by the British government in Malaya for their radical anti-British manifesto and for collaborating with the Malayan Communist party (MCP) which was formed at the end of 1930 and which conducted an aggressive campaign against the British authorities. Among the political parties or political organisations banned were AWAS, MCP, PKMM, API (Angkatan Pemuda Insaf), the Malayan Democratic Union and AMCJA (All Malaya Council for Joint Action or *Majlis Tindakan Bersama Seluruh Tanah Melayu*). With the collapse of AWAS, the women went their own separate ways. Aishah Ghani later became a member of the women's division of UNMO, the *Kaum Ibu* in 1950. Sakinah joined the Pan Malayan Islamic Party (PMIP) formed in 1954, after her marriage to the chairman of the party, Datuk Asri. Samsiah Fakeh went underground and became member of the Malayan Communist Party Army in Pahang, a branch of the tenth regiment of the Malayan National Liberation. Seh as instrumental in directing the political interests of many Malay nationalists including Ahmad Boestaman (whom she married), Wahi Anwar, Abdullah C.D. and Rashid Maidin, all of whom were exposed to Islamic teachings in Indonesia and who became the most revolutionary Malay patriots of the time. A recent report confirmed her second marriage to Ibrahim Mohammed, the head of the Jakarta based Malayan National Liberation League (MNLL) in the late 1960s. She is now believed to be in china with friends and her son Kamaruddin Ibrahim (*New Straits Times,* 10 August 1987). The Indonesian political experience derived from Islamic education was equally strong in other women's movements which began in Malaya. In 1944, Khatijah Sidek, a Minangkabau Sumatran woman married to a Malay, formed the Women's Military Voluntary Corps or the *Badan Sukarela Tentera Wanita* known more commonly as *Puteri Kesatria.* Later, she started a movement called the *Taman Didikan Puteri Kesatria* concerned mainly with training children to join the army as well as to develop technical skills and expertise as teachers and informal community leaders. Although she began these movements in Sumatra, she became more involved with the activities of the radical Malay intellectuals mentioned earlier, particularly Dr. Burhanuddin who was propagating the notion of *Melayu Raya* in response to he *Indonesia Raya* movement which aimed to see the Malays and Indonesians united as a cohesive militant force against

British and Dutch rule respectively. Her attempt to set up a branch of the *Taman Didikan Puteri Kesatria* in Singapore was a cover to excite stronger nationalist sentiments in Malay women. Her subsequent marriage to a Malay in Johore, Dr. Hamzah, and imprisonment by the British in Singapore, between 1948 and 1950, intensified her determination to develop a women's movement in Malaya. However, the *Kaum Ibu* in UMNO for *UMNO Baru,* (see *New Straits Times,* 14 February 1988), was the only legitimate venue for Malay Women to voice their political sentiments. However, her Indonesian Minangkabau origin and reputation as an aggressive fighter alienated her from the other women in the organisation. The *Kaum Ibu* chairperson Ibu Zain was unwilling to accept her in the organisation. Finally, in April 1953, she was accepted as a member in *Kaum Ibu* and immediately pursued her efforts to elevate the status of *Kaum Ibu* in UMNO by asking for greater female representation in the UMNO General Assembly and more female candidates for the proposed General Elections in 1955.

In an interview before her death in 1981 *(Nadi Insan),* she stated that MNO had treated her badly. She was an embarrassment to the party, having a police record as a former political detainee in Singapore. She was, she said, 'like an old Koran book *(Qur'an buruk)* ready to be thrown away after much use'. Increasing disagreements with members of the *Kaum Ibu* and Tunku Abdul Rahman, the Chairman of UMNO and first Prime Minister of Malaya, led to her final expulsion from the party in August 1956. The same year she joined the PMIP Party (now PAS, Parti Islam SeMalaysia) then under the leadership of Dr. Burhanuddin and Ustaz Zulkifli Mohd. Together they swept to victory in the 1959 General Elections and won the state of Kelantan and Terengganu. However, she left the party when it developed a provincial 'state' character under the leadership of Datuk Asri (now President of Hamim, a party within *Barisan Nasional*), but continued with her social activities to improve the socio-economic status of Muslim women in Malaysia through the Muslim Voluntary Organisation, PERKIM, at Johore.

Islamic education gave Malay women the impetus to develop strong anti-colonial sentiments and to fight the British. They were extremely committed to political ideals. In contrast, the formal female leaders who laid the foundations to the *Kaum Ibu* organisation within UMNO were mostly wives of existing leaders of UMNO who were encouraged by their husbands to take an active interest in the affairs of the party mainly to enhance their own political careers (Manderson, 1980; Karim, 1983). The earlier group of women nationalists (AWAS) opposed the Sultanate system as a legitimate basis of authority in the state. The early *Kaum Ibu* women however, did not have any direct connection with the militant activities of the Indonesian nationalists who were fighting the Dutch. The kind of female leadership that was considered acceptable in the *Kaum Ibu* was one based on a congenial system of co-operation and harmony, not only with their male counterparts within the UMNO party but also with the British authorities in Malaya.

The women were from conventional middle class or upper middle class backgrounds some of whom were already members of voluntary British associations like the Women's Institute. They were content assisting their husbands in their careers by campaigning in villages and towns and holding charities and bazaars to collect funds for their party. When the *Kaum Ibu* was later expanded to include more female participation from the grass roots, the women were more interested in developing their own leadership potential and strength rather than being appendages to their husbands' careers; this new tide of feeling culminated in the *Pergerakan Kaum Ibu* UMNO in 1949 when *Kaum Ibu* became the women's branch of the UMNO party. Everywhere *Kaum Ibu* branches attracted those who were already formerly educated in Malay in Arabic, or professionally trained as primary or secondary school teachers. Aishah Ghani became known as the first 'grass roots' leader within the *Kaum Ibu.* Although she was not part of the elitist circle of wives of Malay politicians who turned to politics through their husbands' influence, she took up journalism and this, combined with her experiences in AWAS and PKMM, gave her considerable advantage over the other women. The wives of civil servants who were more urban based wee attracted to the multi-ethnic cosmopolitan Western based organisations such as the Women's Institute and Welfare Associations and developed a free voluntary spirit that was not politically oriented in any way. Indeed, they were dissociated from political activity, since their husbands were loyal to the British civil service and adverse to formal or grass-root political movements of any kind. These women formed the backbone of leadership of voluntary welfare movements. Differences in priorities and interests eventually drew them away from their Malay coutnerparts. It can be said that voluntary organisations attracted women who were urban-based and Western educated and who could socialise with the wives of British expatriates freely without prejudice, while the *Kaum Ibu* attracted rural Malay women who were not necessarily English educated, but were concerned to see Malaya being ruled by Malays rather than English administrators.

It is possibly for this reason that Malay women remain a minority group among voluntary social workers in the country. Since the politicisation process of Malay women began at an early state in the political development of the nation, they were channelled into political organisations much earlier and more extensively than women from Chinese and Indian communities in Malaya. While the majority of the members of the *Kaum Ibu* were rural women, the organisation's leadership on the national, state and district levels became dominated by women who were already professionally trained in teaching, broadcasting or journalism. Significantly, Tan Sri Fatimah Hashim's appointment to the UMNO Supreme Council in 1959 was closely associated with her husband's successful political career in UMNO and legal career as Deputy Public Prosecutor in Ipoh, and later as Attorney General. His close associate, Tunku Abdul Rahman, saw her leadership potential in the Kaum Ibu and appointed her as the *Kaum Ibu* representative in the Supreme Council. Although she was part of the 'elite circle' within the *Kaum Ibu,* she realised the need for grass-root interlinkages and participation and made a tremendous impact on rural women in and out of Johore. The transference of the *Kaum Ibu* leadership from Tan Sri Fatimah Hashim to Datin Paduka Aishah Ghani in 1972, demonstrated a significant change in the formal female leadership pattern within the *Kaum Ibu;* for Aishah Ghani's post was elected, not appointed and she had extensive support from the ordinary members. Reviewing Malay women's leadership development in processual terms, it is possible to say that although women's direct participation in, and contribution to, national-level politics emerged rather late in Malaysian history, it is not so much a consequence of cultural constraints as a result of developments in Malaysia's political history itself. Ideas of nationalism and nation-building were only conceptualised in the early forties when surrounding Southeast Asian communities, particularly the Achinese in

Indonesia, fortified Islam as a political tool against the Dutch. The spirit of nationalism which used Islam to develop internal resistance against colonial aggressors was similar to other nationalist movements in West Asia. Malay women were involved in the campaign for independence almost at the same time as men.

When women leaders from political organisations are compared to voluntary community workers or voluntary social welfare workers, significant differences can be discerned in the values of these two categories of leaders. Women who choose to do voluntary social work are normally politically neutral or, even if they choose to join a political organisation, remain back-benchers, rendering support, assistance and guidance whenever it is needed. They normally have a deep sense of commitment and responsibility to the organisation and although personal differences often arise, these are seldom allowed to develop into long term factions or feuds. There are also less opportunities for fame, wealth or power through social work.

Some became attracted to voluntary welfare or social work, mainly because they were housewives from middle and upper class families who had surplus time on their hands. While they were not inclined politically, they were eager to utilise their time more effectively and the main venues open for such women were in voluntary social work. They were also for the most part urban and spent a considerable amount of their own finances in travelling, contributions and donations. Such women became highly dedicated social workers. They had similar skills as women politicians in rallying mass support, public speaking and debating except that they did not have the same access to mass media. Maintaining the appropriate social connections and social networks with other women of the same socio-economic background was also important, not so much to uphold or expand on existing power structures but to gain more recognition and importance for the organisation or agency they represented. Younger members of these organisation show great reverence and support for their leaders who have devoted many more years to the agency or organisation. The idea of challenging seniority and eldership is not as obvious as in political parties. In some organisations like the Women's Institute or the National Council for Women's Organisations, some of these leaders have consistently and regularly held leadership positions over a decade. Long serving members normally tend to be elected as leaders and are seldom displaced by the younger members.

It is possible to say that the leadership patterns in these organisations are more stable and predictable than those seen in political organisations but their very stability reduces competitiveness and as such does not encourage the emergence of new dynamic leaders.

In the government's efforts to improve grass-roots participation in community development and politics, women became a major target group for political mobilisation, particularly in rural areas. Here, the main strategy for encouraging women's active participation in community or national issues was channeling collective action through formal government organisations. These organisations also formed the lowest hierarchical level of information dissemination in the country. Some of these institutions were controlled by ministries which channelled relevant public information and social services through a hierarchy of Government personnel.

KEMAS, administered within the Ministry of Agriculture, provides a multitude of social services and facilities which theoretically aim at improving the socio-economic livelihood of poorer women in rural areas. Its close association with the activities of the *Wanita UMNO* also makes it an appendage of the most powerful women's organisation in the country. Membership within these two organisations usually overlaps so that KEMAS propagates the same ideology and politics as *Wanita UMNO.* Since the political and socioeconomic interests of both organisations are so closely intertwined, the goals of KEMAS to uplift the social position and economic livelihood of women are not always achieved. Women who are politically neutral or opposed to the goals and interests of *Wanita UMNO* are reluctant to participate in the activities of the organisation, either from personal conviction or opposition from family or kinsmen who are aligned to other political parties. Because these political differences often arise, a high percentage of women in rural areas do not participate in the activities of KEMAS. The activities or programmes that are organised through KEMAS reinforce rather than restructure the traditional patterns of socio-economic activities performed by rural women. Although these programmes cannot assist the ordinary woman to develop her full potential in public life, the administrative personnel of KEMAS *(penyelia)* often use it as a launching pad for a political career in *Wanita UMNO.* The participants of KEMAS programmes, however, merely gain new domestic skills which have the cumulative effect of increasing their consumption of material goods and demands for home gadgets and equipment beyond what they can afford. Generally, little training is provided in the field of social or community management. Courses on leadership development are seldom organised.

Otome Hutheesing, in evaluating the KEMAS Family Development Programmes writes:

> 'Programmes as shaped by KEMAS cater to a thin layer of educated young women and touch the *grass-tops* rather than the grass-roots. They fulfill the needs of the young female who because of her education has largely become unproductive rather than developing or increasing production' (1981:18).

Further, one more women's organisation which has penetrated a considerable number of villages in Kedah is *Karyaneka,* a subsidiary agency within KEMAS. This organisation is concerned with improving the economic livelihood of women by encouraging income-generating activities that can be developed within the village itself (Ahmad, 1982). Here, the notion of income-generation through village workshops is to utilise existing natural resources in the production of handicrafts and household goods that can appeal to the urban elites and foreigners. The making of embroidered cushion covers, pot-rests and food covers and some other aesthetically appealing handicrafts seem to be the focus of *Karyaneka* activities in Kedah. Ideally, other than handicraft training, women are also supposed to develop business and managerial skills.

The current position of Malay women in political parties like PAS which use Islam as their ideological strategy is significantly different from the time when Islam was part of a strategy for nationalism. In PAS, women are only used to assist men in their campaigning and are not allowed to stand for elections. This strategy of male leadership and female domestication is reinforced by the party's concept of 'restructuring society' in accordance with an Islamic state system. Its political manifesto rejects Malay *adat* as a legitimate basis of social organisation and together with it, leadership roles in women. It is probably for this reason that PAS has never been able to win massive support from Malay women the way MNO has over last three decades.

Before the 1982 elections, PAS's stronghold in the state of Terengganu, particularly in usila and Marang, was accompanied by the marked increase in female activity in fund-raising work geared towards the production of goods like the *mini telekung* or *tudung* (veil), skull-caps *(ketayap)*, cassette tape recordings of speeches or *ceramah* of PAS leaders and pre-packed food items. Also, in the *ceramah* (lectures, political speeches) organised by PAS before the elections, the audience comprised substantial numbers of women, sometimes even as large as the men. In a particular *ceramah* delivered by stad Haji Hadi Awang, a highly skillful orator and charismatic politician from Rusila, Terengganu, the audience comprised about 20,000, more than half of whom were women. As before, women maintained an active interest in political affairs. Yet they were banned from direct participation in politics, at the state and national levels. In the August 1986 elections, PAS's defeat in Terengganu and Kelantan clearly demonstrated the limitations of an Islamic rhetoric which spoke of the Islamisation of an multi-ethnic community and the non-involvement of women in public lie. Although Barisan Nasional's control of mass media was a contributory factor, *Barisan* women in their anti-PAS campaigns used the strategy of women's unequal political representation, withdrawal of voting rights for women and veiling to discourage women from joining the PAS camp. These anti-PAS campaigns were rather successful, as the results of the elections showed. PAS won only a single Parliamentary seat out of 177 (148) went to Barisan) and 13 in State Legislative Councils (out of 351). In comparison, the Chinese Opposition did better, in DAP, which fielded candidates for 24 Parliamentary seats and 37 state seats (New Straits Times, 5 August 1986).

In the decades after Independence, Malaysian Malay

women leaders had already established themselves as national politicians in their own right long before urban western educated Malaysian Chinese and Indian women asserted their political rights.

Of the three major ethnic groups in Peninsular Malaysia, Malay progress in establishing a women's movement within the political party system was indeed the fastest and most successful. Within the Alliance, now renamed Barisan nasional, the *Kaum Ibu* developed its own independent executive structure within the party under the name of Wanita UMNO, in 1972, long before Chinese or Indian women wee able to do so. Within the Malayan Chinese Association (MCA), the Chinese branch of the National Front, the women's branch was established as an independent unit, only in 1981 while the women of the Malayan Indian Congress (MIC) are still subsumed under the dominant male leadership of the party. No women candidates for State and Parliamentary seats have been fielded by the MIC in any national elections. Wanita UMNO had also fielded more women candidates in the national elections, than any other party within the Barisan or the Opposition. In the August 1986 elections, Wanita UMNO fielded 23 nominees, 15 for State seats and eight for Parliamentary seats. In contrast, Wanita MCA fielded only four, and Gerakan (Chinese dominated party in Barisan) for only one State seat. Significantly, all but one of the Wanita UMNO candidates won with substantial majorities against their male contestants in PAS. All women, including an independent candidate, contested in predominantly rural areas. One of the file of the non-Malay (Chinese) candidates in barisan lost her seat to the Democratic Action Party (DAP) in Lahat, Perak. The independent candidate also lost the election. The Malayan Indian Congress (MIC) did not nominate any woman for State or Parliamentary seats.

All in all, women candidates fared well, winning 24 of the 29 seats contested. Wanita MNO's Datin Paduka Hajjah Zaleha Ismail obtained a record majority (against both male and female candidates) of 31,472 votes in the parliamentary constituency of Selayang, Selangor. In Wanita UNMO, the new nominees to the political scene comprised a mix of professionals and housewives. Although these women stood on the safe UMNO ticket, it is apparent that backing from fellow members in Wanita UMNO and from the 49.7 per cent female electorate were important factors contributing to their political success.

It must, however, be said that only a few women have succeeded in the political sphere. Like their male counterparts, they continue to use kinship, family and affinal networks as a basis of support.

The majority of these politicians were between 41-55 years (52.4%). 35.2 per cent were between 21-40 years, while 12.4 per cent fell in the age group of 56 years and above (see Table 3.7). The young demographic profile is related to the demographic structure of Malaysia, where 65 per cent of the population is below 40 years. Most of the women politicians (68.6%) are married and have children, while 18 per cent are married. Only two women in sample reported separation. One was a divorcee, and 11 widows.

Generally these politicians appeared to maintain very stable family units, with spouses rendering some assistance in child-care and domestic work. It is important to note that despite high divorce rate among Muslims, not many divorces have joined politics. All the women politicians from the Tamil group were either marked or widowed. Similarly all Chinese women politicians were married. One could conclude that family stability is possibly a necessary foundation for a political career, particularly for women. Family stability usually accompanies visible forms of support, co-operation and reciprocity without which a woman might not be able to compete successfully for a political career. The majority of women maintained nuclear families (95%), but assistance and support came from multiple sources, including spouses, children parents, and siblings.

The majority of women politicians (61%) belong to the low educated group (secondary or below). 31.4 per cent had completed tertiary training in teaching college and technical institutes, while 7.6 per cent had basic university education. The majority, 53.3 per cent were holding salaried positions or running independent businesses, 18.1 per cent had given up their jobs to pursue a full career as politician, 28.6 per cent respondents reported as 'housewives'.

The data on work and employment status seems to contradict with their descriptions of the 'self' in relation to the family. When they referred to themselves as 'housewives', it was obvious that what they meant by this was 'home-based' activities, i.e. to be based in the home from where domestic work and some form of commercial activity is generated. Furthermore, the statement that they were pursuing full careers as politicians was based on the assumption that they were no longer 'salaried'. The men of their families continued to have independent earnings through a skilful use of political resources. Hence it shows only 16.2 per cent women who were completely dependent on their husband's earnings. The majority (38.1%) were employed (salaried) in the public sector and a smaller number (15.2%) in the private sector. Twenty per cent of the respondents stated that they were entrepreneurs or engaged in home-based commercial enterprises, while 10.5 per cent said that they were involved in work related to the political organisation or committees from which they derived some income.

The income distribution of women politicians covered a normal wide range with no indication of skewing in any direction. The majority (28.6%) earned incomes of M501—M$1,000 with an insignificant decrease of 27.6 per cent in the income level below, and 14.3 per cent increase in the income level above. The smallest income group of M$300 and below was the least represented (13.3%). This coincided with the Malaysian poverty line. Generally, rural households earned an average of M$300—M$500 monthly. The average of M$501—M$1,000 reflects a relatively higher average monthly income than that obtained in an average rural household. Furthermore, the percentage of 14.3 in the M$1,000 and above income bracket was more than double the percentage of household within this income bracket at the national level in rural areas. Politicians in this income bracket are probably entrepreneurs or salaried, working mainly in urban areas outside their village or town of origin.

Considering that the average educational attainment was secondary school, high academic achievement seemed to be the least important factor for success in politics. Nevertheless, political mobility is related to academic achievement for, almost all women politicians at the national level are graduates. For the majority of women in the sample, early interest in politics was a factor which balanced against their average educational achievement. The majority showed an interest in politics before the age of 40 (94.3%) and 32.4 per cent before the age of 21. For most of them, interest in politics developed from secondary school while they were exposed to issues relating to poverty and development, nationalism and patriotism. The majority

(60.9%) said that an underlying motive for participation was a need to prove personal success and excellence in an openly competitive political environment, while the rest were driven by considerations of social justice and welfare, relating to issues of poverty, development, or ethnic representation.

The final push or decision to enter politics came from friends (35.2%) or the family (34.3%) though 24.8 per cent reaffirmed that they were completely self-motivated and needed no encouragement from anyone. A very small number said that they were personally approached by politicians to enter politics.

The importance of friendship as a motivating factor needs further elaboration. A majority (71.4%) stated that as students, they had the normal number of friends with only 15.2 per cent stating that their friendship circle was unusually large. Most friendships were crystallised in extra-circular activities within the school, college, or the university. They were particularly active in associations (29.5%) and sports (25.7) although a large number said that classroom friendships and informal social activities (36.2%) were just as important.

An important factor in their friendship network is the free association with members of the opposite sex, from school to the university. They were not constrained by social values, anxiety or inhibition and faced very little opposition from family or friends. A very small number (15.2%) said that they socialised only with women, while the majority confirmed a free association with both sexes (46.7%).

From this one can conclude that women politicians enjoy a wide network of friendships with men and women which becomes an important source for personality development. A friendly disposition or and extrovert personality, interest in extra-curricular activity and confidence in intersexual mixing provided the ingredients to political socialisation at a later stage.

Remarkably, family socialisation in politics in childhood does not seem to be so strong. 32.4 per cent of the women politicians interviewer had lost their fathers and another 35.2 per cent their mothers, yet a general response was that even when they were alive, they received no particular encouragement from their parents to venture into politics. Most parents (more than 50%) had only completed basic primary or secondary school education and were more interested to see their children develop a strong professional orientation in a more conventional field like teaching, business, economics, or law.

However, the prospects of having a daughter as a politician did not evoke any objection from parents (71.4%). Only 14.3 per cent faced objection from both parents: 4.8 per from their fathers and 9.5 per cent from their mothers. A large number of women politicians had siblings who were in politics (26.6%); they also had relatives outside the immediate nuclear family (36.2%) who were in politics. Fathers or mothers displayed very little interest in politics and were generally inactive.

In conclusion, it appears that women who were able to carve out a political career for themselves had husbands who were in a non-competitive field. Family dissonance may be a possible consequence of extensive political interests among spouses. To be motivated to compete, a woman needs a strong support system from her spouse, siblings and kinsmen to make a success of her career, without which she would encounter considerable difficulties in balancing her rules and task within the household and without.

A majority of the women (78.1%) stated that they did not have any domestic help and had to attend to domestic tasks themselves. However, when they were busy with political work, the family tended to take over most of their domestic tasks.

Children were the most important source of help. This implied that children were not only more self-reliant when their mothers were busy, they also helped with housework such as cleaning, cooking and sweeping. Husbands were also an important source of help (20%) and assisted in the weekly purchase of groceries, fresh vegetables and meat, basic cooking, sending and fetching children from the school and supervision of meals. Women obtained an equal amount of support from their mothers who assisted in child-care and household supervision. Those who had access to relatives said that they would send their young children to the homes of their sisters or aunts when they were busy and fetch them in the afternoon or evenings. Poor kinsmen from villages were also an important source of help.

The support and co-operation of the family was further demonstrated in their reactions and responses to news of a political victory, in the context of a successful nomination or election to a position or seat. Only 10.5 per cent said that they felt worried and anxious, for fear of receiving objections from their spouses or children. The majority (more than 70%) felt elated, proud and confident to receive the challenge. Actual reaction of family members appeared to be consistent with these felt emotions. Twenty-one per cent said that they received full support from their family; another 27.6 per cent said they received encouragement. 26.7 per cent did not show any positive or negative reaction and took it normally, without such concern.

Participation in politics for most of the respondents has not weakened the family unit, in terms of improper supervision of children, drop in children's school-performance, or reactionary counter-measures from husbands (e.g. polygamy, adultery, dissociation from family etc.). For the politicians, a lot of their work necessitated maintaining a close working relationship with men but this did not impose any major problems of a personal kind. Most women, however, said that they had to work equally closely with men and women (61.9%) since they obtained their support from both sexes rather than from one. However, the majority (75.2%) said that they were not committed to participate in women's associations since they were members of the executive council of their political party (12.4%) or committee members at the district and state level (12.4%).

On the issues of public policy, a majority felt that women could bring about changes in the government (81.0%) by taking an active interest in political issues, articulating their opinions and concerns in a free and uninhibited way and exercising their right to vote. The general view was positive, with 75.2 per cent believing that there was little or no sexual discrimination in politics. 64.8 per cent believed that government officers were beginning to show more consideration for women, particularly in the direction of policy and welfare. Many women politicians viewed their future positively. They were satisfied with what they were doing and would not quit politics (55.2%). Only 7.6 per cent were disillusioned because they felt that they were not getting anywhere. Some (17.1%) stated that they had personal conflicts and were uncertain about their future. A high majority felt that their political standing would be stronger if women were viewed to be as effective and capable as men and were given equal representation in all walks of public life. This required a positive change in attitude and perception, particularly among high ranking government officials, male politicians, and the public. Malaysian Society continues to view the politician's role as 'masculine' and it was important to show that women could be concerned for women and men, and perform in a non-aggressive way without being 'masculinised'. Religion, in particular Islam, was not seen as an obstacle. Women's domestic responsibilities were not viewed as a problem though a significant number (37.1%) felt that women who did not receive support or encouragement from their husbands would probably not be able to participate at all.

An even smaller number, 0.5 per cent farmers on rented land. The small percentage of farmers reflected the declining participation of rural Malay women in agriculture and their re-employment in unskilled and semi-skilled occupations in the manufacturing sector. Significantly, a rather high percentage, 12.8 per cent was looking for work but remained unemployed 22.4 per cent of respondents who were not actively looking for work referred to themselves as 'housewives' although it was evident that a significant proportion of these women had independent incomes of their own obtained from home-based work. Those who had managed to expand home-based work into individual businesses (5.9%) or family businesses (2.9%) no longer referred to themselves as 'housewives' even when these businesses were administered from the home. Thus stability in work, self-reliance and economic independence were the criteria used by Malaysian women to express their economic productivity beyond what they conceive to be their 'normal day-to-day' domestic functions within the family and household. Income patterns tended to conform to national lower middle income levels, at M$1,000 (US $370) or less. This included 47.5 per cent of the sample population. A relatively smaller number stated their income at more than M$1,000 (12.3%) while 40.3 per cent were unable to give a proper response to the question, either because they were receiving money from their husbands or were reluctant to disclose differences between income earned and income received. Women in business mostly quoted low monthly earnings or less than M$1,000. Comparing income to education, it might be possible to assume that for the majority, low earnings were related to low educational attainment. 55.2 per cent had done secondary school and 17.3 per cent primary school. Women who graduated from polytechnical institutes and colleges accounted for only 7.5 per cent while 11.2 per cent had university degrees.

The tendency for Malaysians to take their voting rights more seriously with advancing age appears to be a significant finding of this survey. Also voting patterns reflect a fairly inactive passive population within the younger age groups most significantly for those within the youthful category of 22-31 years. This is also the only age group which has a relatively higher percentage of non-voters (50.3%) and a larger percentage of highly educated. A majority of the respondents (80%) were reluctant to disclose their reasons for not voting. Many said that it was a highly personal decision which needed no explanation. However, since these women did not provide non-political reasons for not voting (such as physical distance, lack of transport, insufficient time, health and family commitments) it was obvious that the decision to refrain from voting was politically motivated, possibly relating to low confidence or disenchantment with the political process. Many of the younger respondents said that within their respective constituencies, voting or not voting for a particular candidate would not change their life in any way. They could not foresee a brighter future for themselves or their families. The disillusionment of women in the manufacturing sector has been highlighted in earlier studies (Ong, 1987; Karim, 1987) and this sentiment is possibly echoed in young school-leavers who, lacking better alternatives in employment, become production workers or enter the service sector for low paying jobs. For these women, the prospects of economic advancement and a more stable future seem low. The youthful population of non-voters does not appear to be sufficiently politically conscientised to know that voting is an effective way to press for changes. The choice of refraining from voting, even if politically motivated, is passive rather than active and seems to be more prevalent in the younger age groups. Significantly, the remaining 20 per cent who did not vote cited reasons such as distance, illness, lack of transport.

Once respondent said that she did not like the candidates on account of differences in political ideology. Two admitted that the candidates were of a different ethnicity and felt that voting would not get them anywhere. The majority of women voters stated that they voted for the candidates rather than the party although many added that they felt more reassured if the candidate was of a similar ethnicity and stood for the same issues they believed in.

The vote for a candidate rather than for a political party does not mean that the two are mutually exclusive. Though political parties represent different ideological interests, in the context of Malaysian politics, these interest are substantively ethnic or communal, the maintenance of ethnic identity or unity, the upliftment of a particular community vis-a-vis others, increasing rights for one ethnic community against another etc. Political parties which are ideologically concerned with class imbalances (*Parti Rakyat*) do not seem to generate much support. Hence when women stated that they voted for the candidate rather than the party, they were also suggesting that the candidate reflected the ideological biases of a particular party which they most closely identified with.

Here ethnic consciousness plays a major role in determining self-identity and group alliances. The strength of support for the present government party, the Barisan Nasional or National front, lies in its ability to absorb and embrace the various structural contradictions in Malaysian society. Although it is a coalition of many ethnic and non-ethnic based parties the strongest are ethnic-based (United Malay National Organisation, Malayan Chinese Association, Malayan Indian Congress). People appear to vote for candidates who ideologically support a multi-ethnic stance but in reality obtain their candidacy, support and popularity through a particular ethnic membership. The coalition appears to be multi-ethnic but in practice it derives its strength from maintaining clear ethnic boundaries which are constantly fused with sentiments of ethnic consciousness.

Notably, 31.5 per cent of the respondents stated that they voted for the candidate because they were in agreement with the political ideology of the candidate. 29.3 per cent saw a similar line of support for social interests, (usually communal). Reasons of a personal nature (self-interest, family interest, personality etc.) seem to be insignificant and when added up comprised less than 20 per cent of the total number of voters. Of the 81 or 21.6 per cent 'Not relevant' cases, 7 or 1.9 per cent did not vote while 74 or 19.7 per cent claimed to have voted merely for the political party, irrespective of the candidate's qualities.

Voters who claimed to cast their votes according to party interest rather than candidacy were those who felt that ethnicity and personality were of secondary importance. This covers voters who, for example, voted for the Barisan Nasional even if the candidate standing in their constituency belonged to a different ethnic group, or was considered to be of doubtful reputation and calibre. Alternatively, if included those who voted for a party like Party Rakyat merely because its socialist ideology did not differentiate people on ethnic lines.

Generally, it appears that Malaysian women do not regard personal or ideological factors, such as personality, calibre, and reputation as sufficient reasons to support a particular candidate. Regardless of those factors, the most important considerations are the political issues or ideas the candidate stands for as reflected in the party ideology upheld by the candidate. Since most of these issues or ideas uphold ethnic or communal consciousness, the 'personal' side of the candidacy is automatically taken care of. In situations when two or more candidates belonging to the same ethnic group stand on different party tickets, the personality factors become even less important. Voters make the choice by asking who can best advance the interest of the community through the formal political machinery.

That minorities tend to choose opposition parties standing for minority interests rather than minority parties standing within a multi-ethnic coalition is reflective of an increasingly important trend of political consciousness — the view that minority interests are best advanced through an aggressive front of 'outsiders', rather than a conciliatory front of 'insiders'. This explains the increasing support given by the Chinese Malaysians to the Democratic Action Party (DAP) rather than to the Malaysian Chinese Association (MCA) in areas where the majority populace are the Chinese. Though the DAP does not only admit Chinese membership, it is dominated by the Chinese and receives its support mainly from the Chinese voters. Its strength lies in its ability to oppose the government on issues relating to the special position of the *bumiputeras* or indigeneous Malay majority.

Political complexities of Malaysian society usually place ethnic and communal sentiments above gender so that women voters tend to concern themselves with macro issues of political ideology and ethnicity rather than the more homogeneous and universal issue of female representation. The issues of low female political representation always gets pushed aside for the more emotional strategy of *bangsa* (race) or minority rights. More often than not, women voters are unable to sort out priorities between women's political and public representation and the political representation of the community (or ethnicity) as a whole. Political conscientisation in the direction of women's rights is still weak in Malaysia since the democratic process seems to be more oriented towards wider communal ethnic issues which transcend gender.

The majority of women make independent decision in voting. Since the earlier data indicated that women voters placed party ideology and social or communal interest before other factors, it followed that voting was directly related to the wider political interests of the group rather than women. Women were fiercely secretive about the candidate and party they voted for. For this reason, a significant number (26.4%) did not respond to the question which they regarded as an intrusion upon their privacy.

Indeed, the large number who pointed out that their decision was personal and independent were also anxious to indicate that even when family members attempted to influence their decision, they clung on to it for it was something they wanted to do on their own. Significantly, the secrecy of the ballot seemed to be a mechanism for personal and political autonomy. 'Autonomy' was conceived in terms of independent decision-making (as in balloting) rather than the political advancement for women as a whole vis-a-vis men. Incidence of social dissonance in the family and household in rural areas reinforced this argument—divorces on account of husbands forcing their wives to campaign for a party the latter did not support, spouses voting for different political parties, complaints of women attending the rallies (*ceramah*) of a political party and voting for another, etc. This seemed to be parallel to the spirit of personal autonomy in the Malay rural family and household, where spouses maintained an egalitarian pattern of decision-making.

The majority of women voters (56.0%) stated that they were not directly or indirectly involved in any political organisation. They formed their opinions through television reports, circulars, newspapers and rallies. Dialogues, discussions, gossip and rumour-mongering were valuable and inevitable sources of information or misinformation and these usually revolved around key women informants who were interested and anxious to bring home news, on account of their own political commitments and interests. Non-involvement in political organisations did not imply disinterest in politics.

On the contrary, these women felt that they could form a better opinion of candidates if they were politically non-affiliated and uncommitted. The remaining 44.0 per cent who were all members of any political party said that they became party members because they wanted to pursue political interest in a more positive way.

Participation or non-participation in a political party or organisation did not seem to affect interest in politics. The articulation of personal autonomy in terms of social/ communal interests rather than gender can be tested against their opinions of women politicians. The majority (66.9%) felt that there should be more women in politics and more women contesting in the national elections. A smaller percentage (30.7%) disagreed with this idea. Those who felt that more women should be politicians (and contest in the national elections) felt that this was necessary since women politicians were probably more concerned with advancing women's rights than male politicians. They were aware that Malaysian formal politics was dominated by men, in all ethnic groups. Since respondents were not asked about women's rights in relation to ethnic or communal interests, it is difficult to ascertain if this positive response towards women's active participation in politics was articulated within the context of these wider issues. Possibly, since the question called for a hypothetical response to a possible transformation in women's formal power, the most spontaneous response to this was positive.

Hence if women were actively concerned with the politics of Malaysia, it followed that they were anxious to see more women articulating this interest in a more direct and formal way. Yet, this concern did not necessarily imply that they would automatically vote for women to advance their cause. A lot depended on the kind of issue these women stood for and the party they represented.

The majority of respondents said that the sex of the candidate was not the consideration in their vote (41.6%). Only 18.78 per cent said that they would vote for a woman candidate because 'Women must help women' and 'we must support strong women to be strong ourselves'. A significantly high percentage (36.0%) showed preference for male candidates, as men are more 'pushy' and aggressive. Some admitted that they never had a chance to choose. A small number who preferred to support men justified this in terms of women's domesticity. In their view, women should prioritise the family, particularly the education, welfare and safety of their children; family development should be a priority for women and national development a priority for men. Some argued that women were better educators then men. 'What was so important about politics, they said, when the future of their children was at stake?' Significantly, these women did not believe that the political advancement of women was in any way related to their own advancement or that of their children and family.

Significantly, the majority of respondents (53.87%) stated that they would not like to see a member of their family becoming a politician, while 43.2 per cent said that they would. Among reasons given for the former was that they would like their siblings or children to launch themselves in stable high-paying professions. Some said that it was too time-consuming and that politicians usually ended up playing 'dirty'. Politics was characterised by many as 'dishonest', 'dirty', 'unstable' and 'insincere'. A few said that the politicians were more interested in power games than in serving the community. They attributed part of this dishonesty to the rhetorical style of Malaysian politicians, who accused the people of factionalism and conflict when the root causes of 'splitting' were the politicians themselves. They excited sentiments of racism and communalism when they should be working for the good of all.

Those who were positive about a member of their family developing a political career justified this in terms of pride, that a member of their family was actively concerned with helping people in the country. Others said that it would be a good opportunity to get things done quickly since they were tired of red-tape and bureaucracy. Some others admitted that fame and power were important considerations. It appears that both sets of responses do not highlight issues of women's advancement or power, in either a positive or negative way. The diabolical ethics of politics seems to be the most fundamental reason for disenchanment while personal convenience and group advancement are important factors for support.

Significantly, only 37.3 per cent graduates were positive about a member of their family developing a political career, compared to 26.4 per cent non-graduates. Aspirational levels in politics were higher for graduates than non-graduates though the differences were not significant since the majority for both groups still preferred non-involvement. This datum reflects some of the realities of perceptions in Malaysian society, that although success, power and fulfillment are important considerations, women prefer to achieve this in ways other than political.

TO CONCLUDE, IT IS SIGNIFICANT TO NOTE THAT ABOUT the participation of women in politics the women citizens and women politicians have some identical views and some differences of opinion. Firstly, both groups express the need for women to be politically conscientised and they recognise the importance of voting and participation of public life. The achievement of personal autonomy in decision-making is something extremely valued; in Malay society it reflects a cultural preference for bilaterality in social relations. There is a tendency among women to secretly guard their political choice even from their spouses.

On the other hand, opinions, views and decisions about political candidates are circulated in an intimate communication network with other women within the political candidates are circulated in an intimate communication network with other women within the political party, households and neighbourhood so that information at this stage is public and free-floating. However, the final decision-making process is viewed as personal and private rather than public and open it is at this phase in political activity that women exercise secrecy and independence in decision-making.

At a higher level of conceptualisation, interest in politics is expressed in sentiments relating to 'social' interests. In the context of Malaysian society, where many political parties foster ethnicity and communalism or alternatively oppose these verbally but nevertheless attract people of a particular ethnicity, political participation and voting patterns continue to explore priorities of ethnic interests.

This very often override issue of gender although political conscientisation in terms of gender appears to be taking shape. Women politicians who mostly adopt the ideology of the party they belong to do not seem to express their political views in terms of equitable gender relations. They say that they have to take care of the needs of the total population, rather than women in particular. Their allegiance to women seem to be sentimental rather than intellectual although the majority see the need to uplift women as a whole, to strengthen and fortify their own position within the party.

However, as long as Malaysian politics addresses itself to issues of ethnicity and communalism and national integration, in terms of different ethnic parties forming a political alliance where each competes for representation, women citizens and politicians will have problems articulating issues of representation and development in gender rather than ethnic terms. However, a woman politicians with a portfolio for women's development will be able to do this freely and without inhibition. The reluctance for women citizens to encourage family members to venture in politics is upheld by conventional views of 'dirty politics', preference for stable high status professions which are also less taxing in time and energy. These views are obviously not shared by women politicians themselves who speak of their challenging roles in society, their service to the community, and the personal satisfaction achieved where their goals are met. It is important to note that women politicians represent a group which has directly or indirectly transferred some domestic responsibility to husbands, children, mothers and siblings. In a sense, this is what most Malaysian women strive for, without necessarily having to show political or public activity as a reason. Women politicians, like women in other professions, continue to place importance on family stability and unity.

However, the articulation of women's power and autonomy is seldom seen in terms of sharing labour in the domestic sphere but in terms of greater formalisation of legal rights. Sharing and reciprocity in domestic relations is seen as a necessary outcrop of women's professionalisation but formal power is valued for its ability to demonstrate women's political contributions in a more public way. Significantly, the issue of sexual discrimination is not prioritised by both groups, possibly because formal rules of sexual discrimination do not exist in public political activity. Sexual discrimination in employment and labour relations takes place in covert forms in job descriptions which suggest that some jobs are more suitable for men than women, in the majority of promotional exercises when men are given priority over women or informal corporate culture which favours 'maleness' and 'masculinity' to 'femaleness' and 'feminity'.

The articulation of discrimination by women's professional groups and politicians in specific areas of low may indeed change perceptions of women's status in society. Sexual discrimination would be expressed in more concrete terms transcending the communal politics of Malaysian society. Indeed, women citizen and women politicians can together play a leading role in restructuring public opinion and action in the direction of overcoming formal and informal gender discrimination and inequality.

These are four areas which are crucial to the elimination of gender inequality in public and political activity. These are (i) the integration of a national policy for women within national planning; (ii) understanding the basis of formation of social sentiments and attitudes; (iii) restructuring of strategies of leadership, and (iv) inter-organisational co-operation.

A. In terms of national planning approaches, a national policy for women should advocate the following:

(a) planning and implementation approaches which avoid the pitfalls of usual top-down procedures, where centralised and pre-packaged decisions are made about programmes and projects for women, leaving them in the position of passive recipients. Involvement of women in the earlier possible stage of programme or project related to them will help to maximise their contribution to and potential in, those projects and programmes. They can then play a major decision-making role in development and improve their participation in public and political activity.

(b) the necessity to give access to resources to women which are currently denied them. This includes formal education, training in technology, technology transfer, leadership training etc. One of the major obstacles to the full participation of women in public activity is their lack of access to human and environmental resources.

(c) the heightening of awareness at all levels of society of women's contribution to national development. The 'invisibility' of much of women's work is one further reason for their relative neglect in the development process. A National Policy for women must change this invisibility into a clearer appreciation of the many roles a woman play and the depth of her contributions.

In connection with this, chapters in Malaysian Five Year Development Plans should incorporate this information and propose a clearer view of women's role in long-term plans of social, economic and political development.

(d) in line with the above, training for government agents and extension workers should be widened in scope and purpose, to encourage innovative and participatory approaches to community development, with more attention being paid to the potential of women in public and political activity.

B. Malaysia's multi-ethnic and pluralistic social structure clouds more fundamental problems relating to gender inequality in public and political life. Hence it will be necessary to understand the relationships between priorities of sentiments and values.

1. Sexism exists in Malaysian society, yet often, in

public and political activity, it is given secondary importance.

2. Action against discrimination in gender should transcend ethnic differences although priorities should be given to gender relations in sub-cultures of under development, e.g. rural and urban poor, discrimination of unskilled workers and labourers in the estate and plantation sector.
3. Explore the effects of mass media in promoting a sexist image of women and men, so that public programmes can rectify this damage by promoting images of women which are free from existing stereotypes and prejudice. Films and other audio-visual material documenting women's contributions to public and political activity should be produced and distributed on national networks.
4. Legislation which is conducive to the formulation of a non-sexist society will enhance women's participation in and contribution to public and political activity. Women and men must constantly be made aware that legal reforms are always effective if public opinion leads them in a particular direction.
5. Parental and peer-group socialisation may be free from sexual discrimination but the formal code of social relations may be more constraining for women than men, forcing them to evaluate success and achievement in more modest ways. Women have a need to prove success in both spheres unlike men who might place professional achievement before domestic success.

C. In terms of expanding the opportunities for women to find positions of leadership, from which they can exercise a greater and fairer influence on the decisions affecting themselves and the future development of their society, national bodies should actively promote women's participation at all decision-making levels in society and actively work towards producing an atmosphere in which women can play an equal and complementary role to men in all public decisions.

D. In terms of maximising the contribution of women within formal groups, political and non-political organisations should adopt specific policies to improve women's leadership at all levels. Policies should also actively promote continued liaison between women's groups and political organisations at national and international levels to support women's issues in an integrated way. This can be translated into positive long-term strategies aimed at improving women's position in the same direction as men.

II

WOMEN AND POLITICS IN MALAYSIA

Women have been underrepresented in Malaysian politics. Currently less than 10 per cent of all MPs in Parliament are women, yet women constitute almost half of registered voters. In light of the anticipated general election which would inevitably have to address many issues requiring reforms, AM takes the opportunity to tap into the views of two prominent women activists, Zaitun Kassim (Toni) and Dr. Cecilia Ng on the question of women's involvement in politics. Can women make a difference or will the status quo remain unchanged?

AM: Could you describe the nature of women's participation in electoral politics in Malaysia?

Cecilia: There are various levels of participation in electoral politics in Malaysia and women seem to be at the lowest level of participation. That is, they will go all out to mobilise voters, especially during the general elections and of course they will cast their votes. Historically the ruling party has made use of their women, who form about half their total membership, to woo voters, and successfully so. However, how are they rewarded? Do women have much say in terms of decision-making at all levels of government? It is indeed pathetic that women form only 8 per cent of the total number of Parliamentarians in the country.

AM: Why do you think that women are not sufficiently represented in politics?

Toni: There are too few women politicians to begin with. And women's organisations as well as members of the public have found that the few women in office have not sufficiently represented nor made themselves sufficiently accessible in order to address issues that are important to women. Unless they fully understand and speak to women who are affected by the "system", how will they know what the issues are? Even when there have been opportunities to represent women's issues and really push them forward, the response has not been encouraging.

AM: How would women politicians make a difference? Is it a question of "quantity"?

Toni: Clearly, quantity alone is not the answer. You can have women politicians who are not gender-sensitised as well! However, by and large, I feel women are more empathetic and compassionate towards the problems faced by other women. I think women usually find other women more approachable to speak about their problems. Women bring different skills and qualities to organisations, bodies and processes. But critical mass is very important as well. I don't mean just having lots of women in the "wings", as it were, but a critical mass in the upper echelons of the party. It is difficult for a handful of women to make their voices and positions heard without feeling that they will be drowned out or perhaps even ridiculed.

Cecilia: Certainly having more women politicians does not mean that women will automatically speak for women if they are elected. Look at Margaret Thatcher. We must get women who are gender sensitive and who are not afraid to speak out - who will not toe the party line all the time if they feel that an injustice is being done.

AM: As a feminist, how do you define 'politics'?

Cecilia: Politics is about participation in decision making - it is about sharing power - bargaining, negotiating - at all levels and in all issues affecting society. Politics occurs in the family, in the office, at the level of government, even in 'bed', at the level of sexuality - how we relate to each other. Hence it is not true that politics is the domain of politicians - that is a very narrow view of those who want to keep others out of power. All of us are political in one way or another, and today more than ever, we have to actively participate in how our lives are being run, in how we are being governed - to decide what and how we want the country to be.

AM: In that respect then, how important is electoral politics for women to achieve equity?

Toni: Very important, and I believe more and more women are realising exactly why their participation is crucial. Actually, this is not just about the women in this country - I think Malaysians as a whole have, especially in the last year or so, begun to see the critical role that all of us play in determining how this country should be governed. Women need to know how they can affect the governance of this country, and ultimately their issues and interests. We need to assert that if our votes count, then our issues must count as well!

AM: What are the most pressing issues facing women today which need reforms?

Toni: Even issues of violence against women, which women's groups have again and again highlighted through the years and various campaigns, remain an area that has seen relatively small gains. The Domestic Violence Act, for example, took 10 years before it became law. The laws related to rape are completely inadequate, and there is no law on sexual harassment nor does there seem to be plans for one. The lack of commitment to addressing these alone is glaring. The Syariah Court system is another area where despite the numerous complaints that have been received, there has been almost no difference. Women do not want piecemeal and pre-election "solutions". Women want substantive change to laws and their implementation.

Numerous discriminatory laws continue to exist, such as the Immigration Act, the Guardianship Act, or the Income Tax deduction schedules which are based on the assumption that men are the main earners and responsible household heads while women's incomes are supplementary and their roles secondary. These are Acts and policies that are adversely affecting the daily lives of women, and have been voiced repeatedly. But, nothing changes or at best, small steps are taken slowly! The Women's Agenda for Change, which was launched on 23rd May 1999, gives you an idea of what are some of the concerns of women.

AM: You were part of the group which put together the Women's Agenda for Change. Why should politicians support this document?

Cecilia: We hope that they will support the Women's Agenda and will listen to the voices of civil society. They should realise that the electorate, including women, is not ignorant. Today women are more conscious of their rights and if they want the votes of women, then they should support the Agenda, which has the endorsement of more than 100 organisations in the country. Of course they should not be opportunistic and just endorse the Agenda verbally or select issues which are regarded as 'safe' or supposedly 'non-political'. We want them to be committed and to take our demands seriously - not just in terms of women's issues but also in terms of our demands for greater democracy, human rights, for transparency and accountability.

AM: Is gender going to be an important factor in voting patterns in the coming general elections?

Toni: Opinion polls conducted by unbiased, independent bodies - that's what this country needs! It's hard to know exactly how women, or anyone else for that matter, will vote when there are no opinion polls.

Many countries have such polls that can give valuable feedback on what issues are important to the voters. Nonetheless, the feedback we are getting is that women are much more conscious about speaking up about women's issues. In fact, women have become much more politically aware in recent months.

AM: Has there been a call for women from the movement to stand as candidates at the forthcoming general elections? Why is this happening?

Toni: Yes, there has been a call for women to be involved at this level. Not only for women within political parties to stand, but there has also been a call from women's groups for an independent women's candidate. Someone who will *wakil* (represent) the *rakyat* on issues of greater transparency, equality, freedom of speech and expression towards a more democratic system of governance, and especially ensure that issues that are important and relevant to women are actively promoted on the national agenda.

Cecilia: Yes, women's groups are quite disappointed with the track record of our women political leaders. Most of them have not taken women's concerns seriously, and except for the usual expedient political speeches, they have not genuinely committed themselves to advance women's position in the country. It is almost always the women's NGOs who have articulated the struggles of women - be they about rape, sexual harassment, labour exploitation, unionisation, domestic violence etc. Given this situation, yes, there have been discussions among women activists about putting up a women's candidate in the coming elections.

AM: How can women participate more actively in party politics in this country?

Cecilia: Well, they have to come bravely forward and be more active in the parties they choose to be involved in. This is not an easy task at all. For instance, Khatijah Sidek who was heading Kaum Ibu in the 1950s paid a price for her forthrightness - she was summarily expelled! We hope times have changed though.

Toni: Asking how can women participate assumes that it is easy enough for women to participate. Maybe we don't ask often enough "Why do they not participate?". What is it about the structures of political parties that make it so difficult and at times, frightening, to participate in the management and running of the party? Do party processes fully accommodate the needs of women and the multiple roles they are expected to play, which male political members may not be expected to? Political parties should reach out, foster and encourage a more supportive environment if they are truly committed to not only representing the "people", but also the women in their parties.

AM: Do you think that this country can ever be led by a woman?

Cecilia: Why not? But not just any woman. She must be honest, compassionate and have the political integrity to lead. Then she must get the right and competent team to support her. Just because one does not fit the stereotype of a male political animal, this does not mean that one cannot be a Prime Minister.

Toni: A quick scan of the Indian sub-continent countries alone can answer that question. Even now, if we were to ask an Indonesian if it could happen there, they would say "Yes, there is a big possibility", something they would not have thought as possible some years back. The women in this country have the capacity, the strength and the commitment, the passion for and belief in good governance. The space must be created for anyone who believes in justice and equality.

[***Courtesy:*** Aliran Monthly (A.M). We express our gratefulness to AM and also Dr. Maznah Mohammed The interviewer for reproducing this interview herein this chapter.]

REFERENCES

Abdul Majid bin Ahmad Khan. *An analysis of the UMNO Kaum Ibu as a women's political organisation,* Kuala Lumpur.

Current Legislation in Peninsular Malaysia. *Some Thoughts for International Women's Year,* 1975, Kuala Lumpur. Report of the Federation of Women Lawyers, Malaysia.

Dancz, V.H. (1983). *Women's Auxiliaries and Party Politics in Western Malaysia,* Ann Arbor, Microfilms International Michigan.

Gullick, J.M. (1958), *Indigeneous political systems of Western Malaya,* Atlone Press, London.

Karim, W.J., (1982), "An evaluation of participatory research as a method in developing community skills and decision-making", in *CONVERGENCE:* An International Journal of Adult Education, Toronto, Vol. XV, No. 4.

_____, (1983), "May women's movements, leadership processes of change", in *International Social Science Journal,* Paris, No. 98.

_____, (1987), "The status of Malay women in Malaysia", *International journal of sociology of the family,* No. 1, Vol. 17, Illinois.

Lim, K.C. and Menon, L., (1989), *'Problem areas in civil law governing the rights of Muslim women's* in workshop of Syariah and civil law", KANITA and The Women Association of USM, Universiti Sains Malaysia, Penang.

Manderson L., (1980), *Women, politics and change: the Kaum Ibu UMNO. Malaysia, 1945-1972.* Oxford University Press, Kuala Lumpur.

Ong., A (1987), *Spirit of resistance to capitalistic discipline,* New York State University Press, Albany.

Syed Husin Alatas, (1968). *Sociology of corruption,* Singapore, Donald Moore Press.

Syed Husin Ali, (1975). *Malay peasant society and leadership,* Kuala Lumpur, Oxford University Press.

UMNO (n.d.). Malaysia: *Kaum Ibu Movement: Its history and achievements,* UMNO Research Division, Kuala Lumpur.

4

Women in Politics in Thailand

Geographically, Thailand is situated on Mainland Southeast Asia, sharing borders with Malaysia to the South, Myanmar to the West and Northwest, Laos to the Northeast, and Cambodia to the East. The total land area of the country is 513,115 sq. Kilometres. An interesting way to understand the physical characteristics of Thailand is to follow geographer Wolf Donner (1978) who divided Thailand into five 'faces' or areas of study based on differences in agriculture, economy, climate, topography, hydrology, and other factors. In this classification, the Central Region of Thailand extends from the northern part of the peninsula to the foothills of Northern Thailand. It also includes the Western border mountains and parts of the Phetchabun Range in the East. The Antral Region is served by three major rivers—the Chao Phraya, Bang Pakong, and Mae Klong. In fact, an abundant water supply is a distinctive feature of this region. The central plain, along with an ample supply of water, has made rice cultivation possible and easy. Also, the transportation system is greatly enhanced by the rivers and their tributaries which have been further extended as man-made waterways.

Until an increase in population began exerting pressure on land holdings and the availability of natural resources, the Central Region was known for its abundance in natural resources, exemplified in the well-known saying "fish in the water and rice in the field". The second region is the Northeast, which is demarcated by a mountain range. This region suffers from water shortage, and in many areas, from poor soil condition. Culturally, it shares a strong affinity with the people of Laos and, to a much lesser extent, and in a small part, with Cambodia. Although home to many older civilisations (as evidenced by archaeological remains), the region in modern history has been a relatively poor and 'back water' area of Thailand in which environmental conditions are relatively harsh and poverty prevails among its sizeable population.

Further the southern region has a 'Monsoon climate'. A part of it is on the peninsula with the Andaman sea on one side and the Gulf of Thailand on the other. In general, it is blessed with a fertile soil, and rich mineral deposits such as tin as well as income earning rubber and palm oil plantations. Fishing, (Both for consumption and for commercial purposes) is also an important activity. Rice growing is prevalent in the valleys but there are other means of livelihood as well. The fourth region is the Northern part which is characterised by lowlands and dry uplands, and a variations in climate, vegetation, and population composition. The hilltribes make their niches in the mountains, some practicing traditional 'slash and burn' agriculture and others subsisting on growing opium poppies. Until 20 years ago, the northern region was proud of its rich forest, abundance of wild life and its distinctive history and cultural tradition. However, it has reluctantly allowed itself to be incorporated into the central-Thai dominated political state.

The fifth region of the country, according to Wolf Donner, is Bangkok. It stands apart from the rest of the country because of its high concentration of population - a highly urbanised area with an official population count of over 5 million and an unofficial estimate of well over 7 million. Bangkok is urban society par excellence, expanding ceaselessly as migrants from all over the country swarm to the city in search of jobs, education or pleasure. As the seat of political power and social and cultural prestige, the city is also the centre of commerce and finance. Administrative functions and policy making are all centred in Bangkok. In other words, the primacy of Bangkok can never be over stated. Bangkok also exemplifies westernisation and modernisation, inserting dualism into Thai social and cultural realities where tradition and modernity coexist.

Traditionally, Thai women have played an important role in the economy. Presently, the country's population is divided almost evenly between the sexes, with 49.7 per cent female and 51.3 per cent male. The total population is estimated at between 53 and 54 million persons. Although Thailand is undergoing rapid industrialisation and urbanisation, the majority of her people still resides in the rural area. The labour force participation rate of Thai females (67.5%) is less than that of males (77.8%).

Because of urbanisation, modernisation, and a changing economy, the percentage of women in the agricultural sector has dropped from 87.5 per cent in 1960 to 61.3 per cent in 1987; simultaneously the percentage of those entering manufacturing and services has increased. The following chart shows how women earn significantly less than men in various industries.

Status of Women

The sociocultural tradition of Thailand had its genesis in the blending of three cultural traditions: indigenous beliefs and practices prevalent in the local areas, Hindu

Brahmanic as well as Buddhist traditions introduced from India, and Chinese values and beliefs as expressed through Confucianism, Taoism, and Mahayana Buddhism. The prime examples of the admixture of these traditions in Thai life are best seen in culinary and religious practices in everyday life. Thai cooking has dishes which clearly reflect their origins- curry from India, pan-fried dishes from China, and the vegetable and hot sauce *nam prik* dishes from the indigenous tradition. The syncretism of religious practice is another case in point: Buddhist philosophy and beliefs co-exist harmoniously with Hindu rituals and indigenous beliefs. Hence, one gives alms to the monk, propitiates the spirit house, prays to the goddess of mercy *Kwan-In* from the Chinese-Mahayana Buddhism tradition just as one recognizes and pays homage to the spirits that may inhabit trees and anywhere else in the environment. No conflict occurs in the Thai's perception of the philosophical—metaphysical or phenomenological world as flexibility and accommodation are the central principles behind the Thai amalgamation of different cultural influences. Thus, the Thai cultural tradition adapts and adjusts to everchanging conditions but also retains dominant themes from the past.

1. A bilateral kinship structure with a preference for matrilocal residence. However, as one rises in the stratification system, patriarchy and male dominance become more pronounced, as evidenced by male-centred genealogies and a shift towards male-centred kinship reckoning.
2. A sexual division of spheres of dominance. Men are supposed to control activities vis-a-vis the world outside the domestic sphere and women are supposed to control affairs within the home. This division appears clearer as one rises in the social system. In the vocabulary of the upper stratum of society the

'interior' or *Fai Nai* refers to the women of a household led by the wife or major wife of the head of the household.

3. In the Ayuthaya period (15th-18th century), as an extension of the division of the male and female spheres, politics and administration of the state fell into the sphere of male dominance. This was of course reconfirmed and strongly endorsed by the Hindu — Bhramanic concept of god-king divinity which was to become the rationale for the legitimisation of the role and status of absolute monarchy and the organisation of society based on the *sakdi-na* or dignity marks system, two elements which effectively instituted the Thai feudal system. There is no evidence that women were active in politics prior to the Ayuthaya period. Where women figured in political affairs, they did so as a medium of exchange used to foster political alliance or as tributes or offerings to the male leaders in power. As the Sukothai kingdom declined, it was repeatedly challenged by the rising Ayuthya kingdom. Wars between the two states ceased after a Sukothai princess was joined in marriage to the Ayuthaya monarch.

4. Male supremacy in politics as reinforced by the Hindu-Bhramanic tradition gradually spilled over into social organisations in various ways.

   (a) Men's role as head of a household was unchallenged and unquestioned.

   (b) Women became the property of their husbands, or of fathers in the case of unmarried girls. Women could be punished, bought or sold upon the whim of their husbands or fathers.

(c) Polygamy was not only allowed but tacitly approved and endorsed as the symbol of wealth, success, achievement, power and influence.

(d) Women were expected to serve and please their husbands and to raise and nurture their children. Consequently, the art of pleasing and serving men became elaborated through refinements in mannerism and etiquette, fruit and vegetable carving, culinary arts, and the like.

(e) Allowance for male freedom in matters related to sex and sexual practice but stringent restrictions on women. Hence, adultery committed by women was intolerable, and pre-marital sex punishable. An unmarried woman's purity as epitomised by virginity was essential whereas a man's unlimited sexual pursuits and exploits would never be regarded as promiscuous.

Some of the above characteristics were not unique to Thai society. In fact, male chauvinism, male dominance and male supremacy have been common and prevalent in both western and non-western countries. In particular, standard pertaining to sex and sexual norms and practices were applied differentially to men and women. However, patterns of social evolution diverged and one finds today varying degrees of male dominance in different countries.

It is pertinent to note in the Thai socio-cultural context, a paradox has in fact existed. While men were imbued with formal authority, power, and leadership, women were active in economic exchange and in trade. Being charged with the inner domain also meant being in control of the family purse. Thus, women from different social classes were not denied access to, and control of, household spending money. Moreover, petty trade, in the form of buying and selling in the market place, were carried out by women. This poses the paradox that male leadership could not have been absolute because women were in-charge of economic resources and activities. Explanations for this phenomenon tend to dwell on the family and kinship structures, claiming the bilaterality and matrilocal residence were responsible for women controlling the household economy.

Such an explanation, however, is only partly true. A deeper look at the issue tells us that the origin of Thai women's role in the local economy was due largely to the social structural requirements of the *Sakdi Na* system. As commoners were required to perform corvee labour for the king and the state, able men were drafted into services which took them away from their homes for long periods. It was not uncommon for men in corvee service to leave home for a total of six months in a year. The responsibility of tending to household activities (both economic and otherwise) was left to the women. And since they worked in the fields, reared children and disposed of agricultural and other surplus in exchange for items they needed and which they could not produce, Thai women groomed and toughened themselves for a variety of activities including economic exchanges in the market.

Historical conditions have propelled Thai women to assume the double burden of domestic and childcare functions on the one hand and the management of household economy on the other. The paradox continues: if women had a central position in economic production, why were they content to play a subservient role to men? Why did able women allow men to subjugate them and treat them like material items, subject to buying or selling according to the whims of the owner. Why did they allow men to make the major decisions in the family? This is certainly puzzling. However, it we were to examine traditional Thai society, we would see clearly that male supremacy, dominance and chauvinism were strongest among the social and political elite.

At the apex of the society, corvee labour was not a requirement because anyone with noble ancestors was exempted. Money and wealth were made through political power and status; the nobility and loyalty were allowed to extract labour and resources from their clients. Hence, money and power were vested in men who were ennobled and who made their livelihood through their positions. It is in this segment of society that the Indian, and to a lesser degree Chinese, influence of male supremacy and dominance originated. Women in this stratum of society were not subject to the conditions described earlier for common women.

But their dependency on men deepened the requirements for them to serve and please their male counterparts. As the social and political elite strengthened its hold on society, the values and norms that elite society saw as appropriate for itself were disseminated to the rest of society. Greater equality and sharing between men and women of the earlier days (which was perhaps indigenous to the Southeast Asian region) were gradually eroded by the elite culture. Long years of cultural imposition from the elite have supplanted the original more egalitarian male/female relations with the male dominance model.

Apparently, corvee labour, which subjected common male citizens to untold hardship at times, must have had another kind of impact on male/female relations. As beloved sons, husbands, or brothers were forced to leave home on corvee missions, their mothers, wives, sisters and daughters awaited their return with worry and anxiety, because many men never made it home again.

Dangers in the forms of illness, accident or ambush by enemies in the case of war, were common and normal. Thai women must, therefore, have pampered and indulged their men while they were home. This behaviour must, over time, have evolved into a pattern of socialisation in which boys from a young age were indulged by doting females and men were pampered and spoiled by their female kin.

In Thailand, women's participation in politics, both in terms of exercising voting rights and engaging in competition for certain political offices such as Member of the Parliament, has a history of nearly 60 years, since the first national elections in 1933. It was, however not until 1949 that a woman actually competed with men in politics and won a seal in parliament. Subsequently, women in small numbers successfully won seats in parliament. The same was true of appointive political offices such as membership in senate.

Why did so few women successfully participate in Thai politics when no legal barrier prohibited them from doing so? Clearly, there are reasons for this and we hope this study will elucidate some of them. Since, historically, Thai women have held a strong position in the household economy —controlling the family purse strings or having a say in decisions related to spending, and given their visibility in different levels of economic activities and exchanges such as in the market and in certain professions, it is pertinent to examine their low visibility in politics and in public decision-making, as well as to identify the reasons behind their lack of involvement and participation in politics.

Over the past 70 years, urban Thai women have

gradually entered the job market. At first, they did not do so out of pressing economic necessity. But in the last ten years Thai society has seen changes in economic conditions, making it essential for most urban families to have two incomes instead of one. Hence, both in the urban and rural areas, women work to contribute to the maintenance of their families. Increasingly, non-working women are becoming a rarity. Even housewives pitch in to supplement family income in a variety of ways. As women begin to hold their own in business and finance, in the professions, the public sector, and in the service industry, their status vis-a-vis men improves significantly.

At the very least, they are no longer seen as the appendages of men. Women are now admitted, albeit grudgingly, into higher positions in the workplace and at times into decision-makings forums. However, in the area of social values pertaining to the male/female relationship, changes have yet to come about. For one, men do not yet accept the sharing of childrearing, children and house chores with their wives as a duty or responsibility.

This places an extra strenuous burden on working mothers who must single-handedly shoulder responsibilities both at home and at work. Moreover, men still believe that women must be sweet, pleasant and ready and waiting to please and serve. Working women experience stresses and strains at work and are too tried and worn out by the end of the day and cannot muster energy to serve men as they desire.

Many women still cling to the belief that men are the 'front legs' of an elephant; they continue to give them a higher status, and to engage in indulgent behaviour. Double standards in conduct and mindless, egoistical gratification indulged in by men would peter out if women gave up their tolerant attitudes. But since women have been socialised by cultural values that are biased in favour of male dominance, women appear to accept these values. Sadly, they even appear to perpetuate them. In spite of the advances made by women in the work area, they constitute a small minority in the field of politics and administration. And since this is an area which relates directly to policy planning and policy decision-making, it will be worthwhile to study the reasons for this lack of participation and generate workable recommendations for their greater involvement.

Women in Politics

It is worthy to mention that Thai government does not perceive women's participation in politics as an issue requiring special attention. In fact the government is open minded about the issue of women in development and has appointed a permanent National Commission for Women's Affairs with a secretariat to supervise and co-ordinate its work. Ever since the changes of 1932 which brought an end to absolute monarchy, Thailand has embarked on a rocky road to parliamentary democracy, interrupted by autocratic governments.

The first constitution, which was promulgated in 1933, provided for equal rights and participation of women in politics. But in the view of Malee Pruekpongsawalee (1980) and Amara Pongsapich (1988) although there were constitutional provisions and guarantees for women's right to participate in politics, somehow women's participation remained low. In the era immediately prior to 1932, women were not allowed to participate in the affairs of the state. Time and a change of attitudes and values were necessary. It was a long time (16 years) before the first women candidate, the wife of a well-known MP, successfully won a seat in parliament in 1949. Since then, women have contested and won in elections, but never in great numbers. They have been appointed to seats in the Senate. But again, the ratio of women both appointed or elected to political offices, as compared to men, was so low that female representation in politics could be deemed insignificant.

Malee Pruekpongsalee (1986) pointed out that discriminatory laws against women did exist and could be found in the following areas:

(a) Laws pertaining to women's rights to education and training;
(b) Laws pertaining to women's economic rights;
(c) Laws pertaining to family and citizenship rights of women;
(d) Laws pertaining to women's rights over their own bodies; and
(e) Laws pertaining to women's political and administrative rights.

No doubt, women and particularly lawyers, had worked to bring about change and equality before the law, the general political atmosphere since early 1960 did not permit advancement in this area (Kanala Sukhabanij-Khantaprab 1986, Malee Pruekpongsalee 1986, Chantanee Santabuta, Amara Pongsapich 1988). These authors agree, however, that the student revolution of 1973 and the blossoming of democratic ideals and practice in Thailand made it possible to initiate changes in the laws to grant equal rights in different areas for women.

> The promulgation of the 1974 constitution had an explicit clause which guaranteed equality between men and women as prescribed in Article 28.

> Furthermore, Article 236 instructed that all laws and regulations which discriminated against women must be eradicated within two years after the promulgation. Special committees were set up to revise family related laws as well as discriminatory ministerial regulations. [Malee Prueksalee 1986).

Had political event allowed the 1974 Constitution to be upheld, women's cause would have been further advanced. Even in this brief period, positive changes occurred, women were admitted to the judiciary and the public prosecution. But regrettably, the 1974 Constitution was abolished by a bloody Military coup in October 1976. Hence, the revision of discriminatory laws was interrupted. The Constitution presently used was promulgated in 1978 and in it, equality between men and women is not explicitly prescribed

Surprisingly, no supplementary legislation has come into effect pertaining to the rights of women. As mentioned, had the Constitution of 1974 been allowed to be used, supplementary legislations may have been a reality today. A significant even took place in 1982, when the revision of the Local Administration Act of 1914 came into effect which made women eligible to compete in the local election of village leader an commune (sub-district) leader. Apart from this, the admission of women to the Judiciary and Public Prosecution department was the other significant change in lieu of supplementary legislations. A proposed legislation for women to retain their family names after marriage was not passed by Parliament. One significant amendment to the law of Royal Succession was successfully carried out which stipulated that a female person—a princes—is permitted to accede to the throne. It is significant because heretofore only men were allowed to reign.

Women's Movements

Thai society in general is not a highly organisational society. In other words, social groups and social affiliations, particularly in the formal sense, are not numerous. There are few social, economic, political, or even voluntary associations. Professional and business associations patterned after western models have been a relatively recent phenomenon. It remains to be seen how functional and effective these organisations are in the Thai context. The traditional pattern of social affiliation is the patron-client relationship where status difference is the essential component of the relationship and exchange of favour for support and reciprocity are the principles behind this type of relationship.

Inherent in the patron-client relationship are two other organisational principles: (1) that social affiliation is personalistic because personalities and exchanges are the bases upon which such a relationship is maintained over time; and (2) that because of the personalistic nature of this relationship, permanency is not the norm, rather, impermanency and change are natural and expected. Individuals' relationships with one another and their feelings about one another, are subject to constant changes. As vertical and personalistic relationships permeate the entire society, formal organisations are not in great demand and where they exist, are not highly functional or operative. Often they only serve as venues from which their members can form more meaningful personal relationships. In other words, people get more things done through their informal relationships rather than through formal organisations. In the light of the above, we can appreciate the relatively 'few' women's groups with their seemingly non-aggressive and low-profile image. Women's movement has always been constrained by political conditions and climate. As Pongsapich (1988) aptly pointed out, prior to 1855-1935 when the first period of women's moment was identified, Thai women did not organise themselves; individual women, however, did protest against the system or engaged in heroic acts, but on an infrequent basis.

In this period, some women formed social groups to improve their lives and lessen the plight of their sisters. Welfare activities were carried out by some of these groups but there was some confusion over the main thrust of the women's movement. Political contitions and climate prevented this movement from carrying on its main task — that of advancing women's cause for equality with men and for freedom from exploitation. Thus, in the period 1935-1970, the women's movement groups focussed on welfare and benevolent activities. From 1970 until the present time, woemn's gorups were permitted and encouraged by the general democratisation of society (except for the year 1976-1977) to once again direct their interest to issues pertinent to women's advancement and equality in society.

Coupled with the general feminist awakening and movement in the West and subsequently in different parts of the world, the Thai women's movement has drawn inspiration and camaraderie from sister movements elsewhere. Organisations such as Friends of Women, the Association for the Promotion of the Status of women, the Women Information centre, for example are mainstream associations which deal with current issues that women face due to exploitation, inequality and other situations in which they are invariably the victims. However, in comparison to the women's movement in many countries, the Thai women's movement is relatively low key and definitely not radical-feminist. Amara Pongsapich is quite correct in differentiating women's organisations which deal with philanthropic and welfare activities from those whose central concern is women's issues.

As Pongsapich mentioned, women's issues such as prostitution and child labour, inequality and exploitation have neither gained wide attention nor strong and committed support from a broad spectrum of society. Perhaps the degrees of exploitation or inequality are not so severe, or perhaps women have their sphere of dominance and kin as well as a social support system. Nevertheless, these issues need to be raised and the eradication of exploitation and inequality, needs to be systematically implemented.

Women did not participate directly in politics in traditional Thai society. At both the national and local levels, women were excluded from active participation. Indirectly, however, they contributed to political power play, political exchange, alliance formations, and probably behind-the-scene plans and intrigues. Women were offered as tributes to kings and members of the royal family and to high ranking nobles. Princesses were given in marriage in order to foster alliance and to strengthen political ties. The only recorded case where women participate din politics and administration was when a royal princes—Chao Chamma Thevi—was installed as the ruler of a new state which is now the Lampoon province. In other instances, the queen mother or queen was appointed as the regent when the king was not of age or when he was absent from the country (Sukbhanij Khantaprab, 1986). As reported before, the actual participation of women in politics was begun by Mrs. Orapin Chaiyakarm who entered the parliamentary contest as a candidate in the same district that her husband had been serving as a MP. Her victory gave her a place in women's history in Thailand. But statistics show us clearly that women are in a truly minority position in Thai politics. The following table is taken from a paper written by Amara Pongsapich in "Women Leadership in Rural Thailand" 1989.

Statistics on the Number of Women Members of Parliament and Senators

Year	*Female Number*	*%*	*Total*
Members of parliament (election)			
1933	—	—	78
1937	—	—	91
1938	—	—	91
1945	—	—	96
1948	—	—	99
1949 (additional 19 seats were elected)	1	0.85	19
1952	4	3.36	119
1957 (February)	1	0.63	160
1957 (December)	4	2.52	160
1958 (26 Senators resigned and replaced by MPs)	—	—	26
1969	6	2.78	219
1975	3	1.12	269
1976	5	1.79	279
1979	7	2.33	301
1983	13	4.01	324
1986	12	3.46	347
1988	10	2.80	357
Senators (nomination)			
1933	—	—	78
1937	—	—	91
1945	—	—	95
1946	—	—	96
1946	—	—	80
1947	2	2.00	100
1951	1	0.81	123
1957	—	—	123

Statistics on the Number of Women Members of Parliament and Senators

Year	*Female Number*	*%*	*Total*
1959 (Constituent Assembly Members)	—	—	240
1967	—	—	164
1968	—	—	120
1969	—	—	164
1972 (National Legislative Assembly Members I)	—	—	299
1973	18	6.02	299
1975	9	9.00	100
1976 (National Administrative Reform Assembly Members)	18	5.29	340
1977 (National Legislative Assembly Assembly Member II)	10	2.78	360
1979	3	1.33	225
1981	3	1.33	225
1983	4	1.46	243
1985	5	2.06	243
1986	5	1.92	260
1987	5	1.92	260

To provide a broader picture of women's participation at different levels of politics, the following table indicates the distribution of men and women in national, provincial, and municipal parliaments. Again, the percentages of women elected at all three levels were very low, but their percentage was high at the lowest level, low at the national level, and somewhere in between at the provincial or middle level. Does it mean then that women are more acceptable to both male and female voters if they engage in local rather than national politics? Or is it because at the local level, the women candidates are personally known or familiar to the voters and therefore found acceptable by them? These questions need to be empirically tested.

Distribution of Men and Women in National, Provincial, and Municipal Parliaments

		Number ran Number	*%*	*Number elected Number*	*%*	*% elected of total in same sex*
Members of National Parliament						
1979	Female	—	—	6	—	—
	Male	—	—	295	98.00	—
	Total	1,626	100.00	301	100.00	18.51
1983	Female	54	2.87	13	4.01	25.07
	Male	1,826	97.13	311	95.99	17.03
	Total	1,880	100.00	324	100.00	17.23
1986	Female	362	9.40	12	3.22	3.31
	Male	3,451	89.61	355	96.73	10.29
	Total	3,813	100.00	367	100.00	9.62
1988	Female	366	9.20	10	2.80	2.73
	Male	3,612	90.00	347	97.20	9.61
	Total	3,978	100.00	357	100.00	8.97
Members of Provincial Parliament						
1985	Female	239	3.68	78	3.95	32.64
	Male	6,260	96.32	1,896	96.05	30.29
	Total	6,499	100.00	1,974	100.00	30.37
Members of Municipal Parliament						
1985	Female	258	6.75	110	5.87	38.60
	Male	3,937	93.25	1,781	94.18	45.24
	Total	4,222	100.00	1,891	100.00	44.79

Source: Division of Election, Department of Local Administration, Ministry of Interior.

Women's participation in local politics is primarily at the municipal level which is divided into three -sub-categories, city, district and tambon. The municipality as à form of local government was instituted in 1933. Although initially members to the council were both elected and appointed by the Ministry of interior, the revised municipality law of 1955 stipulated that it was through election alone that candidates could enter the municipal council. However, because of subsequent political events from the 1958 military take-over by Sarist Tanarat until 1974, the municipal council members were alternately elected and appointed. Then once again, since the promulgation of the 1974 Constitution, election was stipulated for all levels of the municipality. Within the municipal council selected members belong to the municipal cabinet headed by the municipal mayor. Since 1936, when the first women became a member of the municipal cabinet other women have been either elected or nominated to this position. As for women mayors, the first to be elected to this office was in 1966. The following tables illustrate the involvement of women in local politics in numerical terms.

In addition to local politics at the municipal level, the Thai system includes local offices which are administrative in nature. These include: subdistrict head, subdistrict deputy head, village head village, assistant head, and subdistrict health officer. Entry to the posts of two of these offices is through local elections which, it is hoped, will encourage people's participation and ensure the responsiveness of office holders to those who have elected them. These offices were restricted to male candidates only until 1982, when the Local Administration Act of 1974 was revised to allow women to compete. In the minds of many Thai, these offices and the office holders are 'political' because they have to campaign and get elected, not unlike other political offices. The confusion is understandable because both have a somewhat ambiguous status as semi-politicians, i.e. they have to bargain, negotiate, co-ordinate with higher authorities and with the people, just as politicians are required to. But the nature of their day-to-day work is administrative in that they are the extensions or arms of the Local Administration Department at the lowest level village and subdistrict.

Office holders have a stipend or salary, albeit quite small. They can wear the civil service uniform and once elected, they are entitled to stay in office until they reach the age of 60. Because village heads and subdistrict heads are local people who are closely tied to everyone under their jurisdiction, national politics invariably extends itself into their lives. Politicians and political parties recruit these local leaders to be their campaign agents and canvassers for votes. Because of this, local leaders, who are supposed to be local administrators, often become highly politicised and come to assume the role of political agents and political leaders at the local level as well. The number of women elected to these positions is shown below. Studies show that they have performed well and in general they have been accepted by men as well as by women.

Women politicians in Thailand are few in number and successful political office holders are fewer still. The parliament in 1990 for example, had only ten women members out of a total of 357. In the previous national election in 1986, only 12 women were elected to a house of 347 members, although 362 women competed.

By and large women candidates tend to come from comfortable to well-to-do background. A number in fact, hail from prominent and rich families whose influence and leadership have been well recognised. Aside from economic resources, it is fair to say that serious women candidates possess other qualities which are at par if not superior to those of their male counterparts. To begin with, they are well educated; most of those we interviewed have studied beyond secondary school. Many possess at a least B.A. degree. Three have an M.A. and two have a Ph.D. In addition, other prominent features in the candidates' background may be important, for example, one M.P. is a sister of a former Miss Universe whose fame, popularity and glamour helped to enhance the visibility of the candidate. Her candidacy was greatly strengthened by her famous sister's assistance in the campaign. Another M.P. was a one time TV announcer and actress whose lovely voice and face had endeared her to the public long before she entered politics.

To be in politics is considered risky in any case. Hence, all the women politicians studied stressed that because they had no personal concerns or worries, they felt ready and able to serve the public. Comments such as the following were not uncommon "I have everything that I need in life and even more, therefore I must make myself useful to those who are less fortunate than I" or I" am comfortable and I have no personal needs, I must sacrifice my time and comfort to serve others." Another informant had devoted her life to a religious group.

Women candidates tend to be the older children in families and more often than not they are daughters in a family with few (or no) sons.

Candidates have family members who have been actively involved in politics or have been interested in politics at different levels.

Due to the relative comfort and affluence of their lives, they were provided with good education. Only two candidates mentioned hardship in childhood but in one case it was the death of the mother and in another, wartime economic deprivations. In all other ways, however, they consider themselves more fortunate than their peers. Many have strong and capable mothers whose ability and leadership, albeit not necessarily in politics, were well recognised by their daughters. Fathers who were interested or active in politics, even if only local politics, was another feature shared by some women in our sample.

Apart from some moral proprieties which women politicians were told to observe in their childhood (with regards to talking to or being friendly with the opposite sex, or staying overnight at a friend's house), it is fair to say that the women politicians in our sample were not raised in a tight mould which confined them to stereotypical female specific activities. They were not prohibited from playing sports, or from participating in extracurricular activities. Many in fact felt that they were expected to be strong like boys and that their parents had wished for them to achieve and behave as sons were expected to.

Remarkably, all indications point to close and warm family relationships for most women in our sample. Strong family ties appear to prevail and to serve as an anchor and a source of strength for the women politicians in their political careers. Although many women had been exposed to politics since childhood and youth through their family members and friends, most did not feel a conscious interest in politics when young. On the contrary, most professed to be somewhat uninvolved and uninterested until much later in life. As youngsters, they were good students with a keen interest in school activities. Many were appointed class leaders or deputy leaders in the case of co-educational schools where boys were generally given leadership roles. Involvement in sports competitions, plays and debates was common.

There were occasions for informal leadership too. The strict discipline and rigidity of the formal educational system led some of our women politicians to react to repression: they were mischievous and scorned the 'good' behaviour expected of them. Hence, friendship was important because peer solidarity was an alternative to the teacher-approved role of a good student. Interestingly, the family was a source of support, nurturing and indulgence. While they might not have been treated by the adults in their family as equals or encouraged to give their opinions, they were nevertheless, allowed to be passive participants of adults' discussions which often dealt with political and social issues. As children, they were not excluded, ignored or oppressed.

They were tolerated and loved. Suffice it to say, that our women politicians were strong individuals who cherished their independence and freedom. From the stories they recount, they emerge as rebels against unfairness, injustice, and oppression, talking back to teachers; defending themselves and others against bullies, even male bullies; engaging in passive aggression through non-communication with their mother, etc. What they enjoyed as they grew up was the freedom to choose. Most could not recall incidents when they were forced to do things against their will. Although they may have been persuaded into choosing a field of study or a particular school, the decisions were made gently by parents who believed it to be in their children's best interest. This is a far cry from the forced imposition of parental will. Perhaps because of their relatively privileged social and economic position, women politicians tend to empathise with others who are less advantaged. From a young age they were moved by the plight of others, and helping those in need became, for them, a mission.

Our women politicians did not consciously plan their entry into politics. For some, it was almost an accident. For others, unplanned events propelled them into this course. Although many have family connection in politics none had planned, wished, or intended to be a politician. Let us look at some specific cases:

(a) Father who had always been interested and active in politics (although he had never been a candidate but did have an uncle who had been an (MP) persuaded and convinced daughter to join politics through district level elections. Daughter who was working in a company had been interested in politics but had not planned a political career for herself. After a number of years in politics, she is certain that her father was right and she has never regretted taking the plunge at that time.

(b). As loyal and devoted members of a newly-found reformist political party, two women politicians were quite willing to work for it. They began by showing ability in campaigning for their leader and co-workers and were eventually recruited as candidates themselves. This they reluctantly accepted. While one of them failed to win in one national election, both were elected at the local level.

(c) As a volunteer social worker who was liked and respected, one candidate was surprised and unsure when a party leader asked her to be a candidate from his party. Her acceptance was based in part on the high esteem in which she held this person and in part on her desire to be more effective as a social worker.

(d) Another candidate with many years of work experience in a bank and in the hotel business, was overwhelmed by the offer to stand for election from a party leader whom she deeply respected and liked. After consulting with and securing permission from her brother-in-law who was her immediate boss, she plunged into politics.

(e) As a university instructor, she was overwhelmed and surprised when the newly appointed Prime Minister request that she join his cabinet. With no prior experience in politics and little knowledge of power play, she was reluctant to accept the position. But though the warm support and encouragement from her junior colleagues who were her former students, she accepted the challenge on the condition that they assist her in her task.

(f) Another candidate had reached a dead end in her career when friends of her brother urged her to join politics; that is when she became interested in a field which had never attracted her earlier. But tired of the impasse in her profession, she decided to risk a well-established job for the volatility of politics. She hoped that politics would facilitate her desire to better implement rural health care.

(g) One women politician who had been working as an assistant to her father—an MP—became aware of the needs and problems of her father's constituency. When election time approached, it was decided that her father needed a running mate, and she gladly accepted that position though she was sure of losing the election. When the results of the election came in she was stunned to learn of her victory and the defeat of her father. Now she had to come to terms with the fact that she was a bona-fide MP—a role she had not seriously envisioned for herself. But she affected the challenge and subsequent elections proved that she was a full-fledged politician in her own right.

(h) Years of active participation in social and communal activities in the village and subdistrict had brought recognition to one woman politician as a strong and reliable leader. Her village could depend on her. So could government agent who came to the rural area to propagate development. She was forever eager and willing to organise people for community activities. When the election law for local government was changed and women were allowed to hold office, she was immediately elected as village head; subsequently she qualified to compete for the post of subdistrict head, a post which she also on easily.

(i) A successful business woman, a happy and contended wife and mother of four children, one politician was inducted by her friends into the political fray. Although not unfamiliar with the political world because her material grandfather was a prominent politician, she felt that politics would be a challenge and a means to help others and to contribute to society. Heretofore she had worked hard only for herself and her family. She admitted that when she took the plunge, she was quite ignorant of the true nature of Thai politics, and it was campaigning the election that opened her eyes to its workings and realities.

Such cases and others indicate that women's entry into

politics was neither premeditated nor looked forward to with great eagerness and anticipation. Women tend not to groom themselves for politics, but when the conditions and timing are right, energetic, active, educated and privileged women do join. Initially they are neophytes to the realities of the game, somewhat wide-eyed but with good intentions of serving society to the best of their ability.

They do not admit to having personal or ulterior motives and tend to view politics more as a vehicle for contribution to society and less as a venue for personal gains. Unconsciously, however, politics may satisfy other needs—such as social recognition fame and glamour, or the feeling of being useful to and needed by the public. In any event, there is little evidence to indicate that entry into politics is the response to a need for power.

Most of the women politicians we studied have had a relatively short career in politics when compared to their male counterparts. None had begun her working life as a politician. Therefore a female veteran in politics has necessarily spent fewer years in office than male veterans. As for the political career history of women politicians, the overall picture is one of gradual and incremental change; a slow but steady ascendency to better positions in parliament. No one had any special or dramatic career jumps in politics. As for the women minister who has been a many-term MP, it is her rightful due to be appointed minister from her party's quota in the coalition government. Even in her case, it was her supporters' pleas that made her accept the ministerial position. Previously, she had stated that she was not interested in such posts. Generally, women politicians tend to assume a low profile during their first years in politics; they spend their time and energy on 'learning the ropes,' so to speak. Close relationships and ties with their constituencies tend to be maintained and further developed. Meanwhile, as they learn about the intricacies of politics and the actual workings of parliament, they gain more confidence and began to assume positions and assignments of greater responsibility. The appear to be humble and quite willing to step aside for their male colleagues in vying for positions of 'importance." For instance, membership in certain committees, such as the budget committee is considered more powerful and prestigious than others.

Women politicians recounted that they did not fight for this much sought-after membership or for the positions of chair or secretary of committees in parliament. In local politics, a woman politician willingly cedes the position of chair to a much older, although possibly less educated, male peer out decorum and respect for his seniority.

One veteran MP has been elected repeatedly with a high percentage of votes since she embarked on a political career. As described in the previous section, her entry into politics was somewhat of a coincidence—her concerns and effort as a social worker plus her former career as a television personality made her a desirable candidate for a young party. When she joined the party and began parliamentary work, she kept a low profile, and did not assert herself when it came to competition for resources or rewards. Through diligence, patience and particularly constant and consistent interactions with her constituency, she built up a solid base. Her peers in parliament, see her as a rational, humble, nice, hard working and reliable person. To her constituency, she is like an angel or goddess of mercy. Several times she willingly relinquished her right to sit on certain committees as gesture of good will and compromise to her male colleagues. Given her overwhelming popularity in her district, her image of diligence, rationality and generosity and her non-aggressive personality, she became a deputy leader—the highest position that a woman politician has attained in her party. There is little doubt that should her party join the government coalition, she would be entitled to a ministerial position. As she says, she will assert herself when the time is right. For example, when she made it known that she wanted the chair of a certain committee, no one argued and the chair was hers.

The second case is interesting because it not only provides us with a glimpse into a political career, but also gives us an insight into the limits of that career. As stated in the previous section, one respondent decided to go into politics after having fought hard in a different profession. She began as a nurse, but switched to academia and aught public health. Further studies abroad equipped her to teach, do research, and supervise health extension projects. Nevertheless, because medical doctors reign supreme in the university, she was not allowed to shed her former identity as a nurse.

Her Ph.D. degree meant little to the physician professors who discriminated against her not because she was a woman but because she was not a physician and ought therefore to play a subservient role to doctors. Discouraged because she found she was reaching a dead-end, she took up the offer of a friend of her brother's to go into politics. In fact, she received more than one offer because the period following the 14 October 1973 revolution; democratic enthusiasm was in full gear and political parties mushroomed over night.

Her first foray into politics did not yield her a seat in parliament. But her background and certainly her Ph.D. degree gave her status in her party. She became advisor to the party leader and later was appointed advisor to the Prime Minister on behalf of her party. In this capacity, prepared herself carefully on issues where her opinion was requested. Her earnest desire to be useful and helpful and her unbounded energy in pursuit of truth gave her the confidence to be frank and express her opinions honestly. Her reputation as a hard working as conscientious advisor grew. In the next election, she stood as an independent for parliament and won a seat. Subsequently, she had to join a political party as the new election law stipulated. In the course of her career she changed political parties a number of times. In one government, she was a deputy minister—a period in which she gained special insights into top-level politics.

Being forthright about her feelings and principles, she did not observe the norms of non-interference of other ministries in cabinet meetings. Nor did she follow strictly the rules of political bargaining and compromises, a fact which she feels, makes her sort of a pariah among her peers in the government. In retrospect, she believed that her reputation as a straight, uncompromising, principled cabinet member was a drawback to her political career since other politicians were reluctant to include her in their inner circle of political allies.

When her party was in opposition, she felt no discrimination or ostracism because she was useful in preparing and researching thoroughly on issues in which the government had failed. Her opinions, when contrary to those of the ruling party, could serve a bullets fired against the government. But when and should her party join the government, there will be a different situation altogether. She is well aware that her desirability as a colleague in government is not great, as evidenced by the exclusion of her name on her party's list of cabinet members for a shadow government.

Her reputation as an uncompromising, straightforward and principled politician has not endeared her to those who view politics as a game of power in which maximum personal gain (be it economic or the desire for power or position) is the ultimate goal. With this in mind and because she realised that competing further would incur greater financial loss to her family, she decided not to be a candidate in the last election. It was not an easy decision. She had seniority in her party and in parliament. But knowing that she would not fare well when her party joined the coalition government—i.e. — she would not be given a ministerial position, and that she would not b able to replace the monetary investment she had made in her campaign as she was not prepared to use her position to enrich herself, she decided to withdraw herself from active politics. She was not a businesswoman, but derives no sense of gratification from her work. We do not know yet if her political career has come to an end or if she is only taking a temporary respite.

Elected women politicians tend to devote their full-time and energy to politics. Since some of them are married, they must use their time wisely in order not to allow their home life be disrupted Hy politics. As mentioned earlier, women politicians tend to come from comfortable and even well-to-do social backgrounds, they are therefore relieved from housework, childcare, and other chores related to housekeeping.

However, married women politicians stress two points: (1) their relationship with their children is close and warm; and (2) their husbands or someone else in the family, their mothers, for instance, devotee a lot of time to their children to compensate for their absence from home.

Unmarried women politicians expressed the feeling that this status probably allowed them more time, energy and undivided attention for their career in politics.

No doubt, politicians are not forbidden to engage in business or do other work, and in fact most male politicians do so, women appear to take their career in politics seriously by devoting great deal of time to it. Only one woman in our sample discussed her intention to improve her economic status. Others do not feel this need because (1) they were relatively comfortable economically; (2) if they are married, they are not the sole or major breadwinners, and if they are not married, there is no urgent compulsion to amass wealth; (3) they live somewhat simply and are not motivated to build an economic empire. Ambitions male politicians may feel the need to have a large economic base to support a large political following. Women at the local level appear to be preoccupied with improving the basic conditions of daily life among the people. Their functions are dual; (1) scrutinising and prioritizing budget allocations for their districts; and (2) acting as the intermediary between people living in a district and the appropriate person, authority or agency whose services is required by the people. For instance, infrastructural needs are important and central to people. Roads, bridges, electricity, and water are the most common of these infrastructural needs. Women politicians at this level know these needs well and try to co-ordinate with the appropriate agency/agencies to deliver needed goods and services.

They can turn to higher politicians such as the Governor of the Bangkok Metropolitan Administration, members of the BMA council or responsible members of the parliament. Women members of parliament are preoccupied with the functions discussed above as well as, for example, catering to the needs, wishes, and demands of the people of their respective constituencies. But in addition, they must spend time working on committees and concern themselves with introducing appropriate legislations. Veteran women MPs are more involved in studying social issues in order to effectively alleviate problems through better legislation. It is fair to say that in general, women politicians are not immersed in jockeying, bargaining, plotting and scheming for personal power. They appear to leave the wheeling and dealing for power and positions to their male counterparts.

One politician in our sample is different in that she herself has not sought political office. But her role as a politician is importantly because she was a co-founder of an important party and she is currently a member of its Central Executive Board. This woman leader's work in politics relates to party building and party expansion. Women politicians do not have a life-long interest in politics. They are individualists-courageous and outstanding either in social welfare activities or in daring to be different from others.

They are leaders to their friends and some are rebels who defied authority. Above all, they are most definitely fighters, having proved this either in their earlier careers or in their defense of the less privileged. Working as volunteers in organisation other than political parties taught them ways of working with the people and trained them in organisational skills. How well-informed are they on social and political issues and on world affairs and politics? Since most women politicians were not initially interested in politics, they did not spend much time in their early years thinking about such matters, nor were they able to discuss politics with a wide range of people.

As most of them did not study Political Science or Social Science in college, fundamental principles and theories of politics are presumably self-taught or learned from veteran politicians. It is little wonder, therefore that women politicians do not probe deeply or linger long on questions such as: what are the means for women to influence government or to effect social change. They agree that parliament is where social change could be initiated, but they appear vague and non-committal on the detailed ways and means to effect this. On the question of whether or not people should vote, they are unanimous: everyone should go to the polls because it is a citizen's right and privilege, and because it strengthens democratic institutions. However, one gets the feeling that they are not really concerned with politics in a holistic sense. They appear more knowledgeable about electoral politics than about its other aspects, and not unlike most Thai, they seem less aware and interested in democratic institution—building or in strengthening political parties and party politics as a means of fostering democracy in society.

Their image of politics is that it is a means of doing good deeds for society and people. To them, an ideal politician is a selfless, benevolent, caring and concerned caretaker of the public. In reality. Women politicians adhere to the definition of the culturally sanctioned role of ruler, giving, helping merciful, benevolent, loving caring, and the other qualities of a god patron. When asked to give an opinion on a woman politicians such as Margaret Thatcher, most respondents expressed positive feelings about her. In particular, they liked her strength, decisiveness, her ability to maintain calm and poise in the face of turmoil and criticism and above all her good domestic life.

Among the Thai women politicians, the respondents showed their esteem for Thanphuying La-iad Pibilsongram and the Minister Supatra Masadit—the former for her pioneering role as a woman politician, (although the fact that her husband was then prime Minister was not mentioned) and the latter for her ability to deal with the press successfully, for her diligence, her courage to tackle problems, her ability to co-exist with male colleagues and be accepted by them. It must be noted, however, that women politicians were more ready and willing to praise non-Thai women politicians than Thai women politicians. A couple of women admitted that they would rather work with men than with women because women were 'nitpickers.' Admiring a person from a distance is perhaps easier than admiring one's equal who may be considered a threat.

Possibly also for this reason, a deceased female politician from the past was more readily cited as an inspiration than a contemporary colleague. Interestingly, a majority of women politicians did not feel gender discrimination. While some admitted that discrimination may exist and may have a strong bearing on women's lives, they denied it themselves. When they described how they had never been appointed class leaders because only boys were allowed to hold that post, they seemed not to have perceived it as discrimination but rather as a normal practice. Or when they had to give in to male colleagues in vying for the same position in a committee, for example, they believed that this was a goodwill gesture, a strategy to form social alliance for the future. If given half a day free from all chores and commitments, how would they spend it? A few said they would relax and catch up on reading. One person said she would sleep and be by herself because she needed the solitude which public life had denied her. Another said she would discuss religion with the learned ones; a third stated that shopping would be a form of relaxation for her and a fourth insisted on visiting her constituency.

All women politicians in our sample believed that there were too few women in politics and related activities. Because of their small number, it was natural, they said, that even fewer women had risen to the top echelons of political parties and government. That is not based on the belief that women have been discriminated against either in social life or in politics.

Only one person believed that such discrimination existed. In fact, women politicians tend to think that the have a decided advantage because their smaller numbers add flavour to political campaigns and to the composition of political partis. Besides, voter appear to be curious and turn out to look at them. Men politicians as yet do not feel threatened by the presence of women; they even seem to welcome women into the fold. Softness, gentleness, good manners, a pleasing personality, good social and public relations are qualities which characterise women politicians, are much appreciated by, but found lacking in, their male counterparts. For this reason, people turn to women politicians to act as intermediaries and mediators in situations of conflict or tension.

Women are better at public relations functions or so it is thought. In any event, women politicians feel that they are assets and not liabilities to their parties. Women voters from the lower and middle classes tend to favour women politicians because they are happy to find their own sex representing them.

Why do women politicians lag behind men? The answers are varied: (1) women are not as ambitious, decisive or one-track minded in vying for power and position as men. Self-limiting factors as expressed by women politicians are timidity, lack of courage and ambitions and reluctance to extend oneself fully for fear of failure and disappointment. Also, their endurance is seen to be lower than men's particularly when it comes to coping with lies, slander, deceit, character assassination, cheating, bullying and outright dishonesty and unfairness. In Thai, there is a saying that a women's facial skin is thin, and therefore they are not considered able to take too many abuses and thus choose not to subject themselves to situations in which they may be slandered. Ability and endurance, plus a lot of ambition and a gutsy manner, will get a female politician quite far or so they believe.

But surely, politics cannot always be easy for these women, they agreed, there are hurdles yet to be crossed. Chief among them are:

1. Safety precautions—women cannot travel everywhere at any hour of the day or night. Some places are difficult for women to get to, such as extremely remote and isolated areas with poor or no roads and which require long and arduous journey, or certain rough sections of town at night.
2. Women follow more hygienic practices such as bathing, washing, a change of fresh clothes, often denied them by the long hours of political campaign. This creates physical discomforts for them.
3. Women are readily and easily accused of misconduct in their relationship with men. If they spend long hours with male colleagues, they may be accused of

sexual relations with them. This stems from a societal attitude which categorises women as sex objects. Younger women are vulnerable to such unidentified accusations like being the mistress or minor wives of their colleagues, and in particular, of their superiors or bosses; women politicians have been accused in this way. In fact, one of our informants who was happily married and a mother of three children was once accused of being the minor wife of her party leader. It is interesting that while men are also implicated in sexual liaisons, their reputation or stature remains untarnished in the eyes of society. Women, however, are invariably hurt and their good names stained by such accusations. This is no doubt due to the double standards that prevail in Thai society. Men are allowed greater freedom and leeway in their sexual practices while women must remain chaste, virtuous, and loyal to their husbands or even lovers.

4. If women politicians do not conform to the model of a gentle, unassertive, good mannered person, their male colleagues may feel somewhat uneasy and may even withdraw or withhold co-operation and assistance to their women colleagues. A veteran female MP said "When I try to state may point and conviction strongly and in no uncertain terms, men call me bossy, interfering, strong headed, opinionated, etc.

Women politicians feel that they are sympathetic to the plight of women and will give their support to legislation in favour of improving the status of women in Thai society. But most of them do not actively work to achieve this. One informant who was working on social issues proposed that more enquiries be made prior to registering a marriage. It was hoped that this would deter the practice of multiple marriage registrations often done by men who lure 'innocent' women into illegal union. She believed that this proposed change would at least provide a little protection for women. In conjunction with this, she had also proposed that the government declare one day a year as Family Day.

Apart from the organisation for women already referred to, no other feminist or women related organisations were mentioned by the women politicians in our sample. Some reiterated that they were not hard-boiled feminists and most said they would readily denounce radical feminism or any women's movement that would openly alienate men from their cause. They preferred gradual and peaceful promotion of women's status, the kind that is non-disruptive to the existing male/female relationship and social structure.

Nevertheless, when asked whom they would choose between two equally competent male and female candidates most answered that they would choose the latter. They would like to see an increase in the number of women in public offices where they are greatly outnumbered by men. They also felt that it was desirable for more women to participate since they could then better represent the needs of women. On the question of whether or not there was an improvement in the government's attitude towards women, the answers were mixed but the general opinion was that a lot more needed to be done. Most respondents voiced their skepticism, even cynicism about affirmative action ever being implemented in Thai society. Moreover, most of them disagreed rather strongly with the view that it should ever be introduced and implemented. Extra or special privileges for women were vehemently denounced because they felt that they should be selected in the same manner as men.

Otherwise, men would have less respect for women politicians. Moreover, non-elected women would not have the pride and prestige that elected women politicians had. All in all, they opposed the emergence of a second class female colleagues because they felt it would surely set back women's effort to participate in politics.

By and large, the women politicians in our sample intend to stay in politics, to continue their careers and to climb up the political hierarchy. Women in local politics plan to learn more in order to compete successfully at the national level. Woman in national politics hoped to be re-elected in order to gain seniority and to be respected by their colleagues. Some women admitted to planning for higher political offices such as those of deputy minister, minister and deputy party leader. However, no one mentioned becoming Prime Minister or Head of their political party-positions tacitly acknowledged, it seems, to be reserved for men. When they were pressed to explain why they did not plan to reach the highest position, their answers could be summarized as follows:

1. Politics means serving and helping the people. It is not an end in itself. Therefore being a MP is quite sufficient. Top positions are for those who are ambitious and skilful in the power game.
2. They are not confident that they can handle or manage well in top positions which are extremely demanding.
3. They do not wish to look or plan so far ahead because such plans appear unrealistic for the moment.

It appears then that women politicians do not live in a

cocoon. They are pragmatic and firmly rooted in the present, concerned about how to get things done and not engaged in grandiose dreams that bring in disappointments and pain if unrealized.

To the question "It there anything the would make them quit politics?" the answers are varied. Some of our informants were quite active in politics, as related earlier. Most insist that they would not quit easily but also add that, to them, politics is not an *obsession* nor a *passion.* It is something that is fulfilling, fun and meaningful. However, they would opt out quite easily if:

(a) the people no longer wanted them to serve, as signified by their poor showing at the polls.

(b) their party is found to be corrupt and mundane, accepting bribes, engaging in dishonesty, etc.

(c) politics badly disrupted their family life and marital relationship.

One informant strongly asserted that politics was so important to her that she would give up her husband, children and even life for it. In her opinion, her party stands for political reform which will inevitably lead to social reform. Therefore, politics is a social cause and the means to realize a better society. However, she said she would quit if and when the people refused to go to the polls to help improve the would. If only 10 per cent of eligible voters went to the poll, she would be discouraged and would readily quit.

So great is their disinterest in politics that many women did not know the names of the members of Parliament from their respective constituencies. The village women were, however, able to mention the name of the health minister, as he hailed from that area and was a very popular figure; but these very women found it difficult to name the Foreign Minister or the Minister of Education. In the case of our sample from the town, those who could mention the names of the ministers cam from the upper middle class, and even there, the percentage of those who gave these names was around 40. In the Bangkok metropolitan area, 10 per cent from the lower class, and 15 per cent from the middle class were able to identify members of the parliament. Only 25 per cent could name the foreign minister. However, the woman minister was known to quite a substantial number. Poor people did not regard politics as relevant and useful. Seventy per cent of the village poor and 67 per cent of the urban poor thought that politics is meant for the urban rich and the educated. They did not think it proper for their men to enter politics, as the amount of money required for doing politics is just not affordable to them. While views differed regarding the politicians, a majority of the respondents from all three localities, perceived politicians as 'dishonest,' 'corrupt,' 'unfair,' and 'insincere,.' They were of the view that politicians will never do anything to improve their communities and solve their problems. Of course, the respondents did qualify their statements by mentioning that not all politicians are alike; there are good an bad politicians—but more bad than good.

In general, women showed a lower sense of political efficacy by answering in the negative all questions designed to elicit their faith in the power of the ballot, or in the political process. They said that it was immaterial whether they participate in the electoral process or not. Things will happen as the politicians will decide. Such feeling was greater among the village women. But all the respondents in the three locales were generally of the view that in recent times the situation of women in Thailand has changed for the better and that they receive good treatment. Their number in the labour force is also growing.

On the hypothetical question of making a choice between a woman candidate and a male candidate, the responses were tilted in favour of the male candidate — politics is the domain of the men, they felt. Respondents also said, in majority, that they vote for the individual and not the party on whose ticket he/she contests. Thus, it is the personality and not the party ideology that is important consideration in voting. Their reason for choosing a particular candidate was that the candidate had proved to be good and reliable or that the party leader was well liked, capable etc. Personality dominates over everything else. Faith in, and liking for, a party leader, therefore, shed a positive light on the candidate's party as well.

Viewed in terms of voting behaviour, it can be said that women in Thailand are high on the political participation index. But this can be misleading. The government makes all efforts to ensure that every person votes, almost as a required duty. In some districts officials persuade, cajole, and even coerce the residents to go to the polls. This leads to a high voting percentage.

A CASE STUDY

Definitiely, the preceding discussion leads us to believe that most women in Thailand—irrespective of their residence (rural or urban) — are apolitical. But there are exceptions. One such exception is Aunt Noy, a lower class woman living in Bangkok. Her strong interest in, and her commitment to politics make her a special case worthy of being described. Her life may perhaps give us an insight into the very subject of our study.

Aunt Noy is a small built, 59-year-old woman with snowy white hair, slightly blackened teeth, and cracked, dry lips with permanent stains left by her chewing betel nut with lime. At fist glance, she resembles a multitude of older women in Thai society: small, frail looking, simply dressed, aging prematurely from hard work and yet short of money. But underneath Aunt Noy is a dynamic personality, a woman of a strong character and will, of unwavering courage and determination, of fighting spirit, and strong leadership qualities. Her strong voice reverberates though the crowd as she instructs, persuades, and cajoles her audience into following her orders. In order words, she is an informal local leader who acts as a broker—a go-between—between the people in the local community and the 'external' world.

The local community is a lane (or Soi in Thai) off a road that has only lately become an important artery of Bangkok. In this Soi, there are a number of large and medium-sized houses with private compounds. The people residing in them are middle class and upper middle class. But the community to which Aunt Noy belongs a composed of rows and rows of tiny houses standing next to each other in a most congested manner. These shanties are made of make-shift and even discarded materials, giving an appearance of transience, impermanence, and of physical dilapidation. This is what one would immediately identify as a slum area. Needless to say, the residents do not own the land that they live on. Because of the widespread poverty in this area, having a roof over one's head is the only essential need. Everything else is a luxury.

Population density and a large number of eligible voters have generated interest in the community within a certain political party and, as a result, political field workers have attempted to organise and mobilise its support. This is where Noy found her calling.

She responded to politics by establishing herself as a local agent for the aforementioned party. Through her, campaign messages and news were passed on to the people. She gathered their complaints and desires for the improvement of living conditions. She prioritised the residents' First of demands and presented them to the party via its field workers. The role of Noy as an agent and broker for the community has yielded positive results. The party, which won overwhelming support from her community, reciprocated by building a small, concrete walkway in between the rows of houses. Prior to the construction of this permanent structure, residents had to make do with rickety wood planks that served as a tiny pathway. Her effort gained her honour and prestige. Not only did she feel that she had helped her community, but she was introduced to members of the party leadership, She has been a devoted fan of the party leader ever since he had shifted his loyalties from another party and founded one himself. Her admiration for him is based on his ability to convey his honesty and sincerity.

She did not mind that he and his party had a slim chance of forming the government, because she realised that he received little support from the military and that other parties would not like to include him in the coalition. But her faith in him and his party was firm. As a registered party member, she feels that she should enjoy a privileged status. Therefore, when election time arrives, she is always prepared to act as a vote canvasser and a campaign worker—tasks which she claims she has performed very well. Imagine her disappointment in the last election in 1988, when her party did not approach her to do anything special. Out of loyalty to the party and its leader, she campaigned for the candidates as the same.

However, she could not understand why they did not come to her with special instructions as they had always done. Her pride and joy derived from having met leaders, and especially the top leader. This little personal touch gave her the strength and energy she needed to continue working and giving support to other. In what ways is Noy different from other women? Clearly, her involvement in politics indicates that she is strong and not unwilling to assume a leadership position. In fact, active participation in social and community life comes naturally to her. Noy's leadership qualities were manifest in many different ways. She is gregarious and knows the community and its members. People talk to her and tell her about their lives and problems. The police in charge of this area discovered that she was an informal leader. They contacted her for information and tips on crime and the security of the neighbourhood. Again, she accepted willingly this role as a intermediary between the authority and the people. Likewise when the community itself, or even the wealthier people in the lane, had problems such as theft, they solicited her assistance and advice. She was successful in negotiating for the return of lost items or in reporting and turning in drug addicts and petty criminals to the police. Having assumed the role of an informal leader, she was compelled to be generous to her followers. Although not a woman of means, she devoted a major portion of her income to the public. She would feed community members as often as she could afford it. One year, she made a vow that if she made a handsome profit from the sale of durians, she would spend it on her youngest son's ordination. Fortunately she did make a lot of money that year, and gave a grand feast on the occasion of her son's ordination.

Her neighbours can not fault her for lack of generosity and this has also strengthened her position as an informal leader. In the Thai context, a leader must be ready and willing to give and to provide for his (or her) followers. Noy is also generous in contributing towards religious merit-making. She divides her extra income among different types of religious donations. In her words, by donating to charity she is contributing towards a better future life. But religious merit-making is also considered a social virtue and is well regarded in Thai society. A religious person is seen as a person of high moral character and principle. This enhances a person's standing in the community. Leaders, it is felt, should also possess good moral qualities.

Thus we begin to understand the various factors which contributed to Noy's role as an informal community leader.

What about her personal life? We discover that it is also far from ordinary. She came from a low income family. Her mother, substantially better-off than her father, was related to a lesser noble of the feudal days. Before she completed fourth grade, her life was shattered by the separation of her parents. Her mother was unwilling to share the same roof with a woman his father was bringing in as a minor wife. His reason for taking another wife was her mother's inability to provide him with a male child. As ill luck would have it, her father had a total of eight daughters but no sons from the two wives.

When her parents separated, Noy remained with her father. However, when she finished forth grade, her father disregarded her principal's plea to let her continue her schooling and placed her instead in a doctor's home/clinic in Ayuthaya province to work as a child-servant. In fact, her status was that of an indentured servant for her father collected all her wages. But she did not complain. She felt that it was her filial duty to serve her father; besides her basic needs were provided by her employer.

While working for this doctor she discovered that he performed abortions on women and she was forced to assist in this supposedly de-meritorious act by cleaning up afterwards and burying the aborted embryos. Once, while digging in the ground to bury a fetus, she discovered a pot of buried treasures; old jewellery and gold. It was a windfall for her and she believed that the clinic must have been built on a one-time temple ground. Over the next few years. She worked very hard. During this period, she was in love with a performer from a likay company. But nothing came of that infatuation. When she was about 18, the Doctor raped her. In desperation, she ran away looking for her mother. Humiliated, confused and pregnant, she decided she could not bear to go to her father and the stepmother since they had given her this employment. By the time she found her mother her mother had remarried, but for a brief period during her late pregnancy and childbirth her mother gave her refuge.

After her child was born, misfortune struck her once again. Her stepfather raped her this time. The blow was too severe for her mother and she died of a broken heart. Noy then left to seek work on her own. She found a strenuous job in the railways, as helper to the engine driver in the train. When she stumbled upon the opportunity to change her job, she seized it. She preferred to be a hawker selling cloth. Then she fell in love and got married. Meanwhile, her son was traced by his natural father and was taken back to Ayuthaya. The marriage produced two sons. Her business prospered and she inherited a little sum of money from a piece of land that her mother had left her. Her life was good. She felt that she would never be poor again. But then she discovered that her husband was a professional pick-pocket and the fact struck her like a bolt of lightning. She had often wondered about his work. How did he work odd hours and bring home irregular sums of money? But he had explained that he was a salesman and that his earnings come strictly from commissions. Now, he ignored her repeated pleas to give up this criminal life. His brushes with the law increased as the proportion of her wealth and income she spent to defend him decreased. Totally disenchanted, she decided that she should leave her husband.

No matter how much she begged him, he refused to grant her a divorce and insisted that he still loved. Her. Finally, in desperation, her older cousin and her cousin-in-law developed a plan: they would create a situation which would force her husband to divorce her. Her cousin-in-law pretended to be her lover and took her to stay with them. This convinced her husband, who finally agreed to a divorce.

What was to follow was not what she had anticipated. While staying with her cousin's family immediately after the divorce, her cousin-in-law forced himself sexually on her. As a result, she became his minor wife and also bore all the responsibilities of raising the household. She was a small-scale entrepreneur, selling different things and later making desserts and sweets for sale. Business prospered for a while. She bore this husband four sons and raised two sons from her previous marriage, as well as a few other children, belonging to her husband and her cousin—his first wife.

She struggled to rise these more than ten children with the aim of giving them the best possible education. She was strict in their upbringing, never lax in disciplining them.

Her cousin was in-charge of cooking and cleaning for the family while Noy brought in the money for everyone. Although there was a tacit understanding of the division of labour between the two wives in the family, and all children were supposed to be treated alike, life was not totally harmonious. Occasionally her husband strayed into a series of affairs and flirtations with other women which brought a lot of pain. When her sons grew up, she used her connections with the 'external' world to seek patrons to place them in jobs that she felt were desirable.

The saddest moment in her life was when she learned about her best loved son's death in a motorcycle accident. Even as she told us the story which had happened many years before, she broke down and sobbed.

Politics in the Thai context denotes primarily the electoral process. For people, politics is what politicians do in order to be elected so that they can have positions, money and power. Elections are central to the careers of the women politicians. Hence, they make every effort to establish and maintain a good relationship with their voters.

Politics in the Thai context denotes primarily the electoral process. For people, politics is what politicians do in order to be elected so that they can have positions, money and power. Elections are central to the careers of the women politicians. Hence, they make every effort to establish and maintain a good relationship with their voters.

Politics also means that exchange of favours. People expect their politicians to do concrete things for their community in exchange for their support. Women politicians feel strongly that it is their duty and responsibility to respond to their voters by providing assistance and services which translated easily into social welfare acts or programmes.

It is at this point that some women politicians may be diverted from the role of a politician to the role of a social welfare worker. Difficult boiled politics may require one to be in the midst of power struggles and competitions which often involve arm-twisting and negotiating, as well as compromising, bargaining and exchanging favours. A successful politician must set his/her priorities correctly in order to maintain control over everything, including his/her position towards other members of his/her party.

On examining the literature on women and politics in other countries and comparing their findings to the situation in Thailand, common hindrances and obstacles to women's participation in politics were observed. These are: male dominance, role limitations imposed on women as mother and wife, socialisation factors, women's acceptance of male hegemony, women's lack of technological skills and knowledge, which is a disadvantage in dealing with information (Kirkpatrick: 1979, Currell: 1974, Elliott: 1977, Millett: 1971). However, on further comparison, other characteristics peculiar to Thailand begin to appear. A significant number of Thai women who have been recruited into politics appear to share the following features: they are related to known male politicians either by blood or marriage. In other words, they have inherited political legitimacy from their male kin and this has facilitated their entry into politics. Moreover, some of them were drawn into politics not because they were native to their constituency, because their education and social class influenced their public behaviour or even because their parents had a leading role in inculcating in them a strong sense of public spirit and public responsibility, as Kirkpatrick has argued. On the contrary, they were recruited inspite of all of these factors. In the Thai case, wealth is a decided advantage and some of our women politicians are quite wealthy. How women are recruited into politics may depend more on their socio-economic background and their stature in society. Well-known women or public personalities tend to be favoured as candidates by political parties.

No party wishes to build up the career of unknown woman because merely fielding a woman candidate is already seen as risky. In local politics, the Thai situation is somewhat similar to the West; local candidates have a slight advantage over non-local ones. The data on municipal elections discussed in this paper, show this clearly. But in the Thai context, money is a crucial factor, irrespective of the level at which women would like to participate. Without it, the struggle is very difficult indeed. In local politics in Malaysia, successful women leaders tend to come from the families of civil servants and tend to be educated. They also use education as a tool for achieving their position in politics (Manderson: 1980). However, women who successfully achieve election to political and administrative positions in Thailand, have a different background. Often they have strong family backing. Education is neither a special criterion nor a tool in the realisation of their political ambition.

Political women in Thailand tend to learn about politics from men, rather than from other women. For one thing, there are many more men than women in politics. But women politicians are not especially close or attached to one another. Little camaraderie or sense of sisterhood is felt by women who pursue the same career. In fact, women politicians admitted that men were good mentors and no special reason to seek advice or help from their *consoeurs*. Perhaps, as one woman politician insisted, a suppressed competitiveness, mingled with a little jealousy or even hostility, exists between women more than between men and women.

Do women politicians perform their tasks well or adequately? Our investigation suggests that they take their work seriously. Most of them are committed to their work; they are hardworking, and responsive to the needs and wants of their voters. By and large, no complaints about their performance are made by either men or women. If anything, they elicited praise for their diligence, empathy, sensitivity, good human relations, ability to co-ordinate and negotiate, along with 'softness,' gentelness and good manners. The women politicians also evaluate their own performance, or strong points, in the same way. But has their presence significantly advanced women's position in Thai politics and the evolution of Thai politics in general? Perhaps not that much. Not only they present numbers as compared to male politicians, but they are not a single cohesive group. Women politicians are also divided along party lines, and therefore they do not act in unison to produce a joint 'impact.'

REFERENCES

Amara Pongsapich (ed), 1986, *Women Issues Book of Readings,* Bangkok. Institute of Social Research, Chulalongkorn University.

——, 1988, *Occasional Papers on Women in Thailand.* Women's Studies Programme, Chulalongkorn University, Publication No. 3.

——, 1989 *Women Leadership in Rural Area.* A paper prepared for Women's Conferences and Leadership Development Programme, Bangkok, Thailand.

Apichai Janeteerawong, 1989, *Relationship between Backgrounds of Women Politicians and Political Recruitment: a Study of Members of Thai Municipal Councils.* A thesis submitted to Chulalongkorn University, Department of Government.

Aphichart Chamratrittirong and Thephi Bandhumedha, 1989, *Problems and Obstacles of Local Women Leaders: A Group*

Discussion Research Methodology. Department of Local Administration, Ministry of Interior.

Bhassorn Limanonda, 1985, *Research Report on Local Women Leaders: an Analysis of Census Data*. Department of Local Administration, Ministry of Interior.

Carolyn M. Elliot, 1977, "Theories of Development: an Assessment" in *Women and National Development: the Complexities of Change*. Chicago: the University of Chicago Press.

Jean J. Kirkpatrick, 1979, *Political Women*. Princeton: the Eagleton Institute of Politics, Rutgers University.

Kanala Sukhabanij-Khantaprab and Pongsak Pongpaew, 1984, *Thai Women Intellectuals: A Study on the Socio-Political Attitudes of Women Professors at Chulalongkom University, Srinakharinwirot University at Prasanmit and NIDA*. A research report presented to Chulalongkorn University.

Kanala Sukhabanij-Khantaprab, 1986, "Women and Thai Politics" in *Women's Issues a Book of Readings,* edited by Amara Pongsapich. Bangkok: Institute of Social Research, Chulalongkorn University.

Kate Millett, 1971, *Sexual Politics*. New York: Equinox Books, Doubleday and Comp. Inc.

Lenore Manderson, 1980, *Women Politics and Change*. London: Oxford University Press.

Malee Pruekpongsawalee, 1986, "Women and Law" in *Women's Issues a Book of Readings,* edited by Amara Pongsapich. Bangkok: Institute of Social Research, Chulalongkorn University.

Prathip Chongsubthum, 1985, *Women Leadership in the Thai Local Administration: A Study of the Role of Women Village and Tumbon Chiefs Throughout the Country in the Year 1985:* A master's thesis submitted to Chulalongkorn University. Department of Government, Faculty of Political Science.

Pongrit Khongprasit, 1985, *Research Report on Local Women Leaders:* an Analysis of Interviews and Mailed Questionnaires.

Smira Chittaladakorn, 1985, *Women Leadership in Thai Local Administration.* A Ph.D. thesis submitted to Chulalongkorn University, Political Science Programme.

Suteera Thompson, et al., 1988, Concept paper: *The Role of Thai Women in Development.* Women in Development Project, Thailand Development Research Institute Foundation.

Suteera Thomson, 1989, *Integrating Grassroots Women's Concerns into Mainstream Agriculture and Development in Thailand.* A paper presented to UNIFEM's Series of Briefings on Putting Women in the mainstream: Experience from Asia.

5

Women Leadership in Australia

MODERN Australia comprises a land area of 7,682,300 square kilometres, and land mass 50 per cent grater than Europe or approximately the same size as USA (excluding Alaska). The island continent is relatively flat; approximately 87 per cent of its total land mass is below 500 metres. Additionally, the continent is quite dry with 50 per cent of the area having a median rainfall of less than 300 milimetres per year. Many of the inland areas with very low rainfall are desert. Regions with the highest rainfall are the mountainous area of Tasmania, the semi-tropical east cost of Queensland, the Snowy Mountains region of NSW and pockets of Victoria. There is a fairly high incidence of flooding in the north and eastern coastal areas. Similarly drought have had severe economic consequences for primary industry. Due to the absence of mountain masses, extreme cold temperatures are not as low compared to other continents. On the other hand, high maximum temperatures are reached, up to 50°C over the inland.

Australia is a relatively rich nation. The country is one of the world's major commodity producers. Wool and wheat, and to a lesser extent, meat and dairy products, represent a large component of Australia's overseas exports. Since the 1960s, development of Australia's extensive mineral resources has complemented agricultural exports. While resource development is often located in remote regions of the North or the interior, Australia's manufacturing industries are concentrated in the South-eastern corner of the continent. In the past, these industries were protected from high tariff barriers but there is now strong encouragement from both state and federal governments for improved export competitiveness and expansion into the high tech areas. Likewise, the tertiary sector has looked towards export in the health, education, communications, and tourism areas.

The political geography of Australia reflects its colonial origins when the continent was divided up into six autonomous colonies. These colonies federated in 1901 of form the Commonwealth of Australia. It is a federal system with a national government based in Canberra, and six state governments of New South Wales (NSW), Victoria, Western Australia (WA), South Australia (SA), Queensland and Tasmania, was well as two territories, the Northern Territory (NT) and the Australian Capital Territory (ACT). Local government forms the third layer of government in Australia but, traditionally, it has not been as strong a force as in other nations.

Australia is not a densely populated nation. Over the past century, Australia has experienced rapid but variable population growth. The first significant period of population growth was during the gold rushes of the 1850s and during the subsequent economic diversification and pastoral expansion. The second period of growth followed the two great wars. The population is increasing at a rapid rate and was approximately 19 million by 2000.

From the 1860s through to the late 1940s, natural increase was the major engine of population growth. In the post-World War II era, this trend was reversed. The federal government sponsored a massive immigration programme from northern and southern European countries to help meet labour needs in Australia's post-war reconstruction. After federation and prior to the 1950s, the White Australia policy meant that British overseas born were predominant among immigrants. The removal of immigration restrictions, however, has seen the diversification in the overseas born population of Australia. Immigration has contributed to the increasingly multi-cultural nature of Australian society.

The Australian population is heavily concentrated in capital cities and in a few others cities on the eastern and southern coasts. The population has been characterised by a rural to urban drift. In 1921, for example, over 37 per cent of the population lived in rural areas but this had dropped to 14.5 per cent in 1986. This trend reflects increased industrialisation over the past century and the decline of the family farm.

During the early years of settlement there was a heavy concentration of young males in the Australian population. But gradually the situation was changed, and in 1981 the female population of Australia exceeded males. Among the older age groups there is a more pronounced bias towards females. An important characteristic of the Australian population is that it is aging. The median age of the population has increased from about 20 years in the 1880s to 31 years in the 1980s. Furthermore, the proportion of the population aged 65 and over has increased significantly whereas the proportion of the population aged less than 15 has dropped. From the 1950s, there has been a decline in the level of fertility although the absolute number of births has been increasing. This is in part due to the availability of oral contraceptives from the 1950s, women in the 1980s are more likely to defer and restrict child-rearing to the middle range of their reproductive years. The Australian population has consequently 'aged' with the effects of declining birth rates and improvements in life expectancy. This phenomenon is of particular significance to women since they tend to have longer life expectancy.

As a consequence, sate and federal policies in regard to housing, social security, and especially health and other welfare services are likely to have disproportionate effect on women. Policy formulation will tend to be more sensitive to their needs. Since 1911, Household formation has exceeded population growth and the number of people per household has dropped. The number of one and two person households has grown due to reductions in completed family size, the availability of mortgage financing by instalments since the 1920s, and demographic factors such as the baby boom years after 1047 which lead to high rates of household formation in the late 1960s and 1970s.

Higher life expectancy has also increased the incidence of older couples and persons remaining in separate households. From the beginning of the century there have been three noticeable patterns in marriage statistics. Firstly, a far higher proportion of the population was marrying, secondly, the age range of marriage narrowed with a preference for marriage at younger ages, and thirdly, the differences of ages between the sexes was reduced. Prior to World War II, almost 25 per cent of the population never married. After the war there was a much greater incidence of marriage which translated into births in the favourable boom years of the 1960s.

Since the early 1970s additional marriage patterns have emerged. The number of marriages in which neither party has been married has fallen. Secondly, the median age of first marriage has risen. There has been a steady rise in divorces over most of last century. A rapid increase commenced with the Family Law Act of 1974. Furthermore, the duration of marriages that end in divorce has shortened while there is an increasing tendency for divorce to occur in the earlier years of marriage and at earlier ages. The increase in divorce, greater numbers of teenage pregnancy and the availability of supporting parents benefit have led to the growth of single parent families. In 1987, they represented 9 per cent of the total number of families.

Australia is a predominantly white and English speaking nation. With white, settlement, aboriginal society was greatly devastated. It began to reassert itself since the 1960s. Multicultural policies of the government initiated in the 1970s have acknowledged diverse cultural backgrounds of the people who have immigrated to Australia such as the Greek, Italian and Vietnamese communities. Even so, the major political, judicial, educational and cultural institutions in Australia continue to be dominated by the Anglo-Celtic majority.

Woman and Government in Australia

From the turn of the 20th century, women have participated in government in Australia. Following federation, the government of the newly formed Commonwealth of Australia passed the *Commonwealth Franchise Act 1902* allowing most women to both vote and stand in the federal election of 1903. The crown colonies of South Australia and Western Australia granted women the vote before federation, and the states of New South Wales, Tasmania, Queensland and Victoria also passed legislation allowing women to participate in government at the state and local levels following federation. Indigenous Australian women did not achieve suffrage at all levels of government and in all states and territories until 1962.

Although Australia was the first country to allow women to stand in elections, women were not successful at a federal election until 1943. In general women have been slow to enter all levels of politics in Australia. Most states are yet to have a female Premier and neither of the main political parties has had a federal parliamentary female leader.

Women's Suffrage

Women's suffrage groups began to appear in the Australian political landscape in the 1880s. The first, the Victorian Women's Suffrage Society, was formed by Henrietta Dugdale in Victoria in 1884. The organisations involved in the suffrage movement varied across the colonies. A unified body, the Australian Women's Suffrage Society was formed in 1889, the societies aims were to educate women and men about a women's right to vote and stand for parliament. Key figures in the Australian suffrage movement included, from South Australia Mary Lee and Catherine Helen Spence, in Western Australia Edith Cowan, from New South Wales Maybanke Anderson, Louisa Lawson, Dora Montefiore and Rose Scott, Tasmanians Alicia O'Shea Petersen and Jessie Rooke, Queenslander Emma Miller, and Victorians Annette Bear-Crawford, Henrietta Dugdale, Vida Goldstein, Alice Henry and Annie Lowe.

In 1861 land-owning South Australian women were able to vote in local elections. In 1894, South Australia became the second jurisdiction in the world extend franchise to women and the first to allow women to stand for State Parliament. South Australian women voted for the first time in the 1896 South Australian House of Assembly election. In 1897 Catherine Helen Spence became the first woman political candidate when she ran for election to the National Australasian Convention as one of ten delegates, but came 22nd out of 33 candidates. In 1899 Western

Australian women achieved voting rights for State elections but not the right to stand for State Parliament. In 1901 women from both South and Western Australia voted in the 1901 federal election.

The Introduction of Women's Political Tights in Australia

Parliament	*Right to vote (a)*	*Right to stand*	*First elected to lower house*	*First elected to upper house*
Commonwealth	1902 (b)	1902	1943, Enid Lyons	1943, Dorothy Tangney
State				
South Australia	1894	1894	1959, Joyce Steele	1959, Jessie Cooper
Western Australia	1899	1920	1921, Edith Cowan	1954, Ruby Hutchison
New South Wales	1902	1918	1925, Millicent Preston-Stanley	1952 (c), Gertrude Melville
Tasmania	1903	1921	1955, Mabel Miller and Amelia Best	1948, Margaret McIntyre
Queensland	1905	1915	1929, Irene Longman	n.a.
Victoria	1908	1923	1933, Millie Peacock	1979, Gracia Baylor, Joan Coxsedge

(a) The dates for the right to vote at State level refer to equal rights for women and men, but not necessarily universal rights;

(b) Women in SA and WA were able to vote in the 1901 federal election;

(c) Two women, Catherine Green and Ellen Webster, had been appointed to the upper house in 1931.

On 12 June 1902 the *Commonwealth Franchise Act* came into effect, granting most Australian women the right to vote and stand in Commonwealth elections. Franchise of Indigenous Australians at the federal level was not universal until 1962, and voting by Indigenous Australians was not compulsory until 1984. The first election at which women used both the right to vote and stand for election was held 16 December 1903. Four women stood for election: Selina Sarah Elizabeth Anderson stood for election to the House of Representatives for the Division of Dalley; and Vida Goldstein, Nellie Alma Martel and Mary Ann Moore ran for Senate positions; none were successful.

Following the inclusion of women in the 1903 election, many Australian women and the Australian government, led by Prime Minister Alfred Deakin, used their experience to promote women's suffrage in the United Kingdom and elsewhere. 'Trust the Women Mother, As I Have Done', banner painted by Dora Meeson was carried at the head of the Australian and New Zealand Women Voters' Committee contingent in the Women's Suffrage Coronation March in London on 17 June 1911.

New South Wales, Tasmania, Queensland and Victoria followed the lead of the other states in allowing women to vote, and later to stand for election. Victoria, the last state to grant women's suffrage, had briefly allowed women to vote when the *Electoral Act* 1863 enfranchised all ratepayers listed on local municipal rolls. Women in Victoria voted in the 1864 general election. The legislative mistake was quickly repaired in 1865, it took 19 private members' bills from 1889 until Victorian women gained the vote in 1908, and were able to exercise the vote in 1911. Women in the Northern Territory and the Australian Capital Territory were, as federal subjects, eligible to vote at the federal level from their establishment. By the time the territories achieved self-government in 1978 and 1989 respectively, they did not need to enact specific legislation to enable the women's vote.

Women's participation in local government in Australia

	Right to vote (a)	Right to stand	First elected
State			
South Australia	1861	1914	1919, Grace Benny
Western Australia	1876	1919	1920, Elizabeth Clapham
Victoria	1903	1914	1920, Mary Rogers
Queensland	1879	1920	1925, Ellen Kent-Hughes

City of Brisbane	1924	1924	1949, Petronel White
Tasmania			
Rural	1893	1911	1957, Florence Vivien Pendrigh
Hobart City Council	1893	1902	1952, Mabel Miller
Launceston City Council	1894	1945	1950, Dorothy Edwards
New South Wales			
Sydney City Council	1900	1918	1965, Joan Mercia Pilone
Municipalities and Shires	1906	1918	1928, Lilian Fowler

(a) The right to vote in local elections was not necessarily universal since there were property ownership restrictions on the right to vote in many local jurisdictions. Modified from Sawer, 2001

The right to vote in local government elections was granted later in most jurisdictions than it was at the state and federal levels. The right to vote in local elections was also not automatic, as property ownership qualifications limited the eligibility to vote and stand for local elections.

Women in Government

Commonwealth Government

In most countries, women entered parliament soon after gaining the right to stand. The first women successfully elected to the Commonwealth government were both elected in 1943, 40 years after they were able. The major Australian political parties did not support any female candidates until the Second World War, until this time all female candidates were independent or backed by minor political parties. In 1943 and with major party backing, Dame Enid Lyons was elected to the House of Representatives as the member for the Division of Darwin, which was located in Tasmania, and Dorothy Tangney was elected to the Australian Senate representing Western Australia. In 1949 Enid Lyons became the first female cabinet member, however her appointment as Vice-President of the Executive Council did not involve the administration of any department. In 1966 Senator Dame Annabelle Rankin became the first woman with a federal portfolio when she became Minister for Housing. In 1975 Senator Margaret Guilfoyle was the first female cabinet minister with a portfolio, Education.

In 1983 Ros Kelly was the first woman to give birth while an MP. In 1986 there were two firsts, Joan Child became the first female Speaker of the House of Representatives and Janine Haines became the first woman to lead a parliamentary party when she became head of the Australian Democrats. Margaret Reid became the first female President of the Senate in 1996.

Kathy Sullivan, with a total service of 27 years, is the longest-serving female federal parliamentarian. She was the first woman to have served in both the Senate and the House of Representatives.

In the Forty-First Parliament of Australia there are 23 female senators and 37 women in the House of Representatives.

Commonwealth Public Service

The *Commonwealth Public Service Act 1902* stated that every female officer was "deemed to have retired from the Commonwealth service upon her marriage". The very great majority of women were effectively blocked from non-secretarial positions in the Commonwealth Public Service. In 1949 women were allowed into the clerical division of the service but they remained restricted by the marriage rule. In 1966 Australia became the last democratic countries to lift the ban on married women in the public service.

State Government

The first woman elected to a state parliament was

Western Australian Edith Cowan when she was elected to the Western Australian Legislative Assembly in 1921. Millicent Preston-Stanley was elected to the New South Wales Legislative Assembly in 1925, Irene Longman was elected to the Queensland Legislative Assembly in 1929 and Millie Peacock was elected to the Victorian Legislative Assembly in 1933. Ironically, South Australia as the first state to allow women to sit in state parliament, was also the last to have a female sitting member when Joyce Steele and Jessie Cooper were elected on the same day in 1959. Both the Australian Capital Territory Legislative Assembly and Northern Territory Legislative Assembly had women in their inaugural Parliaments. Women were not elected to the Upper House of state parliaments until after World War II.

In 1989 Rosemary Follett became the first female head of government in Australia, as Chief Minister of the Australian Capital Territory. Carmen Lawrence was the first female premier of an Australian state when she took office in February 1990. She was followed by the appointment of Joan Kirner as Premier of Victoria in 1990. Clare Martin was Chief Minister of the Northern Territory from 2001 to 2007. Anna Bligh became Premier of Queensland in 2007 when Peter Beattie retired. In 2008, she became the first woman in Australia to be elected Premier.

The Queensland Legislative Assembly currently has the highest female parliamentary representation in Australia and the third highest in the world with 30 out of 89 Members being women.

Local Government

The first woman elected to a local government authority in Australia was Grace Benny, who was elected to the

Brighton Council in South Australia in 1919. Mary Rogers was elected to Richmond City Council, Victoria in 1920 and Elizabeth Clapham was elected to Western Australia's Cottesloe Town Council. Queensland's first female councillor was Dr Ellen Kent-Hughes, elected to Kingaroy Shire Council in 1925. New South Wales' first female alderman was Lilian Fowler, elected in 1928 to Newtown Municipal Council; she was later to become Australia's first woman mayor. New South Wales also produced Australia's first female Lord Mayor, Alderman Joy Cummings, who was elected to Newcastle City Council in 1974. Dorothy E Edwards, Tasmania's first alderman, was elected to Launceston City Council in 1950.

In 1951 the Australian Local Government Women's Association (ALGWA) was formed. A unique organisation, it is an association of local government women helping other women to join them.

In 1975 Western Australia and the Northern Territory elected their first women mayors, Councillor Evelyn H. Parker of Subiaco and Dr Ella Stack of Darwin City respectively.

In the 1980s women began to hold the position of Lord Mayor in the capital cities for the first time, including:

(a) Brisbane - Sallyanne Atkinson (1985-91)

(b) Hobart - Doone Kennedy (1986-96)

(c) Melbourne - Lecki Ord (1987-88) and Winsome McCaughey (1988-89)

(d) Sydney - Lucy Turnbull (2003-04) and Clover Moore (2004-).

The recent developments are as follows: in the first

instance, a small but significant number of the women politicians have become Ministers and Senior Parliamentary Officers at both the Federal and the State levels; secondly, a small but growing number of non-labour women have been elected to Australian Parliaments to complicate the model of ALP hegemony at least in the numerical sense and; thirdly, many of the 'second wave' of women politicians of the 1970s have been in Parliament long enough now to have themselves developed or changed and to have observed changes around them. These three developments have not yet from fully charted or analysed. Marian Sawer and myself have, in various articles and papers, commented on some of these changes. The 1984 Federal elections, for example, saw an increase in the numbers of women candidates fielded by the Liberal Party some of whom were elected to the Federal parliament. The views of some of these women belied the notion that women politicians will necessarily share a feminist or even a female consciousness.

Many of the Liberal Party's women candidates in 1984, for example, disagreed with the existence of separate and identifiable *women's* issues. They urged too that politics should be blind to gender differences. A number, but by no means all, of these women supported a variant of free market ideology which advocated *inter alia* the cutting of government services to women and children. It is clearly not the case that the election of more women to Australian Parliaments will necessarily lead to an increase in expenditure by governments on services to women and children.

Furthermore, some ALP women Members of Parliaments (MPs) as well as many anti-Labour women MPs are quite wary of the feminist label. It is still, however, a very important research issue to address the question of the similarities and differences amongst women MPs of all parties towards their own position as 'political' women as well as towards the position of women in Australian politics and society. This question has underpinned my analysis of the three major developments for women in Australian politics during the 1980s. The answer to this question will formulated in the third section and will rely heavily on the results of the interviews with women politicians; as a preliminary to this, and before a more extensive examination of the history of the women's involvement in Australian politics in section two.

Some salient features of Australia's political landscape are described, and some comments are offered about the ways in which this influenced the methodology for this study. Australia has been labelled variously as a *small rich industrial country,* a *lucky country* and a *workingman's paradise.* If we take these three aphorisms together we end up with a small advanced capitalist country with some kind of equalitarian heart. These labels are all relative. Australia was widely seen as a 'workingman's paradise' over a 100 years ago in contrast with the 'old world.' The invention and early adoption of the secret ballot (1956) and the 'early' adoption of universal suffrage (1902) — except for the Aborigines—for the Federal Parliament were widely seen as progressive or at least experimental moves.

Labour parties were formed in the colonies of New South Wales and Queensland in the wake of the 'great strikes' of the 1890s. These Parties, however, were blind to the question of sex discrimination and were vehemently opposed to 'coloured' immigration, ostensibly on the grounds of job competition. Religion was to became a major factor as well. After a major split in 1916 over military conscription the Australian Labour Party became predominantly a Catholic Party of the Irish variety.

Political parties took firm hold in Australian politics in the twentieth century. The dominance of a so-called two-and-a-half party system was ensured by the introduction of compulsory voting for Federal and State elections and with the introduction too of the preferential (i.e. alternate) voting system for the single-member constituencies of the House of Representatives.

The strength of parties is reflected by three main indicators. First, independent Members of the Federal House of Representatives have been very scarce indeed since the Second World War. The ALP has faced the anti-Labour team of the Liberal and National (junior partner) Parties. Secondly, Party solidarity within the Federal parliament is at a premium. Labour Party MPs are not allowed to vote against the Party's line unless on a specifically designated 'conscience' vote—Liberal Party MPs do not have such formal restrictions but voting against the party, or 'crossing the floor' as it is known, is fairly unusual. Persistent offenders are liable for punishments such as losing the Party's endorsement at the next election. Thirdly, on the labour side of politics at least, internal party factions are highly developed. Internal party divisions are not particularly novel or unusual.

The fact that the ALP has undergone three major splits during this century provides ample testimony to the prevalence of divisions. The significant feature of the operation of party factions, 1980s style, for the ALP is that ordinary party members and Parliamentary Party members alike are tied to a particular variant of the Party's policy as well as to the Party's policy more generally. The Parties themselves are still essentially Federal-style organisations. The State branches are the primary unit of the organisation. The Liberal Party's Federal Secretariat has no power to direct the State branches. The various State branches organise politically and electorally for the State and for the Federal elections. The State branches are responsible for the selection and the re-selection of Parliamentary candidates. In recent times, however, the ALP's head office, its National Executive, has intervened in the selection process.

REMARKABLY, position of women in Australian society has been secondary to that of men. Scholars such as Dixon (1977) and Summers (1975) argue that Australia's early cultural history is marked by a dual perception of women. Summers has characterised women's position as that of either 'Damned whores and god's police." Prior to the 1840s, women in the convict colonial society were viewed as shores, and objects of sexual gratification. From the 1850s, the bourgeois family became a more common form of social organisation and the 'god's police' stereotype of women as mothers and wives with the moral guardianship of, and civilising influence on, society ascended.

The early suffragists espoused this latter view of womanhood. Complementary to the dual image of women in society was the mateship tradition. Men socialise as work mates and companions in the pub. On the one hand, there is a nostalgic view of mateship as egalitarian and democratic, linked, with the notion that the ALP is an innovative social democratic force. On the other hand, the mateship tradition has been criticised by Dixson as one-sided, leaving out men's relationships with women. Women are regarded as sexual providers, not people to converse or work with and are excluded from being mates.

These cultural traits have persevered to the present day and are evident in Australian social and political institutions, in particular, the sexist portrayal of women in advertising. While the Australian labour movements has had great influence in advancing the rights of workers, this strength has not been specifically used to enhance the political rights of women. Women were regarded as no more than workers, not as political participants. By the turn of the century, the unions were committed to industrial arbitration. In 1907, the Harvester Judgement was handed down by the Federal Arbitration Court. It enshrined the concept of a "fair and reasonable wage" which has been a major factor for the persistence of low wages for women.

Essentially, the Tribunal set wages according to the principle that men were the wage earners of a family with a dependent spouse and children. Wages consequently were meant to provide for a man, wife and three children in `frugal comfort.' There were patriarchal assumptions about the proper place of women in the demand that a living wage provides for a man and his dependents, that women be paid less than men (since they would marry eventually), and that women be kept out of certain industries. Women in Australian society are expected to take responsibility for domestic labour, specially childcare

Those women who do work outside the home often have the of two jobs—domestic and paid work. Such expectations can "negatively affect women's attitudes to education, training and work force participation." Such expectations are reinforced by theories (largely discredited) that working mothers have detrimental outcomes for their children who are `denied' the healthy development that can only be provided by a full time mother. Over the past century there have been extensions of the concept of citizenship along with modification and expansion of women's legal rights and improved social justice programmes. From the 1970s a number of changes have been initiated that have greatly altered the position of women in society.

Nevertheless, while women have the same legal, civil and political rights as men, patriarchal power is still evident and major inequities persist.

The differences in the social and economic standing between the sexes is most evident in the workplace. The workforce participation of women has increased significantly since the 1950s. For example, in 1954, 13 per cent of married women with dependent children were in the paid workforce; this steadily increased to 29 per cent in 1966, 43 per cent in 1981, and 47 per cent in 1989 (Edgar, 1989:21).

Policies have been developed by the federal government to protect and enhance women's rights in the workforce such as the 1972 Equal Pay wage case, maternity leave provisions, the Sex Discrimination Act of 1984, and the Affirmative Action Legislation of 1986. Aside from legislation, there are other programmes such as improving the opportunities for girls leaving school to go into male dominated trades such as carpentry and plumbing. For the special needs of migrant women, the federal government funds the Adult Migrant Education Programme. Non-English speaking women who do not learn English when they first reach Australia embark on a cycle of isolation. Lack of English language skills had further implications in restricted social and economic opportunities for these women.

Migrant women tend to be locked into these low status, low paid jobs. As they often experience language and cultural problems they are particularly vulnerable to exploitation. Despite such provisions, the Australian labour market is characterised by a high degree of sex segmentation. Women are concentrated in service industries, predominantly as clerks or as salespersons and personnel staff. Women are under-represented in the professions and tend to clump in 'soft' areas such as education, health and welfare.

Even in these areas, very few women attain managerial positions. To some degree, work-force segmentation originates with the education system. There are many more girls studying domestic sciences, literature, history languages and secretarial courses whereas boys have concentrated on manual courses, physics, maths, economics and chemistry. Furthermore, boys are more likely to go on to apprenticeships or technical and vocational training than girls. Until the 1950s, universities were male dominated, but expansion of the higher education system in the 1960s and the abolition of fees in 1974 led to an influx of women. Nevertheless, women are concentrated in the Arts and Social Sciences while men are more predominant in the physical and biological sciences.

Fewer women go on to graduate study; the academia is thus, male dominated. Women represent just over 27 per cent of all academic staff employed in Australian higher education institutions. Women who do pursue an academic career are often congregated in the lower career grades. While 53 per cent of male academics are senior lecturers, readers of professors, only 22 per cent of women academics attain such positions (*Australian Financial Review*, 5.12.1989).

In general, women's work-force participation brings lower pay, poorer conditions, less mobility and limited provision for training and promotion, compared to traditional male areas of employment.

Unemployment, and under employment, is also higher among women than men but is not accurately reflected in labour market statistics. There are considerable numbers of married or cohabitating women for whom there is no incentive to register as unemployed with the Commonwealth Employment Service as their spouse's income excludes them from social security benefits. There are also more women in part-time and casual work than men. While such work may be conducive a family responsibilities, it is disadvantageous in terms of lower pay, access to promotion and superannuation provision. Demanding better work conditions for part-time and casual work is difficult to pursue.

Part-time and out-workers are not highly unionised; the unions have made little effort to improve their situation. One of the fastest growing areas of employment for women, however, has been the public sector at both federal and state levels. This has translated into high female union membership but has not meant proportionate female participation in union activities or leadership. Poverty in Australia is increasingly feminised with recession and economic downturn since the 1970s. Part-time workers are often the first to be laid off. Furthermore, as many women work intermittently and generally have lower earning power than men, they are less likely to earn a living wage.

Single parent families are particularly hard hit. Over 80 per cent of single parent families are headed by women and these women are often dependent on social security payments that are well below the poverty line (Outhwaite et al. 1988). Their problems are compounded by the failure of many fathers to pay maintenance. Single parents who do have jobs are in a much better position, but even so, they have to pay the high costs of child-care.

Aged women are also at a disadvantaged in the poverty stakes. As they have often had fractured working lives, they have had less opportunity than men to benefit from superannuation schemes that would have made their retirement more comfortable. The position of aged women will became increasingly important towards the end of the last century as the population ages and as the number of aged women reliant on social security increases.

Voluntary work will be of increasing importance as Australian society ages. With decreasing fertility and the changing pattern of women's lives, there will be fewer offspring to care for the elderly, and longer spans in women's lives that will be free from family and work responsibilities. In an era of economic recession and fiscal restraint of government in the welfare areas, self-help and voluntary work of women for aged women is necessarily on the rise.

Government Policies Towards Women's Participation in Politics

1. Constitutional Provisions

There are no constitutional provisions as such regarding women. Women and men are treated equally under the Constitution and do not merit separate reference. From 1902, the Constitution gave Australian women the right to vote and stand for election in federal elections. Universal suffrage at a federal level preceded the initiative of the majority of states.

2. Supplementary Legislations

Manhood suffrage had been extended by the various state governments during the 1860s, some four decades before women would attain equal political rights. Even so, Australia led the world in extending the franchise to women. In 1894, South Australia was the first state to extend the vote followed by Western Australia in 1899. New South Wales extended the vote to women in the lower house in 1902, Tasmania in 1903, Queensland in 1905 and Victoria in 1908. A number of restrictions against women often remained. Many states extended only the vote for the lower house while other states did not allow women to stand for election until much later dates.

For example, it was not until 1920 that Western Australian women could stand for election to the state parliament. In 1921, Dame Edith Cowan in Western Australia became the first Australian women to be elected to parliament. At the federal level, there was an even greater time lag between gaining political rights and actually gaining political representation. In 1943, Dame Enid Lyons was elected to the Senate and Dorothy Tangney to the House of Representatives. In local government, the first women councillor, Cr. Benny in South Australia was elected in 1919. At local governmental level, there are similarly no special provisions for women's representation on committees. Women remain poorly represented at this level.

This is despite the formation, in 1957, of the Australian Local Government Women's Association to promote women's participation at this level. In 1989, women represented only 13 per cent of elected representatives in local government and 29 per cent of employees. Women in senior management positions and employment are concentrated in the community services field. Local government in Australia has broadening responsibility in childcare, care of the aged, sport facilities and libraries, and occasionally economic assistance for housing. These are services heavily used by women. In 1989, the federal Office of Local Government conducted a national review of local government labour markets. Amongst other things, it investigated measures for improving the position of women in the local government work-force.

The Local Government Scholarship Scheme has been used to provide financial assistance for officers and elected members of small and remote councils to attend courses at the Australian Centre for Local Government Studies. Over the two year period—1987-1989 all women who applied received a scholarship. These local government programmes reflect government policies that are related to women's work-force participation and do not represent specific policies to aid women into elected positions. Nevertheless, such programmes may have an indirect influence of bringing to the attention of women their potential role in political affairs and encouraging them to pursue such aims.

With universal suffrage, there has not been a need for specific government policies on women's participation in politics as they have the same rights as everyone to vote and stand for election. That women have not gained equal representation as men in political office has been explained away by claims that "women are not suited to politics" or that "women do not come forward." Federal and state government policies that are directed towards women have addressed only the inequities faced by women in education and the work-force. There is no machinery, instituted by government, that exists specifically to help women into politics. Australia is characterised by a strong two party system. The ALP emerged during the 1890s as the political wing of the labour movement.

It has been opposed by parties representing business, industrial and land owning interests, the present day manifestation of which is the Liberal Party and the National party. Party politics has coalesced along class cleavages. In the main, political parties predated women's suffrage and political organisation. The parties were male dominated with established power in the political system and used various structures at hand, such as preselection processes, to exclude women from competition. Socio-cultural factors also worked to define women in a domestic rather than public role. To the present day, women have not formed a separate political bloc. Party structures and discipline are so strong that there are limited avenues for cross party caucusing. The political parties are not bound by any state or federal provisions regarding the status of women, other that those provisions that apply to all organisations. In essence, the political parties regulate themselves in regard to women's participation. In the 1970s and 1980s, the political parties have been more willing to recognise both women's issues and women as candidates.

The above discussion is not to suggest that government in Australia do not have specific policies in instruments related to women. In Australia, there is a longer history of workplace machinery than political rights machinery with state intervention in industrial relations through wage setting and arbitration machinery. These structures reflect the strength and influence of the labour movement.

In general, since the 1970s, state and federal governments have been more aware of womens' needs and have enacted changes to improve the situation of women. At a state level this has included increased funding for women's health and counselling centres. At the federal level, there were the reforms initiated by the Whitlam Government, such as equal pay, and Hawke Government legislation. This includes the Sex Discrimination Act 1984, the Public Service Reform Act 1984, the Affirmative Action (Equal Opportunity for Women) Act 1986, and the Equal Employment Opportunity (Commonwealth Authorities) Act 1987 which have improved women's opportunities in job advertising, recruitment, training and service conditions. At both levels, structures have been created for undertaking research into women's affairs, advising cabinet, and informing the population of policy developments.

Women in Politics

The Women's Movement

In the Australian context there is frequent reference to first and second wave feminism, that is, two periods of highly visible womens' political activism. The first wave revolved around the suffrage movements of the turn of the century and the second wave arouse during the 1960s. There is however, a growing body of literature to suggest that women have been politically active in the intervening period, albeit in different forms. The struggle for the vote was the focus of the first wave of women's political participation. Suffrage was regarded by early activists as essential to attain legislation that would reinforce the family and extend the moral virtues of family life into the public sphere. Early feminist concerns were to gain equal pay for equal work, to raise the age of consent for girls, and to improve women's working conditions. The early feminists, however, did not seek to alter women's traditional role as wives, mothers, and homemakers but sought to enhance the position of women in the home. The means to doing this was through suffrage which would bestow formal political equality on men and women. Most of the women suffragists believed that their gender had special qualities—of gentleness, nurturing, patience and moral virtue—which made them an essential foundation for family life.

The woman in the home represented goodness and right, a constant inspiration to men in the public sphere. Suffrage, they argued, would strengthen the role of women in the home by giving them "an equal standard" with men. It was the opposite view to male critics who argued that the vote would make women less womanly and undermine the family and marriage. The suffragists did not seek to transform the social and economic role of women. Rather, their philosophy can be characterised as `domestic feminism' limited to the home (Searle, 1989).

Notably, first wave of the women's movement was largely middle class in character. Those women who were unmarried, educated and had domestic help had the time to pursue this cause. Suffrage was pursued through lobbying by the suffragist organisations and the Women's Christian Temperance Union. The Temperance groups were wary of the socialist principles of some groups such as women's Political Association in Victoria led by Vida Goldstein.

Other women felt that alliance with Temperance and its concern with religion and opposition to alcohol would lose women support among men. Temperance had greater financial and organisational resources than suffrage groups. While there were differences between the two they worked closely together for the vote. There were also differences between working and middle class women. Whilst both suffered inequities because of their sex, their class experiences were vastly different. The grievances expressed by middle class women were more often gender linked whereas the concerns of working class women were related more to immediate class issues of wages and working conditions. The labour movement, however, was not very sympathetic to the demands by women. Pressure for equal pay ran the risk of undercutting men's jobs and male workers showed hostility to the burgeoning work-force of low paid women. Opposition or lack of support from male trade unions was not uncommon. The labour movement failed to recognised that there was a class-gender conflict. For them, class was the only issue, gender did not come into the realm of consciousness.

Likewise, the political parties were unconscious of gender issues and generally unsympathetic to women's suffrage.

There are two theories for the decline of first wave feminism. Firstly, there is a school which clammed the weaknesses of the suffragist ideology, that is, one based on middle class values that placed women in the home and did not criticise patriarchal structures. A second school defends the suffragist achievements as significant given the constraints of their time.

The more radical demands of the second wave would have been impossible given the prevailing norms at the turn of the century. Certainly, the suffragists succeeded in their objective to gain the vote. Even if the first wave feminists had a limited social programme, equality within the domestic sphere was an important step towards equality within the public sphere. In the interregnum between the first and second wave of feminism, women's organisations continued to flourish. At a National Women's Conference held in 1943, 91 major women's organisations were represented. Such groups included the United Associations of Women (UA established in 1929) and the Council of Action for Equal Pay (1937) both in Sydney, the former representing the broad span of issues affecting women, the latter a single cause group. In this year, the Women for Canberra Movement was established to support women candidates in the 1943 federal election. In the immediate post World War II period, much of the unity and impetus that had been acquired during the war years dissipated as servicemen returned home and women were forced out of jobs by wage cuts and forcible exclusion from some occupations.

Divisions were often political in character: the UA maintained links with communist groups while the Australian Women's Movement Against Socialism, formed in 1944, had indirect links with the Liberal Party.

Remarkably, re-radicalisation of women in the 1960s complemented many changes in women's lives. The 1960s presented increasing rates of women's participation in the work-force and higher education. The women's liberation movement gained momentum in the late 1960s and its message was widely available through books, journals and consciousness raising groups as well as the establishment of high profile women's organisations such as the Women's Electoral Lobby (WEL) in 1972.

Yet, the second wave of feminism was, in the main, ignorant of the first wave of activism. The second wave of feminism, from the late 1960s, to the present day is of a very different character in terms of organisation, political tactics, and ideology. The feminists of the second wave were critical of patriarchal structures in both the public and private spheres and were much more theoretically inclined, articulating critiques of the nuclear family, sexual relations and marriage, housework and childcare. The women's liberation movement is, thus, a more radical expression of feminism in its emphasis on the oppression all women share on account of their gender. The second wave instigated a grass-roots movement.

The early stages of the second wave were dominated by radical feminism in which the new found awareness sought action through non-hierarchical forms. Hierarchy was identified with patriarchy. Women's groups were amorphous and unorganised and initiated activities such as small consciousness raising groups, participated in marches and protests, and started women's health centres, refuges, and counselling units which not only provided services to women in the community, but also contributed greatly to the process of their politicisation. By 1972, the Women's Electoral Lobby (WEL) was formed. Unlike previous women's groups it was highly organised into state branches and a federal office. Through a constitution it was institutionalised, and under its WEL also had spokeswomen auspices several conferences were organised. WEL also had powerful influence on electoral politics. It issued a questionnaire to all candidates in the 1972 election to elicit their views about women's issues. An analysis of their responses were published and given wide coverage in the media.

Since the 1970s, WEL's influence in electoral politics has wanted although it does continue lobbying and other activities. During the 1970s, a breakdown of communication between various women's liberation groups developed., What had commenced as healthy diversity deteriorated into fragmentation and acrimony over 'correct' organisational structures and tactics. The movement lacked internal organisation and co-ordination. Similarly, anti-feminist groups such as Women Who Want to be Women (WWWW) and the anti-abortion Right to Life group, had emerged which began lobbying governments to defend women's roles as the homemaker. With the onset of economic recession from the mid 1970s, conservative views on the role of women struck a chord with the Fraser Government policies that sought to cope with unemployment and cut back welfare spending.

The 1990s had seen diversification and fragmentation of the women's movement. Indeed, it is no longer a united movement with clear objectives, what emerged were a series of feminist networks in pursuit of a variety of objectives at different levels of government and through a variety of institutions. Some demands such as abortion law reform, can be only pursued at a state government level and the ordination of women priests only through the churches. Women's groups have also lost power and prominence. The women's movement has achieved many gains such as equal pay, maternity leave, and EO and AA legislation. More radical proposals are mooted but are more difficult to achieve as they are more controversial and/or expensive, hence not feasible in economic recession.

Coming to women's participation in politic, it is note worthy that there have been a few attempts by women to form their own political block with women candidates seeking election to represent women's issues in parliament. These exercises have had varying degrees of success. Vida Goldstein ran for federal parliament five times between 1903 and 1917. As President of the Women's Political Association and its candidate, she had the resources of this organisation behind her campaigns. While Goldstein believed that the women's movement and the labour movement were natural allies, she distanced herself from the party system. Goldstein was of the view that men, whether they were Labour or non-Labour supporters, were not interested in promoting women's political rights.

Therefore she contested as an independent candidate. She, and others such as Rose Scott who lead the Women's Political Educational League in NSW, distanced themselves from the ALP recognising the male political ideologies and structures of the trade unions and the ALP paid scant attention to the specific needs of women. Within some circles, Goldstein was perceived as a radical having socialist elements in her platform. Schisms formed between her and the WCTU and ALP women activists. During the war, Goldstein adopted a pacifist stance which did not accord with the prevailing mood. Her very poor electoral performance in 1917 led her to retire from politics. The onset of World War II brought the massive mobilisation of women into the workforce. This was followed by women's attempts at political mobilisation. In 1942, the Women for Canberra Movement was established. A manifesto published in 1943 argued that women had not achieved representation in parliament because of the prejudices of preselectors within the political parties.

A fund was established to help women candidates in their campaigns. The organisation encouraged an unprecedented number of women candidates to stand in the 1943 federal elections. In 1974, the Women's Action Alliance was founded. It is a conservative group established in reaction to the philosophy of the women's movement but perceived itself espousing 'moderate feminism.' As it was in favour of increased opportunities for women it also sought to preserve the family and gain recognistion of the social and economic role performed by the full-time homemaker. While it never stood candidates for parliament it was strongly involved in lobbing, letter writing, and petitions and gained the patronage of some prominent conservative politicians. In 1979, WWWW split from WAA to lobby more strenuously for the anti-abortion issue. With other organisations such as Festival of Light and the Right to Life group, WWWW has occasionally participated in coalition tickets for elected positions. Both groups have opposed the work of the national Women's Advisory Council (which was established by the Fraser Government) and WEL.

Women in the Political Parties

Women also join political parties and actively participate in their affairs. However, they have traditionally been consigned to the role of 'political housework,' that is, auxiliary functions of door-knocking and fund raising. Since the 1970s, women have been escaping this role in increasing numbers, gaining higher visibility in party affairs. The ALP has been traditionally viewed as a men's party. Only about a third of its membership is female. Furthermore, because of the trade union link, few women hold positions as full-time party officers. Since very early in ALP organisational history, there have been Labour Women's Organisations within a number of state branches. By the 1970s some of these organisations were being revitalised by an influx of younger women and growing feminist critique of ALP structures.

In states where these organisations were disbanded, women pushed for change through other avenues such as the formation in 1981 of the National Women's Labour Conference. Despite the absence of women ALP had a favourable image among women. In 1972, WEL polled all candidates in the federal election regarding their views on women's issues. The non-Labour candidates did not fare well whereas Labour candidates scored highly given the ALP's promises to reopen the Equal Pay case, to abolish the luxury tax or oral contraceptives, to institute maternity leave provisions, and to create a position of special adviser to the Prime Minister on Women's Affairs. The party had lost much of its appeal by the mid 1970s with prevarication over abortion law reform.

The ALP National Committee of Inquiry was an internal review of the party established after the landslide defeat of the party in the 1977 federal elections. It reported in 1979 that the party was too 'male' and trade union oriented. This image supposedly alienated women voters. Accordingly, the party enacted internal affirmative action procedures to improve women's participation within the party.

For example, it decided that one quarter of all delegates to the ALP's biennial National Conference must be women. Pressure from women also saw the establishment by the National Executive of the ALP of the National Status of

Women Policy Committee which overviews other national policy committees for their impact of women (Moore, 1985). The programme has had considerable impact, particularly in increasing the number of ALP women candidates. The membership the Liberal Party is far more equally balanced than the ALP with roughly equal numbers of men and women. For historical reasons, some party offices are reserved for women. At the time of party's formation, the Australian Women's National League based in Victoria was flourishing organisation which only agreed to submerge itself within the new party for certain recompense. Accordingly, within the Victorian branch the principle of equal representation of men and women on executive bodies was instituted (but not often attained for the highest party positions). Other minimum requirements for positions apply in the NSW branch.

At a state level, Women's Sections, made up of ordinary branch members, were established and the President of each is a delegate to the Federal Council. The Federal Women's Committee discusses resolutions from women in state branches which, if they are passed, are considered by Federal Council. Thus, for example, the Federal Women's Committee voted in favour of the 1987 EEO legislation but support was overturned by the Federal Council. This was done by the Liberals as a tactic to bolster the coalition with its more conservative coalition partner, the National Party. The National Party has not been a supporter of women's issue or specific policies aimed at improving their position. Nor has the party had a good record of women's involvement in the party in offices or as candidates. Within the Australian Democrats, by contrast, women have been a powerful force.

The party has a high female membership and a high proportion of female candidates are fielded. Its leader is

Janine Haines, the first woman parliamentary leader of a political party in Australia. Feminism within the Liberal Party is a weaker force than in the ALP but feminist networks do exist. The Victorian Liberal Feminist Network was established in 1981 to assist women in obtaining pre-selection for women and produced a document advising women how to do so. Similar networks have been established in other states. The views of these women are often contradictory with the general direction of the party in the 1980s with its traditional view of women and emphasis on motherhood, the family and the free market as an alternative to an extensive publicly funded welfare system. The ALP's campaign treatment of women has been far less sexist in the 1980s. Women feature prominently in election advertising, specifically targeted as voters who need to be won over.

ALP market research has pinpointed women between the ages of 25 and 35 as swinging voters. Consequently, women's issues have been adopted by the ALP as part of its election strategies. Prior to the 1980s, the ALP traditionally polled more male voters than women. The Hawke Government set out to reduce this gender gap.,

In the 1983 federal election, approximately 50 per cent of women and 52 per cent of men voted ALP. The slender 2 per cent gender gap difference was attributed to the high profile of women politicians such as Senator Susan Ryan who acquired a cabinet position, and the ALPs commitment to women's issues.

Women as Candidates

In 1987, Catherine Spence in South Australia was the first woman to stand as a political candidate. She was followed in 1903 by Vida Goldstein who stood as an independent Senate candidate in Victoria. Both were unsuccessful. The major parties have not been keen on running women as candidates. Prior to 1939, these parties fielded only three women candidates for federal office, without success. Nor did those women who ran for minor parties or as independents have nay greater success. At a state level, the number of women candidates was higher and prior to 1940, 11 women were elected. 1943 witnessed an upsurge when 19 women stood for the House of Representatives; more than the total of federal women candidates prior to that date. The political mobilisation of women during the 1970s brought increased numbers of women candidates. This was particularly evident in the ALP After it implemented its AA programme. Nevertheless, women have often found themselves in unwinnable or marginal seats. Often these positions serve as an apprenticeship before acquiring preselection for a safe seat.

The pre-selection of candidates is central to understanding why there are so few women in politics. It is however, a much neglected area of study. At pre-selection, women are frequently confronted with male biases such as the myth that women lose votes or certain preconceptions that female candidates should be married, fortyish and with grown-up children. Women are sometimes deemed not 'tough' enough.

On other occasions, they are denied tickets on the pretext that they did not have the right credentials. For example, familiarity with the business world is often considered advantageous within the Liberal Party. Women, however, have traditionally lacked prominence in the business community and do not have the same contacts as men. They are thus automatically disadvantaged in liberal pre-selection contests.

Within the ALP, there are factional battles that precede pre-selection. Alongside the discriminatory practices within the parties, the electoral system also imposes constraints on the opportunities for women candidates. In General, single member electorates have not been conducive to women gaining pre-selection within the party structure. By contrast, in the Senate where a proportional representation system applies, women have not been placed in a one-sided pre-selection contest against a man. The Senate has a greater proportion of women members than the House of Representatives.

Despite the formal political right to stand for election since federation, women have never gained political representation in proportion to their numbers. By the beginning of World War II, only nine women had been elected to state parliaments, but none at a federal level. In 1943, two women entered the federal parliament. Of these 11, six had family political connections as the widows or daughters or male politicians. In many cases, party pre-selectors were content to run female candidates to cash in on the sympathy vote for the bereaved wife or daughter. This phenomenon of 'male equivalence' has persisted in lesser degree, to the present day (Sawer and Simms, 1984: 39).

In fact, these early women parliamentarians were usually older married women with grown-up children who had not been in paid employment for some time. In the main, they did not acquire ministerial position and the majority of them came from the non-Labour side of politics. By the 1980s, the image of the women parliamentarian had changed. On the whole they were younger and had combined a family of young children with paid employment (often in nursing, teaching, or public service occupations).

A larger proportion of these women were singles, divorces, or unmarried.

More women belonged to ALP, although the Australian Democrats were also adding to the complement of women. The 1980s have seen significant changes in the number of women in the federal parliament. In December 1962, there were 15 MPs in Australia; by December 1989 the number rose to 101. From 1980 to 1983, the number of women MPs jumped from just under 2.5 per cent of the total number of MPs to nearly 5 per cent. During the 1984 federal election, there were 158 women candidates. Of this group, 22 were elected out of a total of 196 vacant positions. Women represented 11.2 per cent of the total. In 1987, there were 122 women candidates, of which 26 were elected. Again women represented 11.6 per cent of the total elected (224).

While the number of women parliamentarians went on increasing since World War II, only a few have obtained cabinet positions or similarly elevated office, until the 1980s.

When discussing women's participation in politics, there is a methodological difficulty of defining the 'political.' Women's organisations have been predominantly involved in legal matters such as abortion, marriage and custody laws and social welfare issues such as women's health. In the Australian context, politics has often been construed very narrowly as the legislative process, party competition, and organised lobby groups which seek to influence the processes and institutions of governing. While women are gaining increased visibility, they he been, and remain severely under-represented in these processes and institutions. The formal arena of politics, the public sphere of political office and leadership has seen few women. Nevertheless, women have been active in political parties, pressure groups and political movements although, as noted above, this has often been 'political housework' which has less public visibility than leadership positions. Furthermore, the practice of defining women's issues such as domestic violence and child welfare as private/familial or community issues rather than as political and public (that is, "the personal is the political"), has had implications for research on women's political involvement. Women are ignored, hence they become invisible in the formal processes of government. As a consequence, women's political activism is shrouded.

They are excluded from political analysis by a very narrow definition of politics. Much of the research conducted on Australian women has related to their traditional roles in the family and community. There would also appear to be a larger body of literature on women in the work-force and education than in politics. The literature on women's participation in the formal area of politics has only grown as women's presence has increased. One response to the observation that women in the political system have not been subject to indepth analysis is that this reflects the lack of women's participation in the formal arena of politics. There is rarely recognition, however, that gender roles have a crucial determinant on women's lack of ambition in this sphere.

In fact, feminist theory and studies is a burgeoning body of literature but within the discipline of political science it remains a sub culture, or on the margins of mainstream analyses. There has been research, more of a sociological nature, into women's position in early Australian society as the work of Dixson (1977) and Summers (1975) testify. Similarly, there has been a good deal of historical research into the first wave of feminism which can be found in book length studies (for example, Searle, 1988) and in edited collections (Grieve and Grimshaw, 1981; Simms, 1984).

Much of this literature has only been produced since the onset of the second wave of feminism and the rediscovery of the first wave. There is a considerable amount of literature about the women's movement and political activism of the second wave (see *inter alia,* Sewer and Simms, 1984; Simms, 1984). Within the public policy literature there is increasing attention to women's issues as a sub theme on topics such as equal pay, affirmative action, abortion law reform and childcare. Nonetheless, policy analysis often remains unconscious of feminist debates regarding the public/private distinction and sex roles.

Policy analysis of a more feminist nature includes, for example, works of (i) Dowse (1989), and Sawer (1985) on affirmative action, (ii) Broom (1984) on social justice issues, and (iii) Connors (1985) on women's advisory machinery in government. In regard to the more specific area of women's participation in the formal arenas of parliament and the political parties the literature is more scarce. Sawer and Simms (1984), Simms (1984) and Clark and White (1983) have conducted in-depth analyses and published book length monographs. In addition, there are numerous articles in Journals. There has been a larger degree of research on women in the political parties.

One strand of the political science literature, in seeking to explain why women having had the vote for so long were not able to gain positions of prominence, has focused on voting patterns. There has been a traditionally held viewpoint that women voters are conservative and relatively uninterested in politics and that they generally acquired their political preferences from their husbands. Evidence since the 1970s, however, reveals a profound reorientation in women's political attitudes and a growing awareness. This is often attributed to women's growing participation in the labour force, financial independence, higher levels of education and the political leadership provided by the women's movement since the 1960s (see Goot and Reid, 1975).

Due to the lack of work on women in Australian politics, there is considerable room for future research. Studies into women's political participation at a local government level is scarce and in want of further attention (but see Cooney, 1982). Similarly, the study of women as political candidates is a new territory currently being traversed by an Australia-wide Candidates Study under the auspices of the Australian National University. There are three main centres of research on women's issues generally, and participation in politics, specifically. Women and some male academic researchers in Australian universities and colleges would form the major component. In some institutions there are women's studies units and degree courses. In most history, political science, anthropology and sociology degrees, units can be taken that relate specifically to women. Academic work has been published in book form or in journals such as *Australian Feminist Studies, Meanjin, Refractory Girl* and *Hecate,* and other mainstream journals such as *Politics* and *Australian Quarterly.* Additionally, state and federal bureaucracies undertaken research into the status of women. The Women's Bureau was set up in the 1960s. Its current work involves achieving higher female participation in the work-force and publicising existing legislative and award provisions that restrict women's employment. The Bureau is linked to a network of women's organisations, women trade unionists, government advisory committees and the wider bureaucracy undertaking basic research on the women's work-force and producing a newsletter, *Women and Work.* The Office of the Status of Women has a wider brief in the board scope of women's issues. It commissions work and publishes various reports on the status of women. An example is the Women' Budget Statement. A world first, the statement lists the spending of federal government departments on programmes and policies which affect women. It has been important in bringing to the attention of the bureaucracy, the differential impact on women of macro-economic policies.

A number of pressure groups also investigate women's issues. Women's Electoral Lobby (WEL) is the prime example. It publishes a newsletter, arranges conferences, and invites speakers. The political parties also occasionally sponsor conferences, commission market research, and undertake internal reviews of matters concerning women as voters and political participants.

Women politicians in Australia are increasing in number at both the federal and the state levels. Traditionally in Australia the pathway to Parliament has been through the main political parties. Since the World War II the two major political groupings, the Labour Party on the one side the two non-Labour (or conservative) parties on the other, have dominated the Parliaments of Australia. In this period, for example, one independent candidate was elected to the House of Representatives. Endorsement by one of the major political groupings was essential for a political career. The several attempts to form women's political parties have failed in the face of the hegemony of the two major political groupings. For the political apprentice it is not enough to have the endorsement of one of the major parties. It is also necessary to be selected for a 'winnable' seat. In this vein it should be noted that it has bene traditional in Australia for the parties to select women to contest 'unwinable' seats. Women have been over-represented amongst what I term the 'flag-wavers,' namely those who carry their party's banner into hostile territory.

Australia's House of Representatives is elected on the basis of single-member constituencies, with the so-called preferential (i.e. alternate) voting system. Research has demonstrated that systems employing single-member constituencies are not particularly hospitable to women and members of ethnic minorities. Women MPs constituted only 6 per cent of the House of Representatives. The contrast here is with the Australian Senate. Originally set up under the Australian Constitution (1901) as a states house, each state (or territory) constitutes one constituency. Since 1949 the Senate has been elected on the basis of proportional representation (PR).

This has led to representation based on a more accurate reflection of the votes cast contrasted with the previous 'winner takes all' system. Consequently, minor parties have often held the balance of power. The results of this system have confirmed the conventional view, namely that PR leads to the parties seeking more 'balanced' and representative lists. In February 1990 women comprised 22 per cent of all Senators. In 1980 and 1983 significant swings to the Australian Labour Party (ALP) result in an increase in the numbers of Labour women MPs. The 1983 Federal Elections resulted in the greatest number of women Federal MPs on record (six MHRs and 13 Senators). All six MHRs were from the ALP as were seven of the 13 Senators. Three of the MHRs had been elected in 1980. The ALP's record number of women candidates was accompanied by a feminist-oriented policy on women. The policy was called

The ALP and Women: Towards Equality. It was based on a paper produced by the ALP's Senator Susan Ryan in 1980.

Senator Ryan was elected before the cohorts of 1980 and 1983 but could be said to have inspired them. A leading feminist activist before her selection as a top-ranking candidate for the Senate in the ACT for the 1975 elections, she quickly became the public face of Labor feminism. She lobbied around three major issues, as follows: in the first instance the need for the ALP to court the women's vote which it had traditionally ignored; secondly, the need for the ALP to increase the number of women candidates in order to achieve the first-named goal; and, thirdly, the requirement for the ALP to develop policies that would improve the position of women in the economy and in the society and also increase the size of the female ALP vote. Senator Ryan's background prefigured those of many of the cohorts of 1980 and 1983. She had been a teacher and a feminist activist (in the Women's Electoral Lobby) before her selection for a safe position on the ALP's Senate ticket in 1975. From a working class Irish-Catholic background she has become upwardly-mobile through the education system. She had gained post-graduate qualifications.

The 1980 elections were to see an increase in the number of women candidates and MPs but did not see a major stress of women's issues. According to Marian Sawer, "the missing female voters which had cost the ALP so many federal elections were to be attracted through women candidates rather than a stress on women's issues.... The ALP's attitude to its female candidates remained ambivalent, despite the attempt to make electoral mileage out of them. There was no such ambivalence on the part of the Liberal Party.

An anonymous Liberal Minister drew Laurie Oake's (a leading journalist) attention to a photograph in ***The Australian*** depicting the women ALP candidates and commented as follows: "Everyone of them is worth at least a couple of per cent to us.... Women won't vote for women candidates for a start. They're doing us a favour by nominating women" (in Simms, 1984: 95-96).

The Liberal Party responded by running on its record on women's issues as it had fielded far fewer women candidates for winnable seats and winnable positions on Senate tickets. By the 1983 Federal election the Liberal Party had begun to campaign around the mainly as an issue, and paid little attention to the separate interests and needs of women.

In contrast, the Labour leader — Bob Hawke — promised that if elected his government would enact legislation outlawing discrimination on the grounds of sex and implement affirmative action in the public and the private sector.

The Liberal Party context was quite different with a 'family' rather than a 'women's' policy and with no women MHRs. There had been a handful of women Senators since the early 1970s who reflected the normal middle class private sector background that was and remains typical of Liberal MPs, more generally. One woman Senator only had a background in feminist politics (WEL). Additionally, the Liberal Party's coalition partner, the National Party, had endorsed Mrs. Flo Bjelke-Peterson for the half-Senate elections in 1981. (In Australia, Senators have staggered terms). Mrs. Bjelke-Peterson was very much in the mould of the traditional woman politician before the 1970s. She was an older woman with a grown-up family whose husband was a leading political figure and the Premier of the State of Queensland. The 1984 Federal elections saw an increase in the number of women MPs with two new Members of the House of Representatives (including one who moved from the Senate) and an increase of one in the number of women in the Senate with several new faces. After the 1984 election there was a decline in the number, of Labour women Senators and an increase in the number of non-Labour women Senators. These newly elected Liberal women were to prove a distinctive breed.

Younger than the traditional Liberal women MP they were also well-educated professional women who had achieved selection and election on their own merit. Unlike the majority of Labour women they tended to adopt a non-feminist or gender-blind approach to the world. They had achieved on their own merits, consequently other women could as well. The other group to increase its representation in the Senate was the peace group. Senator Jo Vallentine was elected under the Nuclear Disarmament banner in 1984.

One the non-Labour side of politics, the Liberal and the National parties campaigned on a 'families first' approach. It is interesting to note, therefore, that the non-Labour side increased its female representation at the same time as it emphasised the family or private role for women.

During the 1980s the Liberal Party has been divided between the so-called 'wets' (progressives) and the 'dries' (conservatives). The labels were taken in the early 1980s from Mrs. Thatcher's Conservative Party. In general, the Australian 'dries' have tended to combine *laissez-faire* economics (including low taxation policies) with pro-family social policies. The 'wets,' in contrast, have been more in favour of using the resources of government to assist the community and have favoured individual rather than family-based taxation policies.

At the time of the 1984 Federal elections the non-Labour taxation policies included elements favoured by both dries and wets. In the vein, the non-Labour parties proposed so-called 'income splitting' (which allows married couples to split their income and thus acts as a disincentive for married women to enter the paid work-force) with the tax deductibility of child-care expenditure (favoured by the wets and by the Liberal Party's own Feminist Liberal Network).

The trends first observed during the 1984 elections were quite pronounced at the 1987 elections. The Liberal Party increased its number of female Senators, who bore similar characteristics to the class of 1984.

Senator Amanda Vanstone who had been first elected in 1984 was promoted to the second position on the Liberal Party's Senate ticket in South Australia for the 1987 elections. She had earlier in the year opposed the Hawke Government's Equal Opportunity Bill. In doing so, she was supporting the decision of her Party's leadership. It is interesting to note that several of her male colleagues had crossed the floor of the Senate to support the Bill in defiance of the Party's decision. The two new Liberal women Senators were the high-profile Bronwyn Bishop (the first Liberal woman to be elected to the federal parliament from New South Wales) and Dr. Kay Patterson, a college lecturer from Victoria.

The ALP, in contrast had no new women selected for winnable positions on its Senate tickets. There were, however, two new faces in the Lower House (the House of Representatives) bringing the total number of ALP women

MHRs to eight. The two women were relatively young (40 when elected) and both were school teachers.

The ALP campaigned strongly on its record particularly on economic issues but also had a special launch of its women's policy. Senator Susan Ryan undertook a leading role on women's issues and launched the ALP's women's policies. Increasingly, however, women's policies were presented in economic terms, as the major issues of the campaign was which team would better manage the economy.

The non-Labour parties campaigned strongly on family policies. It promised 'income-splitting' and a child-care allowance, as part of its new tax policy. The allowance, however, was for couples and not for single parents with dependent children.

Feminist issues, along with environmental concerns, were a strong presence in the 'major' Australian minor party, namely the Australian Democrats (ADs). After the 1987 elections the ADs had three women Senators and significantly the first woman leader of any Australian political party, Senator Janine Haines:

> Senator Powell (ADs—Victoria) said the Democrats, the first party in Australian history to be led to the polls by a woman, were receiving strong female support because of the "prominence given to women in the Democrats and the party's stress on equality for women" (*Canberra Times,* 8 June 1987).

It is interesting to note that Senator Haines was formerly a school teacher before entering the Senate in 1977 via a casual vacancy (i.e. as a mid-term replacement for a Senator from the same party). Senator Haines' rise to prominence was to be counter-balanced by the decline in Senator Ryan's fortune. In the aftermath of the 1987 elections she was demoted within Cabinet and subsequently resigned before the year was out.

In March 1990 Australian's went to the polls again and the Hawke Government was re-elected for an historic fourth term. As we have seen the 1983 Federal elections were significant for women resulting in a 50 per cent increase in the numbers of women Federal MPs from just under 2.5 per cent to almost 5 per cent. Each subsequent election (1984 and 1987) also saw an increase in female representation. At a state level there have also been 'key' elections. For Victoria it was 1982 for Western Australia it was 1983, and for New South Wales it was 1988. For the state parliaments not examined in detail for this study, there have also been 'key' elections. For South Australia it was 1982 but the numbers involved (three) were less significant than in Victoria and we have also not seen a subsequent increase in numbers of women in the South Australian State Parliament or in the State Cabinet. 1989 was an important year for the electors of Tasmania and of Queensland. The Tasmanian Parliament now has two women Green Independents who were part of an important process whereby Tasmania gained a Government based on an historic accord between the ALP and the Green Independents.

One of the women Green Independents, Christine Milne, had gained national prominence as a leading environment activist. The electors of Queensland overwhelmingly rejected the conservative National Party Government at the state elections of November 1989. Several women were elected as the result of a massive swing to the Labour Party. One woman was elected to the Cabinet of Labour Premier, Wayne Goss. The major 'waves' of women MPs elected in the 1980s, as we have already noted, did not come from the non-Labour ranks. In the April 1982 Victorian State elections a group of women was elected as part of the general swing to the Labour Party.

The tenor of this group's values is summed up in the following statement from one of their number who wished to demonstrate:

> .... how a woman politician and her women colleagues can remain committed to improving opportunities for women and girls through persuading the parliamentary party to take initiatives which benefit women and by remaining in close touch with women outside parliament [Simms, 1984: 93].

Three members of the group elected in 1982 went on to become Labour Ministers. There are three striking features about this group. In the first instance the leading lights were from the Socialist Left faction of the Party. Faction is important as a source of power and position for individual women as well as men and also as a guide to a person's views and attitudes. Secondly, several members of this group were not factionalised and were originally selected in constituencies which the ALP did not expect to win. One such woman, in an interview with me in 1989, stated that her selection was a low key and untroubled process until the results of an opinion poll suggested that 'her' constituency would be winnable for the Labour Party. These women tended to be political amateurs and relatively recent converts to Labour Party politics.

Running in outer suburban Melbourne they were some distance away from the machine politics of downtown Melbourne or of any of the major regional Trade Union Councils. Several of this group are still in the Parliament. Thirdly, members of this group have, in retrospect, been seen as pioneers and/or models. For example there had been no women members of the Victorian Parliament at all in the 1950s and the first half of the 1960s. One (a Liberal—the Hon Dorothy Goble) was elected to the Legislative Assembly in 1967 and then a further three in the 1970s, after the Hon. Dorothy Goble's retirement in 1976. There were no women at all in the Victorian Legislative Council until 1979, when both major parties selected a woman for winnable provinces.

Joan Coxsedge, MLC claimed that it was extremely tough being one of the 'first' women. Many women elected since the mid-1080s have pointed out that the pioneer women of the 1970s and of the 1982 elections had to tear down the barriers. One of the successful candidates from the 1982 elections listed the disadvantages and advantages as foilows (Simms, 1984: 92):

Disadvantages	:	'Weaker access to established power network, pubs and politicians etc.: lack of accumulated income; family strains of three or four gobs'
Advantage	:	'Links with community groups; understanding of issues; support network from women; recognition of importance of women's role; media interest (sometimes for the wrong reasons)'

Shifting then to Western Australia we note that the key election was 1983 which saw a pro-Labour swing resulting in the election of a labour government. Subsequent elections, especially the 1986 state election, saw an increase in the ranks of labour women and the election of women to the Cabinet. In fact until the New South Wales state elections of 1988 the vast majority of women Members of the State Parliaments were from the Labour Party. Leaving aside the issue of pro-Labour swings, the ALP's policy of internal affirmative action and the strength of its Socialist Left faction were the major factors in explaining the preponderance of Labor women over non-Labour women. The point about the salience of Labour's internal factions is highlighted by the case of New South Wales. The dominant Labour Right Wing faction had never seen a female member elected to the House of Representatives from New South Wales until the Federal elections of March 1990.

The only women ALP MHR from New South Wales, Jeanette McHugh (elected in 1983), is from the Socialist Left faction. Women were never a presence in the State Labour Cabinets (Labour was in office from 1976 until 1988). The New South Wales Right wing faction is identified strongly with the Irish-Catholic based Machine politics of the old-style Labour Party. State and Federal Parliamentary members of this faction have opposed the availability of abortion and have expressed traditional views on the role of women. The most important background feature of women Parliamentarians in Australia is their political party. Other factors such as, for Labour Party women, their membership of a faction, are also significant. To these features was added the fact that many of the women were elected at 'key' elections. For some this has meant the consequent achievement of ministerial office. Many of these women have achieved 'firsts.' In the 1980s we have seen the 'first' Labour women Federal Cabinet Minister, the 'first' woman Speaker of the Federal House of Representatively, the 'first' woman State Premier and the 'first woman Chief Minister of a Federal Territory. It is interesting to note that when interviewed most of the women Parliamentarians elected in the early 1980s reported both obstacles and a high level of media attention. Women elected in slightly later period claimed that things were easier for them because of the efforts of the earlier trailblazers. Many of the ALP women, for example, mention Senator Susan Ryan and Senator Pat Giles both as role models and women who have given assistance.

Coming to the current group of Australian women Parliamentarians the distinction between the 'early' women and the 'subsequent' women is quite significant., The majority of the women interviewed were tertiary-educated and in full-time employment before entering Parliament. Most had not grown up in political households but had been politicised by major events. For many on the Labour side this event was Australia's involvement in the Viet Nam War. In this sense, the political socialisation of the adult years had been more striking than any processes in the family during the childhood years. There was no significant evidence for strong political identification with the father, nor for major rebellions against the family structure. Family was an important variable when the Parliamentarians were discussing their current lives rather than when examining their early years. One Minister noted: "My husband has learned to cook since I became a Minister." Many mentioned the domestic strains caused by the "long hours and tedium" of the job. Most women had been 'supported' and 'encouraged' by their families at the onset of their Parliamentary careers. When asked what they would do with unexpected free time many of the women mentioned "spending time with their family' or going somewhere with their family" or taking 'grandchildren out." The majority of women, however, listed individual pursuits such as gardening, walking, or simply staying at home and resting.

Surprisingly, however, nearly all of the women interviewed had little or no household help. Some of the women had *no* help in the house and the rest paid someone to come in to do housework for less than half a day a week! Australia, of course, had no servant class and only the very rich have ever had live-in household help. Even so, with an increased in the number of middle-class two-career households there has been an observable increase in the amount of part-time domestic help. The solutions to the problem of combining domestic and political tasks have been tackled in a variety of ways. Several women Parliamentarians mentioned resorting to 'a lot of takeaways' (i.e. carry-out food). One or two others had husbands who took care of the house. Most, however, took the responsibility for the management of family and the household.

This inevitably created difficulties for those who had young children. In the mid 1980s, Mrs. Ros Kelly hit the headlines when she became the first woman Member of the Federal Parliament to have a child whilst in office. She was publicly criticised for this and accused of neglecting her family.

Subsequently other women with young children got elected to Australian Parliaments. Most, however, have older children, or are childless. The majority of women mentioned women's family responsibilities as being a major factor in deterring women from entering politics. Over 90 per cent of the women Parliamentarians interviewed agreed that women were under-represented in Australian politics. Solutions suggested varied from encouraging women to joining parties, through to speaking to girls in school and telling women 'to bite the bullet." A number of Labour women MPs blamed their party speaking of the ALP as a 'male-dominated party with pre-selection battles." Another referred to the fact that there was a "power structure and very organised men [who] won't give up roles of power."

There was evidence of "discrimination in the ministerial stakes as the men all vote for each other."

On this point, it is interesting to note that in 1989 the British Labour Party under Neil Kinnock introduced a system of reserved places for women thus increasing the representation of women in Labour's Shadow Ministry. In Australia, however, both Labour and non-Labour women expressed a horror of 'tokenism.' In this vein, both sides of the political fence opposed the idea of quotas for women in politics. It should be pointed out that in Australia Affirmative Action has been interpreted to mean having goals and targets rather than formal quotas.

The majority of ALP women emphasised the distinction between these two and only two favoured formal quotas. Formal quotas were ruled out by most as being potentially counterproductive leading to resentment among men. Several of the Liberal Party's women made admiring comments about the ALP's policy of Affirmative Action within its own ranks, suggesting that their own Party should borrow the policy. Apparently, there are a lot of 'discouraged' women within the Liberal Party, with the Liberals not 'attuned to the value of women candidates."

Most non-Labour women, however, were opposed to the concept of Affirmative Action or of any kind of positive action. This included several women who had gained 'fast track' selection as candidates at least partly on account of their gender. In fact there were some indications of dissension between those who had to undertake a long and arduous political apprenticeship and those who had gained their endorsements more rapidly and hence more easily. In one state those who had to struggle to achieve selection for winnable seats were more likely to be in favour of Affirmative

Action and those who had gained it more easily tended to oppose it! Ironies and contradictions are not unusual in politics. As well it is arguable that there are additional stresses for women politicians. High visibility is still the norm for women politicians in Australia, particularly for most of the Lower Houses where women are far from achieving the necessary critical mass. Perhaps women political figures have their particular stresses. There are still may signs of sex discrimination in Australia some of which affect women politicians.

Most politicians tend to be competitive and ambitious and are unwilling to accept that factors other than their own merit have helped them achieve political goals. One woman politician, for example, had been very critical of the fact that she had been prevented from opening a credit account with a leading department store yet was unwilling to accept that gender was a factor in politics. She went on to criticise the concept of separate and identifiable women's issues seeing them as "vestiges of the early days" of the women's movement.

Several others referred to small examples of discrimination that they had faced but then proceeded to deny that there were major obstacles to women's participation in politics. There were few feminists in the ranks of the non-Labour parties, if we define feminism in the context of this study as having three main concepts. In the first instance, feminism involves the belief that women are under-represented in Australian parliaments.

Secondly it would tend to embrace the view that there are structures which prevent the full and equal participation of women in politics. Thirdly, feminism would also include the perception that there are issues which affect women differently than men and which require concerted political action by women. According to these criteria then there were significantly more feminist in Labour ranks than among the non-Labour women. This is not a particularly exceptional comments as the non-Labour parties have a philosophy which emphasises economic individualism and, *in some cases* tends to blame people for their misfortunes.

It was more interesting to note the variety that is now increasingly apparent among the Labour party women. I have already referred to the difference between the 'early' women elected at the key elections of the early 1980s and women subsequently elected. One Labour women commented that the 'early women candidates learnt a lot for future women candidates." Three other factors are important sources of difference among Labour women. There is the growing significance of faction. Many women referred to the growing importance of factions. This was condemned by some; others simply noted that they had been effectively forced to join a faction in order to continue with their political careers. One politician observed that the 'factions are getting tougher and nastier for women." Several women, however, emphasized that a mentor within a faction had been responsible for their own good fortunes. And following on from the faction issue, a number of the Labour Party's women Parliamentarians saw themselves eventually as creatures of the political party rather than as activists. These were those who had been adopted by one of the factions. In this group were included those who tended not to be feminists and who had been elected to Parliament relatively recently. The importance of patronage on the Labour-side of politics is reflected in the sheer number of women Members of Parliament who had worked as political officers of one kind or another before being selected as candidates. A small minority of the Labour women have now achieved high political office. Currently there are very few non-Labour women ministers because there are so few non-Labour governments! These ministers have achieved a lot in a very male-dominated community. For some, there have been great costs and constant stresses. For most, they have been forced to adopt particular survival tactics. I was surprised by the number of women—not just ministers but also committee members—who said they were forced to swear and throw tantrums in order to gain a hearing from their male colleagues. In one state a Women's Bill Committee had been established as a more formal source of 'voice' within the Government. Women ministers have not been around long enough for commentators to judge how significant their presence has been for women and for women's issues. There were, however, some signs of optimism. Several women commented that the political parties were now seeking women candidates and that the old view that women were electoral liabilities was past history. Others, from both sides of the political fence, commented that women's issues were now being 'mainstreamed.'

Childcare, it was claimed, was now a mainstream issue as reflected in its appearance on the policies of both political teams during the March 1990 election campaign. One woman claimed that "all issues are people's issues but health and childcare are important for women." A second women stated that "women look at issues differently from men, but men should be more involved, for example in childcare and aged care." From another state, a third woman commented that with maturity came the 'realisation that issues are not just women's issues, but in reality, family issues such as child-minding." No ALP or AD women denied that there were women's issues but several of the non-Labour women did.

Political party remains then the major source of division on political ideas. The salience of party is also reflected in the fact that the majority of women expressed little hope that women MPs from the different parties could co-operate on issues. A minority said that it was possible in theory but happened rarely in practice, or that it could happen with some people, or with some issues only. Where the political party with by far the most women MPs, namely the Australian Labour Party, is itself divided into tightly organised factions there are consequently barriers to co-operation amongst ALP women let alone co-operation amongst women from the different parties.

REFERENCES

Asher, Louise, "The Liberal Party and Women", in *Liberals Face the Future: Essay on Australian Liberalism,*, 1984, pp. 104-116.

Bulter, Garry John and T.D., Mandeville, *Regional Economics: An Australian Introduction,* p. 139, il, University of Queensland Press, 1981, Brisbane.

Clarke, Robert P. and Louise G. White, *Political Analysis: Technique and Practice,* 1983, pp. 285, Brooks, Cole.

Connors, Libby, "Ideologies of Powerlessness: Attitudes to Women and the Working Class in Queensland Schools, 1919-1939," in *Hecate,* Vol. 11, No. 2, 1985, pp. 42-56.

Cooney, Jenny, Sexual Discrimination in Local Government More Widespread than the Halliday Case," in *Australian Municipal Journal,* Vol. 61, April, 1982, pp. 260-262.

Dixson, Mirian, "Some Comparative Constructs for Analysis of the Australian Woman's Movements," in *Melbourne Journal of Politics,* No. 9, 1977, pp. 80-92.

Dowse, Sara, "Keep at it: often and loud: Continuing Need for Government Support of Women's Services," in *Australian Society,* February, 1989, Vol. 8, No. 2, pp. 8-9.

Edgar, Don, "Volunteerism and the Changing Patterns of Women's Lives," in *Current Affairs* Bulletin, April 1989, Vol. 65, No. 11, pp. 19-23.

Goot, Murray and Elisabeth Reid, *Women and voting studies; mindless nations or sexist scientist*? 1975, pp. 44, London Sage Publications.

Grieve, Norma and Patricia Grimshaw (ed.), 1981, *Australian Women: Feminist Perspectives,* p. 33, Oxford University.

Moore, Kate, 1985, "Gains for Women in the ALP (Australian Labour Party)" in *Programme for Change: Affinnative Action in Australia,* pp. 33-50.

Outhwaite, Sue, Margaret Power and Stuart Rosewarne, 1988, *Writing Women Out of the Economy*. (Paper presented at the ANZAAS Centenary Congress, Sydney).

Sawer, Marian, 1984, "Women Candidates Speak," (survey of women candidates in the 1982 Victorian State Election) in *Australian Women and Political System,* pp. 89-93.

——, 1985 January, "The All-Male Election: Despite Pressing issues, Women's Concerns Didn't Rate as Election Vote Catchers" in *Australian Society,* Vol. 4, No. 1, pp. 13-15.

Sawer, Marian and Marian Simms, 1984, *A Woman's Place; Women and Politics in Australia,* pp. 235, il, Allen and Uenwin.

Searle, Betty, 1989 April, "Jessie Street: Feminist and Socialist an Enigma for Her Class," in *Social Alternatives,* Vol. 8, No. 1, pp. 46-47.

——, 1989 Mar/April, "Jessie Street hails socialism and the Red Army," in *Womenspeak,* Vol. 12, No. 2, pp. 8-9.

——, 1988, "Rose Scott," in *Silk and Calico: Class, Gendeer and the Vote,* pp. 77-78.

Simms, Marian, 1984, "The Australian Feminist Experience," *in Australian Women: Feminist Perspectives,* pp. 227-239.

——, 1985 May, "The 1983 Australian Elections: Find the Women?" in *Politics,* Vol. 20, No. 1, pp. 104-112.

——, 1985, "Ideology, interventionism and the Liberal Party's Fall from Grace," in *Essay on Victorian Politics,* pp. 145-156.

——, 1985, "The Dilemmas and Paradoxes of Public Bodies Performing

Commercial Tasks: the Rhetoric of Rationality and the Rejection of Traditional Labour Philosophy on the Role of the State," in *Australian Political Studies Association Conference Proceedings,* Vol. 2, pp. 576-597.

Summers, Anne, 1975, "The Unwritten History of Adela Pankhurst Walsh," in *Women, Class and History,* pp. 388-402.

Wise, Rod, 1977 July, "The Role of Women in the ALP as Policy makers and Candidates." (Paper presented at the Women's Electoral Lobby, Seminar, Sydney), in *Australian Quarterly,* Vol. 49, Sept. 1977, pp. 28-36.

6

Women Leadership in Some South Asian Countries

South Asia also known as cradle of civilizations' lags for behind in the context of women leadership. Though many prominent ladies in the modern course of history have emerged as powerful leaders in different spheres of life in general and politics in particular, the situation and status cannot be said bright.

In Pakistan despite being ruled mostly by military dictators, Benazir Bhutto emerged as successful Prime Minister. Similarly India can boast of having many women leaders like Indira Gandhi as Prime Minister, Pratibha Patil as President of India or Mrs. Meira Kumar as Speaker of Lok Sabha, to name a few at top ranking besides many chief ministers, ministers, party presidents, governors, judges etc. In Sri Lanka the post of President was held by Sirimavo Bhandarnaike etc.

In Bangladesh two women emerged as head of the nation- Begum Khaleda Zia and Sheikh Hasina. In Burma one women was elected as the leader but unfortunately military regime ousted her.

In the present chapter we are giving a brief sketch of women leadership in the special context of Bangladesh, Sri Lanka and Myanmar.

I

WOMEN LEADERSHIP IN BANGLADESH

Women participated extensively in anti-British agitations during the 1930s and 1940s and were an active force during the independence struggle. Since 1972 the Constitution and the legal system have guaranteed equal rights for women to participate in all aspects of public life. The prominence of the well-known opposition party leaders Hasina and Khaleda Zia at first sight indicated a national openness to women's political power. Both, however, were exceptional in Bangladeshi politics. They originally owed their positions to family connections and only later skillfully built their own followings and platforms. Women candidates for political office were a rarity in the 1970s and 1980s, and female participation was labeled anti-Islamic by conservative men throughout the country. Secular provisions in Bangladeshi laws safeguarded the equality of women while "protecting" them and assuming their dependence.

Women running for office have had little success. In the 1979 parliamentary elections, for example, only 17 women were among 2,125 candidates for 300 seats; none of the women won, and only 3 polled over 15 percent of the vote. At the union council level, the 1973 elections returned only one woman chairman, and the 1977 and 1984 elections each returned only four female chairmen. The leaders running the country, recognizing that women suffer disabilities when competing for office against men, reserved thirty seats for women in Parliament. The profiles of the women occupying these seats exemplied the subordinate positions of women in Bangladesh, even those occupying public offices. In the 1979 Parliament, fifteen women members were formerly housewives, and twenty-seven had no prior legislative experience. A study of women nominated to union councils revealed that 60 percent were less than 30 years of age, only 8 percent were over 40 years of age, and only 4 percent had college degrees.

Prior to the 1988 parliamentary elections, the provision for reserved seats for women had been allowed to lapse. The result was that women were left practically without representation at the national level, although there were other forums for political involvement at the local level. In mid-1988 three women sat on union and subdistrict councils. Municipal councils also included women, but the law precluded women from exceeding 10 percent of council membership. Some women's groups, such as the Jatiyo Mohila Sangstha (National Organization for Women), have held major conferences to discuss women's problems and mobilization strategies. Although these women's organizations were the province of middle-class women, they served as training grounds, as did local councils, for a new generation of politically active women.

II

SRI LANKA

Sri Lanka ratified the U.N. Convention on the Elimination of All Forms of Discrimination against Women (CEDAW) on 05th of October 1981. CEDAW articles 7 (b) states that "State parties shall take over all appropriate measures to eliminate discrimination against women in the public and political life of the country by ensuring the right to participate in the formulation and implementation of government policy". Sri Lankan women have been enjoying the right exercise the universal franchise from 1931 and are nearly 53% of the population is women. Sri Lanka also produced the first woman Prime Minister to the World in 1960. Further, women are the major contributors to the country's foreign exchange earnings and Sri Lankan women's literacy rate is higher than other South Asian countries. All these things being true, however, women do not represent themselves enough in political and public decision-making bodies in Sir Lanka. Sri Lanka has the worst record of women's overall participation in national and local legislative bodies in the South-Asian region. Though the majority of women exercise their political rights as voters or campaigners during election times, there was only less than 4.9% of female representation in the parliament in 2005 and in the municipality and local government level participation was 1.7% in 2004. The percentage of women in parliament between the 1930s and the present has never exceeded six percent.

Why Women are Invisible in Politics?

There are various reasons and issues that are inherent in Sri Lankan politics that impeded women's political participation. The political party systems in Sri Lanka are highly male dominated. The gender intensive preferential vote electoral system has discouraged women's participation in elections. Due to stereotyped attitudes prevailing in the society towards women, they are not encouraged to be involved in politics. Further, the lack of child care support system at the community level and women's multiple reproductive roles have taken away a lot of time that could have helped women engage in social networking. Lack of financial resources is also a major impediment for women's political participation. In Sri Lanka, politics is always considered a dirty game. This is quite evident during election times because of high incidence of violence that takes place during election time. The prevailing climate of political violence discourage women in participating politics. In this scenario women are reluctant to participate in politics.

In addition, there are cultural barriers which increase the existing gender gaps. This is because Sri Lanka is a conservative society with strong beliefs in cultural norms and deeply rooted prejudices that reinforce gender stereotyping. There are some inherent problems in the discourse of women and politics. In Sri Lanka there are very few articulated strong independent women since many women are nominated to replace vacancies created by the resignation or death of male relatives. In comparison with other South Asian countries, there is no special quota for women or a special political academy for women to address their training needs and develop skills needed to participate in politics. The proposal for a 25% quota for Sri Lankan women in local bodies was dropped on the grounds that political parties would not be able to find women candidates. Further the lack of opportunity for political training and skills development has been a negative factor that impedes women's political participation.

Without Women No Equality, Development and Peace

The Beijing Platform for action in 1995 declared that without the active participation of women and the incorporation of women's perspective at all levels of decision making, the goals of equality, development and peace cannot be achieved. The rights guaranteed in international conventions states that" women shall be eligible for election to all publicly elected bodies, established by national law, on equal terms with men, without any discrimination. The Beijing Platform for Action 1995 Section 181 says that "Women's equal participation in decision-making is not only a demand for simple justice or democracy but can also be seen as a necessary condition for women's interest to be taken into account. This was further elaborated in 2004

General Assembly 58th Session Resolution 58/142 reaffirming that " women's full and equal participation in the political process and decision making will provide a balance that more accurately reflects the composition of society, is needed to strengthen democracy and promote its proper functioning, plays a pivotal role in furthering women's equal status, including improving women's socio-economic status, and contributes to re-defining political priorities and providing new perspectives on political issues" The Millennium Development Goals *(MDGs)* include female representation in politics as an indication of progress towards the empowerment of women.

In the global development discourse, development requires decisions by those control resources, covering material as well as non-material aspects non material aspects, including political power. The paucity of female legislators means that the interests of women are not adequately represented in the highest body of the State. Unless women gain leadership in the State governance, market and civil society it will be difficult to transform or shape forces of social, political and economic processes to work in favor of women and gender equality.

Despite that 7 decades have passed from the universal franchise for women, women do not represent enough in political bodies. The percentage of women in parliament is little closer to 4%. It is very low percentage at the local government level. After decades of struggle for gender equality women are convinced that they have to be in the places where power exists or be in the position to negotiate a better deal for women. It is high time to urge Sri Lankan government to revisit all existing laws and work on brining necessary changes to existing election laws allowing 33% minimum quota of women in Parliament, half those appointed to the National List be women, 33% minimum quota of women in local government bodies, more women ministers, junior ministers and cabinet ministers, and political parties to increase the nomination of women candidates at all levels. The proposed Women's Act provides a 25% quota for women.

[*Source:* Shamila Daluwatte- Attorney –at-Law –Sri Lanka]

III

MYANMAR

Status of Women in Myanmar

The Constitution of Myanmar guarantee equality before the law "regardless of race, religion, status, or sex. But it does not explicitly prohibit discrimination against women. And although, the government of Myanmar has established two mechanisms to promote women's enjoyment of their human rights, the Maternal Welfare and Child Association, and the Myanmar Women Entrepreneurs Association the leadership of these two bodies is comprised of women who are related or married to high-ranking SPDC officers. Critics say that these organizations have no independent authority or expertise in establishing equality for women. For instance, women in Myanmar continue to have no representation at the national level today. The 19-member SPDC is all male, and there are no women in the 39-member cabinet. Women are not represented in the military. The government even sent an all-male delegation to the 1995 UN Conference on Women in Beijing.

In general women traditionally have enjoyed a high social and economic status and have exercised most of the same basic rights as men. Consistent with traditional culture, women keep their names after marriage and often control family finances. However, women remained under-represented in most traditional male occupations, and women continued to be barred effectively from a few professions, including the military officer corps. The burden of poverty, which is particularly widespread in rural areas, also fell disproportionately on women.

Women in Myanmar have been subjected to a wide range of human rights violations, including political imprisonment, torture and rape, forced labor, and forcible relocation, all at the hands of the military authorities. At the same time women have played an active role in the political and economic life of the country. It is the women who manage the family finances and work alongside their male relatives on family farms and in small businesses.

Women have been at the forefront of the pro-democracy movement which began in 1988, many of whom were also students or female leaders within opposition political parties. This report from Amnesty International details the imprisonment of at least 61 women for political reasons and looks into the conditions of these female political prisoners.

From 1991 to 1992 almost 250,000 Rohingyas from the Arakan state in Burma fled to Bangladesh to escape from forced labor, rape and religious persecution at the hands of Burmese military. Although repatriation was enforced from 1993 to 1997 the outflow continues. According to Bangladeshi officials and NGOs, there are about 100,000 undocumented Rohingyas in Bangladesh taking daily wage jobs as farmers, vendors, rickshaw drivers, and construction workers. Images Asia, a Thailand-based NGO, conducted research on the situation of Rohingya women. The report reveals stories of Rohingya women being trafficked from the camps to Bangladesh and then into Pakistan. The lack of a durable solution to the problem continues to make the Rohingya population vulnerable to abuses, both in Burma and in Bangladesh.

Every day, women and men from Burma cross the border to Thailand to search for work. The ongoing civil war, forced labor and forced relocation have uprooted the lives of many thousands, especially in ethnic areas of Burma. Women enter Thailand under various arrangements. Some already have contacts and know where they are going. Others are brought by agents. Some cross the border without prior arrangement and look for jobs through local friends or taxi drivers. Once women join a brothel or work as domestic help, it becomes very difficult for relatives or NGO workers to stay in touch with them. In theory, migration is a voluntary act that does not involve coercion or deception or detention. But their illegal status puts migrants in a vulnerable position.

Women in Burma have traditionally played a role in society that was equal to men. So it is not very surprising that the National League for Democracy, which won over 80% of the votes in the 1990 election, is led by a woman, Aung San Suu Kyi. But that political party was never allowed to take power, and has been relentlessly persecuted by the ruling military junta, the State Law and Order Restoration Council (SLORC). Women have been actively resisting the brutal dominance of the SLORC, often at great personal danger. Aung San Suu Kyi herself endured over six years of house arrest, and her life has been threatened by SLORC officials, troops and hired mobs. One of her party members, Dr. Ma Thida, a young physician and writer, was sentenced to 20 years in prison for her political views, and is suffering from severe health difficulties.

Like all their fellow citizens, Burma's women face the day-to-day struggles of living under a military dictatorship. But the country's women also face special problems and are often the target of particular abuse. Rape by soldiers is common, and the military has been implicated in the trafficking of Burmese women into prostitution in neighboring Thailand. As many as 40,000 Burmese women, most of them from minority ethnic groups, are believed to be employed in Thai brothels.

Women's rights abuses continue to occur in Burma. The existence and continuation of many of these abuses point directly to the military junta's policies, and their failure to reform either the laws or the economic system.

Women played an active role in Burma's struggle for independence—from British colonial rule and Japanese occupation - and remained an organized force under the post-independence government, 1948-58. Ne Win's seizure of power in 1958 and his military dictatorship strangled the women's and other social movements. But with the explosion of people's movements in 1988, Burmese women rose again.

As is obious from the preceding paragraphs. Women leadership in Myanmar is badly crushed and the status of women is pitiable.

Hereafter we will like to portrary the sketch of one woman leader from Burma who has been awarded Nobel Peace Prize.

AUNG SAN SUU KYI

Aung San Suu Kyi was born on 19 June 1945 in Rangoon. Her father, Aung San, founded the modern Burmese army and negotiated Burma's independence from the United Kingdom in 1947; he was assassinated by his rivals in the same year. She grew up with her mother, Khin Kyi, and two brothers, Aung San Lin and Aung San Oo in Rangoon. Her favourite brother Aung San Lin died at age eight, when he drowned in an ornamental lake in the grounds of the house. Her elder brother emigrated to San Diego, California, becoming a United States citizen. After Lin's death, the family moved to a house by Inya Lake where she met people of very different backgrounds, political views and religions. Suu Kyi was educated in English Catholic schools for much of her childhood in Burma where she was noted as having a talent for learning languages. She is a Theravada Buddhist.

Suu Kyi's mother, Daw Khin Kyi, gained prominence as a political figure in the newly formed Burmese government. She was appointed Burmese ambassador to India and Nepal in 1960, and Aung San Suu Kyi followed her there, graduating from Lady Shri Ram College with a degree in politics in New Delhi in 1964. Suu Kyi continued her education at St Hugh's College, Oxford, obtaining a B.A. degree in Philosophy, Politics, and Economics in 1969. After graduating, she lived in New York City with a family friend and worked at the United Nations for three years, primarily on budget matters, writing daily to her future husband Michael. In 1972, Aung San Suu Kyi married Dr. Michael Aris, a scholar of Tibetan culture, living abroad in Bhutan. The following year she gave birth to their first son, Alexander Aris, in London; their second son, Kim, was born in 1977. Following this, she earned a Ph.D. at the School of Oriental and African Studies, University of London in 1985. She was elected an Honorary Fellow in 1990. For two years she was a Fellow at the Indian Institute of

Advanced Studies (IIAS)in Shimla, India. She also worked for the government of the Union of Burma. In 1988 Suu Kyi returned to Burma at first to tend for her ailing mother but later to lead the pro-democracy movement. Michael's visit in Christmas 1995 turned out to be the last time that he and Suu Kyi met, as Suu Kyi remained in Burma and the Burmese dictatorship denied him any further entry visas. Michael was diagnosed with prostate cancer in 1997 which was later found to be terminal. Despite appeals from prominent figures and organizations, including the United States, UN Secretary General Kofi Annan and Pope John Paul II, the Burmese government would not grant Michael a visa, saying that they did not have the facilities to care for him, and instead urged Aung San Suu Kyi to leave the country to visit him. She was at that time temporarily free from house arrest but was unwilling to depart, fearing that she would be refused re-entry if she left, as she did not trust the junta's assurance that she could return. Aris died on his 53rd birthday on 27 March 1999. Since 1989, when his wife was first placed under house arrest, he had seen her only five times, the last of which was for Christmas in 1995. She also remains separated from her children, who live in the United Kingdom.

On 2 May 2008, after Cyclone Nargis hit Burma, Suu Kyi lost her roof and was living in virtual darkness after losing electricity in her dilapidated lakeside residence. She used candles at night as she was not provided any generator set. Plans to renovate and repair the house were announced in August 2009.

Though Aung San Suu Kyi returned to Burma in 1988 to take care of her ailing mother. By coincidence, in the same year, the long-time leader of the Socialist ruling party, General Ne Win, stepped down, leading to mass demonstrations for democracy on 8 August 1988 (8-8-88, a day seen as auspicious), which were violently suppressed. On 26 August 1988, she addressed half a million people at a mass rally in front of the Shwedagon Pagoda in the capital, calling for a democratic government. However in September, a new military junta took power. Later the same month, the National League for Democracy (NLD) was formed, with Suu Kyi as general secretary. Influenced by both Mahatma Gandhi's philosophy of non-violence and by more specifically Buddhist concepts, Aung San Suu Kyi entered politics to work for democratization, helped found the National League for Democracy on 27 September 1988, and was put under house arrest on 20 July 1989. She was offered freedom if she left the country, but she refused.

One of her most famous speeches is the "Freedom From Fear" speech, which begins, "It is not power that corrupts but fear. Fear of losing power corrupts those who wield it and fear of the scourge of power corrupts those who are subject to it."

1990 General Election

In 1990, the military junta called a general election, which the National League for Democracy won by an overwhelming 82% of the votes. Being the NLD's candidate, Aung San Suu Kyi under normal circumstances would have assumed the office of Prime Minister. Instead, the results were nullified, and the military refused to hand over power. This resulted in an international outcry. Aung San Suu Kyi was placed under house arrest at her home on University Avenue in Rangoon. During her arrest, she was awarded the Sakharov Prize for Freedom of Thought in 1990, and the Nobel Peace Prize the year after. Her sons Alexander and Kim accepted the Nobel Peace Prize on her behalf. Aung San Suu Kyi used the Nobel Peace Prize's 1.3 million USD prize money to establish a health and education trust for the Burmese people.

House Arrest

Aung San Suu Kyi has been placed under house arrest on numerous occasions since she began her political career, totaling 14 of the past 20 years. During these periods, she has been prevented from meeting her party supporters; international visitors, likewise, have been prevented from meeting her. She lives with her two maids and receives visits from her doctor. In an interview, Suu Kyi said that while under house arrest she spent her time reading philosophy, politics and biographies that her husband had sent her. She would also occupy her time by playing the piano and was occasionally allowed visits from foreign diplomats as well as her personal doctor. The media have also been prevented from visiting. In 1998, journalist Maurizio Giuliano, after photographing her, was stopped by customs officials, and all his films, tapes and some notes were confiscated. Suu Kyi met the leader of Burma, General Than Shwe, accompanied by General Khin Nyunt on 20 September 1994, while under house arrest. It was the first meeting since she had been placed in detention. When the military government has released Suu Kyi from house arrest it has made it clear that, if she left the country to visit her family in the United Kingdom, it would not allow her return.

On several occasions, Suu Kyi has been in poor health for severe weakness. Suu Kyi continues to be imprisoned under the 1975 State Protection Act (Article 10 b), which grants the government the power to imprison persons for up to five years without a trial, and the Law to Safeguard the State Against the Dangers of Those Desiring to Cause

Subversive Acts (Article 10 a), as Suu Kyi is "likely to undermine the community peace and stability" of the country. She has appealed against her detention. Many nations and figures have continued to call for her release and that of 2,100 other political prisoners in the country.

The UN has attempted to facilitate dialogue between the junta and Suu Kyi. On 6 May 2002, following secret confidence-building negotiations led by the United Nations, the government released her; a government spokesman said that she was free to move "because we are confident that we can trust each other". Aung San Suu Kyi proclaimed "a new dawn for the country". However on 30 May 2003, a government-sponsored mob attacked her caravan in the northern village of Depayin, murdering and wounding many of her supporters.

Aung San Suu Kyi fled the scene with the help of her driver, Ko Kyaw Soe Lin, but was arrested upon reaching Ye-U. The government imprisoned her at Insein Prison in Rangoon. After she underwent a hysterectomy in September 2003, the government again placed her under house arrest in Rangoon. The results from the UN facilitation have been mixed; Razali Ismail, UN special envoy to Burma, met with Aung San Suu Kyi. Ismail resigned from his post the following year, partly because he was denied re-entry to Burma on several occasions. Several years later in 2006, Ibrahim Gambari, UN Undersecretary-General (USG) of Department of Political Affairs, met with Aung San Suu Kyi, the first visit by a foreign official since 2004. He also met with Suu Kyi later the same year. On 2 October 2007 Gambari returned to talk to her again after seeing Than Shwe and other members of the senior leadership in Naypyitaw. State television broadcast Suu Kyi with Gambari, stating that they had met twice. This was Suu Kyi's first appearance in state media in the four years since her current detention began.

The United Nations Working Group for Arbitrary Detention rendered an Opinion (No. 9 of 2004) that her deprivation of liberty was arbitrary, as being in contravention of Article 9 of the Universal Declaration of Human Rights 1948, and requested that the authorities in Burma set her free, but the authorities have so far ignored this request. Such claims were rejected by Major-General Khin Yi, the national police chief of Burma. On 18 January 2007, the state-run paper *The New Light of Myanmar* accused Suu Kyi of tax evasion for spending her Nobel Prize money outside of the country. The accusation followed the defeat of a US-sponsored United Nations Security Council resolution condemning Burma as a threat to international security; the resolution was defeated because of strong opposition from China, which has strong ties with the military junta (China later voted against the resolution, along with Russia and South Africa). In November 2007 it was reported that Suu Kyi would meet her political allies National League for Democracy along with a government minister. The ruling junta made the official announcement on state TV and radio just hours after the United Nation's special envoy Ibrahim Gambari ended his second visit to Burma. The NLD confirmed that it had received the invitation to hold talks with Ms. Suu Kyi. However, the process delivered few concrete results.

On 3 July 2009, UN Secretary General Ban Ki-moon, arrived in Myanmar on a journey seeking the release of Aung San Suu Kyi and to press the junta for democratic reform. However, on departing from Burma, Ban Ki-moon said he was "disappointed" with the visit after junta leader Than Shwe refused permission for him to visit Suu Kyi, citing her ongoing trial. Ban said he was "deeply disappointed that they have missed a very important opportunity."

Periods Under Detention

(1) 20 July 1989: Placed under house arrest in Rangoon under martial law that allows for detention without charge or trial for three years.

(2) 10 July 1995: Released from house arrest.

(3) 23 September 2000: Placed under house arrest.

(4) 6 May 2002: Released after 19 months.

(5) 30 May 2003: Arrested following the Depayin massacre she was held in secret detention for over 3 months before being returned to house arrest.

(6) 25 May 2007: House arrest extended by one year flouting a direct appeal from U.N. Secretary-General Kofi Annan to General Than Shwe.

(7) 24 October 2007: Reached 12 years under house arrest, solidarity protests held at 12 cities around the world.

(8) 27 May 2008: House arrest extended for another year, illegal under both international law and Burma's own law.

(9) 11 August 2009: House arrest extended for further 18 months because of "violation" arising from the May 2009 trespass incident.

2007 Anti-Government Protests

Protests led by Buddhist monks began on 19 August 2007 following steep fuel price increases, and continued each day, despite the threat of a crackdown by the military.

On Saturday, 22 September 2007, although still under house arrest, Suu Kyi made a brief public appearance at the gate of her residence in Rangoon to accept the blessings of Buddhist monks who were marching in support of human rights. It was reported that she had been moved the following day to Insein Prison (where she had been detained in 2003), but meetings with UN envoy Ibrahim Gambari near her Rangoon home on 30 September and 2 October established that she remained under house arrest.

2009 Trespass Incident

On 3 May 2009, an American man, identified as John William Yettaw, swam across Inya Lake to her house uninvited and was arrested when he made his return trip three days later. He had attempted to make a similar trip two years earlier, but for unknown reasons was turned away. It is unknown what his motives were. On 13 May, Suu Kyi was arrested for violating the terms of her house arrest because the swimmer, who pleaded exhaustion, was allowed to stay in her house for two days before he attempted the swim back. Suu Kyi was later taken to Insein Prison, where she could face up to five years confinement for the intrusion. The trial of Suu Kyi and her two maids began on 18 May and a small number of protesters gathered outside. Diplomats and journalists are barred from attending the trial; however, on one occasion, several diplomats from Russia, Thailand and Singapore and journalists were allowed to meet Suu Kyi. The prosecution had originally planned to call 22 witnesses. It also accused John Yettaw of embarrassing the country. During the ongoing defence case, Suu Kyi said she was innocent. The defence was only allowed to call one witness (out of four), while the prosecution has been permitted to call 14 witnesses. The court rejected two character witnesses, NLD members Tin Oo and Win Tin and only permitted the defense to call a legal expert. According to one unconfirmed report, the junta is planning to, once again, place her in detention, this time in a military base outside the city. In a separate trial, Yettaw said he swam to Suu Kyi's house to warn her that her life was "in danger". The national police chief later confirmed that Yettaw was the "main culprit" in the case filed against Suu Kyi. According to aides, Suu Kyi spent her 64th birthday in jail sharing biryani rice and chocolate cake with her guards.

Her arrest and subsequent trial received worldwide condemnation by the UN Secretary General Ban Ki-moon, the United Nations Security Council, Western governments, South Africa, Japan and the Association of Southeast Asian Nations, of which Burma is a member. The Burmese government strongly condemned the statement, as it created an "unsound tradition" and criticised Thailand for meddling in its internal affairs. The Burmese Foreign Minister Nyan Win was quoted in the state-run newspaper *New Light of Myanmar* as saying that the incident "was trumped up to intensify international pressure on Burma by internal and external anti-government elements who do not wish to see the positive changes in those countries' policies toward Burma". Ban responded to an international campaign by flying to Burma to negotiate, but Than Shwe rejected all of his requests.

On 11 August 2009 the trial concluded with Suu Kyi being sentenced to imprisonment for three years with hard labour. This sentence was commuted by the military rulers to further house arrest of eighteen months. On 14 August, U.S. Senator Jim Webb visited Burma, visiting with junta leader Gen. Than Shwe and later with Suu Kyi. During the visit, Webb negotiated Yettaw's release and deportation from Burma. Following the verdict of the trial, lawyers of Suu Kyi said, they would appeal against the 18-months sentence. On 18 August, United States President Barack Obama asked the country's military leadership to set free all political prisoners, including Aung San Suu Kyi. In her appeal, Aung San Suu Kyi had argued, that the conviction was unwarranted. However, her appeal against the August sentence was rejected by a Burmese court on 2 October, 2009, although the court accepted the argument that the 1974 constitution, under which she had been charged, was null and void, but said the provisions of the 1975 security law, under which she has been kept under house arrest, remained in force. The verdict effectively means, she will be unable to participate in elections scheduled to take place in 2010 - the first in Burma in two decades. Her lawyer stated that her legal team would pursue a new appeal within 60 days.

Aung San Suu Kyi may be released "so she can organise her party," for the upcoming Burmese general election. Though, it is unclear if she will be allowed to run as a candidate.

Burma's relaxing stance, such as releasing political prisoners was influenced in the wake of successful recent diplomatic visits by the US and other Democratic governments, urging of encouraging the Burmese towards democratic reform. President Obama intends to personally advocate on the behalf of all political prisoners especially Aung San Suu Kyi, during the US-Asean Summit of 2009.

Democratic governments hope that successful general elections would be a optimistic indicator of the Burmese governments sincerity towards eventual democracy. The Hatoyama government which spent 2.82 Billion yen in 2008, has promised more Japanese foreign aid to encourage Burma release Aung San Suu Kyi in time for the elections;

and to continue striding towards democracy and the rule of law.

Aung San Suu Kyi has received vocal support from Western nations in Europe, Australia and North and South America, as well as India, Israel, Japan and South Korea. In December 2007, the US House of Representatives voted unanimously 400–0 to award Aung San Suu Kyi the Congressional Gold Medal; the Senate concurred on 25 April 2008.On 6 May 2008, President Bush signed legislation awarding Suu Kyi the Congressional Gold Medal. She is the first recipient in American history to receive the prize while imprisoned. Other non-American recipients of the medal include Sir Winston Churchill, Pope John Paul II, Nelson Mandela, the Dalai Lama and Mother Theresa. More recently, there has been growing criticism of her detention by Burma's neighbours in the Association of Southeast Asian Nations, particularly from Indonesia, Thailand, the Philippines and Singapore. At one point Malaysia warned Burma faced expulsion from ASEAN as a result of the detention of Suu Kyi. Other nations including South Africa, Bangladesh and the Maldives have also called for her release. The United Nations has urged the country to move towards inclusive national reconciliation, the restoration of democracy, and full respect for human rights. In December 2008, the United Nations General Assembly passed a resolution condemning the human rights situation in Burma and calling for Suu Kyi's release – 80 countries voting for the resolution, 25 against and 45 abstentions. Other nations, such as China and Russia are less critical of the regime and prefer to cooperate only on economic matters. Indonesia has urged China to push Burma for reforms. However, Samak Sundaravej, former Prime Minister of Thailand, criticised the amount of support for Suu Kyi, saying that "Europe uses Aung San Suu Kyi as a tool. If it's not related to Aung San Suu Kyi, you can have deeper discussions with Myanmar." U2 supported her on their 2009 U2 360° Tour by encouraging fans to wear masks with her likeness on them during the band's performance of the song "Walk On", which was originally written for her. In 2005, Irish singer songwriter Damian Rice released the single Unplayed Piano in support of Aung San Suu Kyi.

Vietnam, however, does not support calls by other ASEAN member states for Myanmar to free Aung San Suu Kyi, state media reported Friday, 14 August. 2009. The state-run Viet Nam News said Vietnam had no criticism of Myanmar's decision 11 August, 2009 to place Suu Kyi under house arrest for the next 18 months, effectively barring her from elections scheduled for 2010. "It is our view that the Aung San Suu Kyi trial is an internal affair of Myanmar," Vietnamese government spokesman Le Dung stated on the website of the Ministry of Foreign Affairs. In contrast with other ASEAN member states, Dung said Vietnam has always supported Myanmar and hopes it will continue to implement the "roadmap to democracy" outlined by its government.

Nobel Peace Prize

Daw Aung San Suu Kyi was awarded the Nobel Peace Prize in 1991. The decision of the Nobel Committee mentions:

> The Norwegian Nobel Committee has decided to award the Nobel Peace Prize for 1991 to Aung San Suu Kyi of Myanmar (Burma) for her non-violent struggle for democracy and human rights.
>
> ...Suu Kyi's struggle is one of the most extraordinary examples of civil courage in Asia in recent decades.

> She has become an important symbol in the struggle against oppression...
>
> ...In awarding the Nobel Peace Prize for 1991 to Aung San Suu Kyi, the Norwegian Nobel Committee wishes to honour this woman for her unflagging efforts and to show its support for the many people throughout the world who are striving to attain democracy, human rights and ethnic conciliation by peaceful means.
>
> —*Oslo, 14 October 1991*

Nobel Peace prize winners (Archbishop Desmond Tutu, The Dalai Lama, Shirin Ebadi, Adolfo Pérez Esquivel, Mairead Corrigan, Rigoberta Menchú, Prof. Elie Wiesel, Betty Williams, Jody Williams and former U.S. President Jimmy Carter) have called for the rulers of Burma to release Suu Kyi "create the necessary conditions for a genuine dialogue with Daw Aung San Suu Kyi and all concerned parties and ethnic groups in order to achieve an inclusive national reconciliation with the direct support of the United Nations." Some of the money she received as part of the award helps fund London-based charity Prospect Burma, who provide higher education grants to Burmese students.

The Bommersvik Declarations

In Bommersvik, Sweden, in 1995 and 2002, two conventions of the Elected Representatives of the Union of Burma took place and the following two landmark declarations were issued:

Bommersvik Declaration I

In 1995, during the first convention that lasted from 16–23 July, the Representatives issued the Bommersvik Declaration I:

> We, the representatives of the people of Burma, elected in the 27 May 1990 general elections, meeting at the First Convention of Elected Representatives from the liberated areas of Burma, hereby — Warmly welcome the unconditional release of 1991 Nobel Peace laureate Daw Aung San Suu Kyi on 10 July 1995; Thank all who have worked tirelessly and consistently for the release of Daw Aung San Suu Kyi and the cause of democracy in Burma; Applaud Daw Aung San Suu Kyi's determination, in spite of having spent 6 years under house arrest, to continue to work to bring true democracy to Burma; Welcome Daw Aung San Suu Kyi's return to politics to take up the mantle of her father, General Aung San, in Burma's second struggle for independence...
>
> *—The Elected Representatives of the Union of Burma*

Bommersvik Declaration II

In 2002, during the second convention that lasted from 25 February to 1 March, the Representatives issued the Bommersvik Declaration II:

> We, the representatives of the people of Burma, elected in the 27 May 1990 general elections presently serving as members of the National Coalition Government of the Union of Burma and/or the Members of Parliament Union, meeting at the Convention of Elected Representatives held in Bommersvik for the second time, hereby reaffirm — Our Mandate, Position, and Strategic Objectives — that we will never ignore the will of the Burmese people expressed through the May 1990 general elections; - that the military's refusal to honor the election results does not in any way diminish the validity of these results.
>
> *—The Elected Representatives of the Union of Burma*

Awards & Recognitions

(1) Thorolf Rafto Memorial Prize (1990)
(2) Sakharov Prize (1990)
(3) Nobel Peace Prize (1991)
(4) Simon Bolivar International Prize (1992)
(5) Jawaharlal Nehru Award (1993)
(6) Prize For Freedom of the Liberal International (1995)
(7) Honorary Companion of the Order of Australia (1996)
(8) Freedom of Dublin City, Republic of Ireland (1999)
(9) Presidential Medal of Freedom (2000)
(10) UNESCO Madanjeet Singh Prize for the Promotion of Tolerance & Non-Violence (2002)
(11) Gwangju Prize for Human Rights (2004)
(12) Olof Palme Prize (2005)
(13) Doctor of Laws (honoris causa) from Memorial University of Newfoundland (2004)
(14) Freedom from Fear award (2006)
(15) Honorary Canadian citizenship (2007)
(16) Honorary President of the LSESU (2007)
(17) Doctorate of Letters (honoris causa) from Colgate University (2008)
(18) Congressional Gold Medal (2008)
(19) Premi Internacional Catalunya (2008)
(20) Freedom Of Glasgow (2009)
(21) Mahatma Gandhi International Award for Peace and Reconciliation (2009)

[*Source:* Wikipedia].

Bibliography

Abdul Majid bin Ahmad Khan. *An analysis of the UMNO Kaum Ibu as a women's political organisation,* Kuala Lumpur.

Aguilar, Carmencita T., 1987, "The Muslims in Manila Prior to Colonial Control". *Sojourn,* SEACCNA, ISEAS, February 1987.

Alzona, Encarnacion, 1934, *The Filipino Woman: Her Social, Economic and Political Status, 15665-1935.* Manila, Benipayo Press, 1934. 146 leaves.

Amara Pongsapich (ed), 1986, *Women Issues Book of Readings,* Bangkok. Institute of Social Research, Chulalongkorn University.

Angeles, Leonora C., 1989, *Feminism and Nationalism: The Discourse on the Women Question and Politics of the Women Movement in the Philippines.* M.A. Thesis. UP Department of Political Science, 1989.

Aruego, Jose M., 1949, *The Framing of the Philippine Constitutions,* Volume II. Manila, Philippines: University Publishing Co.

Asher, Louise, "The Liberal Party and Women", in *Liberals Face the Future: Essay on Australian Liberalism,,* 1984, pp. 104-116.

Barik, Vandana, 2009, *Women's Education, Gender Equity and Fertility,* Rajat, New Delhi.

Benavides, Enriqueta R., *The Filipino Woman's Social,*

Economic and Political Status. Manila: Cultural Foundation of the Philippines. 17 leaves.

Bulter, Garry John and T.D., Mandeville, *Regional Economics: An Australian Introduction*, p. 139, il, University of Queensland Press, 1981, Brisbane.

Chandra, P., 2005, *Political Dynamics of Women*, Akansha, New Delhi.

Cooney, Jenny, Sexual Discrimination in Local Government More Widespread than the Halliday Case," in *Australian Municipal Journal*, Vol. 61, April, 1982, pp. 260-262.

Cortes, Irene R., 1974, *Women's Rights Under the 1973 Constitution*. Quezon City.

Jean J. Kirkpatrick, 1979, *Political Women*. Princeton: the Eagleton Institute of Politics, Rutgers University.

Kate Millett, 1971, *Sexual Politics*. New York: Equinox Books, Doubleday and Comp. Inc.

Lenore Manderson, 1980, *Women Politics and Change*. London: Oxford University Press.

Mahapatra, S.C., 2005, *Modern Encyclopaedia of Women and Development* (5 vols.), Rajat, New Delhi.

Malayang Kilusan ng Bagong Kababaihan, n.d., Makibaka. Manila.

Moore, Kate, 1985, "Gains for Women in the ALP (Australian Labour Party)" in *Programme for Change: Affinnative Action in Australia*, pp. 33-50.

Ong, A., 1987, *Spirit of Resistance to Capitalistic Discipline*, New York State University Press, Albany.

Paras, Edgardo, 1950, "The Civil Rights of Women in the Philippines". *Centro Escolar University Faculty and Graduate Studies Journal*. pp. 176-200.

Phelan, John, 1956, *The Hispanisation of the Philippines.* Princeton University Press.

Pongrit Khongprasit, 1985, *Research Report on Local Women Leaders: An Analysis of Interviews and Mailed Questionnaires.*

Red, Isagani V., 1974, *Mass Media Exposure and Attitude Towards the Socio-Political Leadership of Women.* Quezon City.

Roy, Ashine, 2003, *Development of Women: An Assessment,* Rajat, New Delhi.

Roy, Ashine, 2003, Women Empowerment and Gender Planning, Rajat, New Delhi.

Roy, R., 2006, *Women's Rights in India,* Akansha, New Delhi.

Romero, Flerida Ruth P., 1979, *Women's Status in Philippine Society.* Quezon City: University of the Philippines Law Center.

Santos, Alfonso, Editor, 1977, *Heroic Virgins and Women Patriots: Female Patriotism During the Japanese Occupation.* Manila: National Book Store.

Sawer, Marian and Marian Simms, 1984, *A Woman's Place; Women and Politics in Australia,* pp. 235, il, Allen and Uenwin.

Sumanlata, 2005, *Women and the Rule of Law,* Akansha, New Delhi.

Syed Husin Ali, (1975). *Malay peasant society and leadership,* Kuala Lumpur, Oxford University Press.

Tapales, Prserfina D., 1984, *Women in the Philippine Bureaucracy: Toward an Alternative Approach to the Study of Political Participation.* Ph.D. dissertation.

UMNO (n.d.). *Malaysia: Kaum Ibu Movement: Its history and achievements,* UMNO Research Division, Kuala Lumpur.

Wise, Rod, 1977 July, "The Role of Women in the ALP as Policy-makers and Candidates." (Paper presented at the Women's Electoral Lobby, Seminar, Sydney), in *Australian Quarterly,* Vol. 49, Sept. 1977, pp. 28-36.

Index